# Living Through Loss

*of related interest*

**Storymaking in Bereavement**
Dragons Fight in the Meadow
*Alida Gersie*
ISBN 1 85302 176 8 pb
ISBN 1 85302 065 6 hb

**Good Grief 1**
Exploring Feelings, Loss and Death with
Under Elevens, 2nd edition
*Barbara Ward and Associates*
ISBN 1 85302 324 8

**Good Grief 2**
Exploring Feelings, Loss and Death with
Over Elevens and Adults
*Barbara Ward and Associates*
ISBN 1 85302 340 X

**Grief in Children**
A Handbook for Adults
*Atle Dyregrov*
ISBN 1 85302 113 X

**The Forgotten Mourners**
Guidelines for Working with Bereaved children
*Sister Margaret Pennells and Susan C. Smith*
ISBN 1 85302 254 0

**Healthy Dying**
*Rob George and Peter Houghton*
ISBN 1 85302 436 8

**Interventions With Bereaved Children**
*Susan C. Smith and Sister Margaret Pennells*
ISBN 1 85302 285 3

**Grief and Powerlessness**
Helping People Regain Control of their Lives
*Ruth Bright*
ISBN 1 85302 386 8

# Living Through Loss
## A Training Guide for Those Supporting People Facing Loss

*Fay W. Jacobsen, Margaret Kindlen and Allison Shoemark*

Jessica Kingsley Publishers
London and Bristol, Pennsylvania

The right of Fay W Jacobsen, Margaret Kindlen and Allison Shoemark to be identified as authors of this work has been asserted by them in accordance with the Copyright, Designs and Patents Act 1988.

First published in the United Kingdom in 1997 by
Jessica Kingsley Publishers Ltd
116 Pentonville Road
London N1 9JB, England
and
1900 Frost Road, Suite 101
Bristol, PA 19007, U S A

Copyright © 1997 Fay W Jacobsen, Margaret Kindlen and Allison Shoemark

**Library of Congress Cataloging in Publication Data**
Jacobsen, Fay W., 1932–
Living through loss: a training guide for those supporting
people facing loss / Fay W. Jacobsen with Margaret Kindlen and
Allison Shoemark
p.   cm.
Includes bibliographical references and index.
ISBN 1-85302-395-7 (pbk. : alk. paper)
1. Bereavement–Psychological aspects. 2. Loss (Psychology)
3. Group counselling–Study and teaching. 4. Counselling–Study and
teaching. I. Kindlen, Margaret. II. Shoemark, Allison.
III. Title.
BF575.G5J33   1997
155.9'37--dc2                                        96-34243
                                                        CIP

**British Library Cataloguing in Publication Data**
Jacobsen, Fay W.
Living through loss : a manual for those working with
issues of terminal illness and bereavement
1.Bereavement  2. Counseling
I. Title II. Kindlen, Margaret III. Shoemark, Allison
362.8

ISBN 1-8532-395-7

Printed and Bound in Great Britain by
Cromwell Press, Melksham, Wiltshire

Every effort has been made to contact copyright holders for their permission to reprint material in this book. The publishers would be grateful to hear from any copyright holder who is not here acknowledged and will undertake to rectify any errors or omissions in future editions of this book.

# Contents

## Part 2: Course Programme and Lesson Plans

# Part 3: Facilitators' Materials

# Part 4: Participants' Materials

# Part 5: References, Further Reading and Resources

# List of Figures

# Acknowledgements

This teaching and learning package is based on experience gained from an initiative by the Scottish Health Education Group (SHEG), which organization was succeeded by the Health Education Board for Scotland (HEBS). We are grateful to HEBS for permission to use the material. This has enabled us to draw on the results of three years of powerful learning.

We had nothing but generosity and support from people at every level within SHEG, and it is therefore difficult to single out individuals for our gratitude. But we would have been lost without the skill and warmth of Christina Coltart and her staff in the library, and Annette Robertson who patiently administered the courses. Helen Mackinnon set the standards of intellectual rigour and integrity which made our association with this work so rich and memorable. We are indebted to her for many of the formulations and much of the structure of Section 1 of this package, which is based in part on an earlier publication (Jacobsen and Mackinnon 1989).

Several individuals have contributed material included in this manual. We thank: Sue Carpenter (hospice social worker) and individuals in the Bereavement Support Group in Morgantown, West Virginia, USA, who contributed to, and commented on, our observation of the process through which their group was successfully launched and maintained; Kate Copp, a MacMillan lecturer in Aberdeen, who contributed two exercises on spirituality; J.M.D., whose poems witness stages on her journey to reclaim herself after suffering sexual abuse as a child; The Jewish Museum, Prague, for permission to print the poem *On a Sunny Evening*, by a child who died in the Terezien concentration camp; The Open University, for permission to reproduce three exercises from its pack P554, *Child Abuse and Neglect*; Kate Robinson, a young artist in Glasgow, who has allowed us to publish three of her poems; Peggy Seeger, for allowing us to print the words of the late Ewan MacColl's song *The Joy of Living*; the Wedgewood Project, West Cumbria, whose banner is included in the design of our cover; and the West Cumberland Hospital, for allowing us to reproduce the text of their leaflet *Helping Children…when Someone Dies. A Guide for Parents*.

We want also to express our sincere appreciation and thanks to many colleagues who participated with us in courses. They were courageous in sharing their pain, and generous in contributing their wisdom, their excitement, their compassion and their skills. Together we have all grown.

*Fay Jacobsen, Margaret Kindlen, Alison Shoemark*

# A Note on Ethical Issues

The course described in this package is designed for training people who already have some basic counselling skills.

Section 4 consists of material that may be photocopied for distribution to course participants. The first of these handouts **(PM 1: Professional and ethical guidelines)** provides advice on how to deal with some sensitive issues that may arise when attempting to use the ideas developed in this training guide. We regard that advice as an essential part of any material that trainers may wish to provide to participants. We have therefore given our permission to reproduce and distribute any other handouts in Section 4, conditional on **PM 1** being one of them.

*Fay Jacobsen, Margaret Kindlen, Alison Shoemark*

# Introduction

## HOW IT STARTED

In 1985, the Scottish Health Education Group (SHEG) solicited suggestions from nurse teachers in Scottish Colleges of Nursing on how it might best contribute to their needs. In response to requests for help and resources to teach basic counselling skills to nurses, SHEG then initiated some pilot courses that culminated in the development of a nine day course, 'Developing Counselling Skills'. This was in three parts. First, a five day course, followed one month later by a further three days, and a follow-up day arranged six months later. This package was taken to major Scottish cities and also to rural areas, including the Outer Hebrides and the Shetland Isles. Many participants were nurse teachers who were expected to teach counselling skills.

## HOW IT DEVELOPED

Another five day course, 'Sharing Counselling Skills', was designed and launched subsequently, in response to further requests. Participants who completed both courses were offered opportunities to co-teach in the continuing 'Developing Counselling Skills' courses. On such occasions, the facilitating team would usually consist of two experienced and two trainee teachers. Hundreds of nurses were thus trained to a primary level of skills, and dozens of nurse teachers reached a higher level of competency. The aim was to equip nurses with sensitive responding skills. At no time was it claimed that this was a complete training in counselling. A detailed training guide on how to run the nine day course was published (Jacobsen and Mackinnon 1989), and SHEG supplied copies to every College of Nursing in Scotland.

Two further five day courses were developed subsequently: 'Counselling for HIV and AIDS' and the course described here, 'Living Through Loss'. (The latter, therefore, includes no material on HIV or AIDS.) Both these courses also travelled all over Scotland.

This manual, *Living Through Loss*, was intended originally as a companion to the earlier publication (Jacobsen and Mackinnon 1989). However, the focus of health education activity in Scotland had changed over the years. Funds for publication of this material were no longer available to SHEG's successor, the Health Education Board for Scotland (HEBS). Therefore, with permission from HEBS, we decided to publish this package independently.

## THE PACKAGE

### Aims

*Living Through Loss* aims to provide a complete manual to train people who have basic counselling skills and who are expected to support others experiencing bereavement or other emotional trauma. The training is centred around the planning and conduct of a five day course with an extra follow-up day.

The aims of the course are to provide opportunities for participants to:

1. Enhance existing counselling skills for working with people facing loss and bereavement.
2. Deepen self-awareness about living through loss.
3. Share personal experiences of grief and bereavement.
4. Explore ways of looking after ourselves and promoting this with our colleagues.
5. Explore some aspects of abuse.
6. Identify relevant resources, including reading materials, which will support and inform about living through loss.
7. Consider how learning can be taken back to the work place and incorporated into our lives.

Originally designed by nurses for nurses, the material in this manual has also been used fruitfully among other 'caring professionals', and with lay hospice volunteers, in Britain and in the USA.

### Structure

The package is arranged in five sections. Section 1 describes the attitudes, values and ideas that have shaped the manual. It includes discussion of how to create a supportive learning environment, how to work with groups, and how to design and plan a course.

Section 2 is a programme for the five day course and follow-up, including detailed day-by-day lesson plans. Opportunities to practise skills are described, and alternative time-table arrangements are suggested.

A standardized format is adopted for the lesson plans: *Title, Time, Timing, Aims, What you need, What you do*. A structured, timed and tightly organized schedule of this kind is sometimes referred to as a *strategic approach*. The idea is to support those who are relatively new to facilitating this type of learning. As confidence grows, and the material and methods become more familiar, facilitators will probably want to introduce their own ideas, creating new materials by responding flexibly to issues as they arise: a *tactical approach*.

The number of participants in a course should not exceed 18. Small-group work, important in many sessions, will then require two facilitators.

Section 3 contains Facilitators' Materials (FM) numbered **FM 1** to **FM 16** for ease of reference. They include information on:

- understanding loss and experiencing growth
- theories of loss and change
- the grieving process
- working with issues of abuse
- the use of poems, for centring or as discussion triggers, with some examples.

Section 4 consists of Participants' Material (PM) numbered **PM 1** to **PM 52**. These are linked to appropriate FMs or lesson plans, or both. With the proviso explained in the 'Note on ethical issues' (page 4) any of these handouts may be photocopied for distribution to course participants.

Section 5 provides references to publications cited in the manual, lists resources and contacts available to course organizers, and includes suggestions for further reading.

Reference to course participants as 'she' in this manual is a convenient abbreviation, reflecting the preponderance of women on most courses. In this context, 'counselling' refers to a variety of levels of active listening and sensitive responding skills. Those organizing and taking care of the course are referred to as 'trainers' or 'facilitators'.

The language and style of expression used in what follows is generally informal and non-didactic. It may appear to be strange, and perhaps even irritating, to some. It reflects the spirit of the experiential approach to learning adopted here, as described in Section 1. The emphasis is on feeling, rather than knowing; on experiencing, rather than understanding; on sharing, rather than reporting or stating; and on being wise and empathic, rather than having knowledge and power.

# Learning to Help People Live Through Loss

## THE LEARNING METHOD

This manual is based on the conviction that the most effective way to learn how to help people confront, and deal creatively, with situations that are highly charged with emotion is to use an 'experiential' approach. Experiential learning is 'learning by doing'. The method is particularly appropriate when learning skills. No one expects to become proficient at using roller-skates, riding a bicycle or flying a jumbo-jet on the strength of a close study of an instruction manual. This is not a criticism of manuals; it is simply an acknowledgement that all such skills involve confronting and working through the fear, anxiety and tension that affect physical and emotional balance. Only then can one expect to use skills safely and effectively.

Exactly the same is true when learning the skills necessary to support those who are terminally ill or bereaved, survivors of disasters or of terrorism (domestic or public), or people faced with the traumatic fall-out from social upheavals, such as endemic unemployment and the attendant undermining of community life. The experiential method of learning aims essentially to provide facilitating structures, such as brainstorming or small-group interactions, which help to focus individuals' attention on an aspect of the topic being explored. The aim is to facilitate participants' self-discovery of:

- their emotional responses to confronting issues of abuse, terminal illness and death
- the skills that they already have to deal with such situations
- what extra skills they may need
- whether they might prefer to avoid working in depth with grief issues at that particular stage in their lives.

Working in small groups facilitates sharing of knowledge and experience. Activities within such groups can include, for example:

- recording and sharing individuals' experiences of loss
- sharing what are one's worst fears of how a situation might go wrong
- imagining how one might respond to the loss of the most important person in one's life.

5

The shared individual experiences provide a basis for the absorption of new information. If that new information is consistent with the group's experience then it is affirmed, validated and more readily retained. Small-group sessions are usually followed by plenary group discussions. Thus the variety of experience is widened and then summarized.

All this presupposes the existence of an appropriate environment in which the learning takes place. In fact, the effectiveness of the experiential method depends critically on that environment, so that its creation and nurturing, as described in what follows, is truly an essential element of the whole approach.

## THE LEARNING ENVIRONMENT

When learning to use roller-skates or to drive a car, a supportive, non-judgemental and respectful environment minimizes stress and fear, and thus promotes smoother development of skills. Such an environment is even more essential when learning how to confront issues that challenge our own fear of pain and of death.

Our culture encourages us to suppress feelings when dealing with emotionally challenging issues. The covert, and sometimes overt, policy of some caring professionals is to keep an emotional distance from clients. To be fair, this is frequently a matter of survival for those working in an unsupportive environment. But maintaining emotional distance requires suppression of feelings, and it is difficult to be selective about which feelings are suppressed. The capacity to feel may thus be numbed, humanity may be diminished, and the effectiveness of work with those suffering loss will then be reduced. Moreover, such suppression of feelings can lead to increasing stress, tension and illness among the practitioners. This seems too high a price to pay for 'professionalism'.

Moreover, even if professionals' empathic responses to those who are grieving are endorsed as proper and desirable, there is rarely, if ever, similar recognition of an important corollary: that support must also be provided for the carers. For those working in this sphere, attachments will frequently be severed by the death of clients. Those supporting grieving relatives may themselves be grieving. Nothing can make this easy or painless. However, familiarity with the process of grief, and an ability to accept and articulate emotions, enables carers to stand alongside clients, recognizing and responding to their needs as well as their own. Both carers and clients are then more likely to travel their parallel roads from grief to growth. The course described in this manual has been designed to help create an environment in which such growth may be achieved.

## PRINCIPLES UNDERLYING EFFECTIVE EXPERIENTIAL LEARNING PRACTICE

The 'ground rules' within which a course will be pursued are introduced to participants at the start of the first day. They are based on six principles:

1. Participation is voluntary and active.
2. People learn through making mistakes.
3. Participants are responsible for their own learning.
4. All in the group are treated and seen as equals.
5. People learn best by co-operating and sharing.
6. Learning can be both fun and painful.

The following paragraphs discuss how these principles may be applied in practice.

## Voluntary and active participation

### CHOOSING TO PARTICIPATE

People attending a course dealing with sensitive issues of loss should have made a considered decision to participate. This implies that potential participants must have had a genuine opportunity to decline without fear of negative consequences. It is important, therefore, that course advertising material includes sufficient information to enable such an informed choice. The application form should be accompanied by a detailed statement that explains to potential participants and their managers the aims and contents of the course, the learning methods that will be used, and the importance of voluntary and active participation.

### RELUCTANT ATTENDANCE

Nevertheless, it may happen occasionally that a participant reveals that she was given little option to decline. The group facilitator may take advantage of this situation by addressing the voluntary participation issue specifically. In particular, it will be helpful to:

- disassociate oneself from the practice of requiring mandatory attendance on courses of this kind
- draw attention to the pre-course information that specified voluntary and willing participation
- make an offer to the participant that, if she chooses to withdraw, the course organizers will provide support by writing to whatever authority she specifies.

If the participant chooses to stay, then it will be helpful to emphasize the particular importance to her of absorbing and using the 'Professional and ethical guidelines' (**PM 1** in Section 4). Such response supports and empowers the individual to make her own decision, and thus goes some way to counteracting the effect of the original denial of that right.

If the issue of voluntary participation is not raised specifically, it will nevertheless be useful to refer to it in general terms.

### ACCOMMODATING PARTICIPANTS' CHOICES

Offering choices empowers participants and enhances learning. The course programme should invite such choices and should provide participants with information to help them make those choices. Active rather than passive involvement is crucial to the notion of taking control of one's own learning, a central idea in the experiential approach. In the present context, this principle is particularly important, since a participant's recent experience of loss may not only inhibit learning, but may also cause anguish.

### THE RIGHT TO OPT OUT

Throughout the conduct of a course, facilitators should stress that participation in any particular activity is voluntary. One should explain that the more active their involvement, the more likely that they will benefit from the course; but participants should not be encouraged to commit themselves to a depth of activity that might push them beyond what they feel is safe for them.

## Learning by making mistakes

We all make mistakes, and mistakes always have within them the potential for learning. For some, mistakes are exploited as opportunities to ask why one took a particular action or behaved in a particular way. This then leads naturally to thoughts about how one might change behaviour or practice to achieve a more successful result. But not everyone learns from their mistakes. For some people, typically those who have absorbed the lesson, from home and work environments, that 'it is not acceptable to make mistakes', the thought of making a mistake may be fraught with tension or even terror. Such tension tends to increase the chance of making a mistake.

At home, in a culture of perfectionism, parents may fail to praise a child's achievements. The result is often an adult who is insecure about whether she ever does anything right. Mistakes may also be used as an opportunity to abuse a child, physically or emotionally, or both. Similar abuse may be experienced again later as an adult, in a working environment, with the additional sanction of demotion or dismissal. In many work situations, making mistakes can be a serious threat to others in the work environment. For someone already tense and anxious, such an atmosphere is likely to increase anxiety levels further.

When asking people to be prepared to make mistakes and to learn from them, one should acknowledge that for some this may be an uncomfortable or even a terrifying thing to do. Facilitators should make it clear that, at this stage, they are asking participants to take the risk only within the very special, secure environment that one aims to create within the course.

## Taking responsibility for one's own learning

Much of what individuals learn when using experiential methods concerns their characteristic ways of responding to situations and to people. These responses are grounded in personal life experiences. Some may choose to share their learning with those around them; others may prefer to reflect upon it privately. These reactions are equally valid. Participants should be encouraged to process their newly acquired insights into their own patterns of behaviour in whatever way feels most appropriate to them.

Experiential learning becomes more effective, and more intense, if participants are able to strike an appropriate balance between taking risks on the one hand, and respecting their own boundaries or emotional limits on the other. But striking such a balance is not a simple matter. Some participants may have been conditioned socially to respect and prioritize the needs of others. Respecting one's own needs is then allotted low priority at best; at worst it may be seen as unacceptable and selfish. Some may have been required to push themselves beyond the limits of their safety and well-being, to fulfil others' expectations, and may have then convinced themselves that their own needs are unimportant. Still others may have learned to struggle for survival in a different way. The lessons of that struggle may have been absorbed as a rule to not take risks, and to guard one's boundaries jealously.

The reality is that individuals differ; only the individual participant is in a position to monitor her own needs and to learn what is appropriate for her. *She has to take responsibility for her learning.*

Thus it is that different participants are likely to learn quite different lessons from what is nominally the same course. For one, the most important thing discovered might be how difficult it is to say 'no' – but how empowering it feels finally to say 'no'. Another may find it exhilarating to have learned to say 'yes'! The important thing is that each participant's unique and individual experience is valued. Trainers need to recognize, endorse and encourage this diversity of positive reactions to the learning experience.

## Participants are equals

### THE PHYSICAL REPRESENTATION OF EQUALITY

It will be clear from the above that in a course of this kind, participants and trainers relate to each other as equals, on a human level, rather than as professionals with hierarchies of seniority, authority and varying levels of achievement. A simple way to demonstrate the importance attached to this principle is in the arrangement of seating for all: chairs, of equal height, in a circle. This removes one intrusive symbol of status pecking orders, and it allows everyone to make eye contact with all. Note people's body language at the start of a course. Often this will demonstrate how vulnerable some people feel when exposed to the gaze of others without the protection of conventional status barriers. Watch how body language changes as the group progresses; the changes seen may help a trainer to judge the growth of the group's cohesion and confidence.

### OVERCOMING HIERARCHIES

Participants may be intimidated when they discover that others attending the same course are colleagues senior to themselves. This is a problem particularly for those from professions where hierarchies are emphasized. Equally, those in senior positions can feel isolated and vulnerable as they anticipate that more will be expected of them by virtue of their seniority; they may feel obliged to pressure themselves so as to justify their imagined position. Initial introductions, on the first day of a course, can help to overcome these problems. Structure this part of the programme so that everyone, trainers included, talks about their personal lives – recreations, hobbies, holidays – rather than about professional issues. In a five day course, it is useful to postpone distribution of the list of participants, with all the information about people's professional status, to (say) day 3. By that time participants usually relate to each other so powerfully as individuals that the information ceases to be a threat. On the contrary, it may be viewed as a resource to form a basis for a future professional support network.

### FACILITATORS ARE EQUAL MEMBERS OF THE GROUP

At the start of a course, participants may accept the idea that they are expected to take responsibility for their own learning; but they are often not prepared for the effect that the learning will have upon them. The experiential approach affects not just the intellect, but also the physical, emotional and social aspects of people's experience. When this process begins to take effect, insecurities and doubts may surface. Some may feel a need to shift responsibility for what is happening to them. They may then look to the facilitators as authority figures to shoulder the burden.

Facilitators beware! A familiar feature of group dynamics is that when group life becomes difficult and stressed, there will be a tendency to develop dependence on an all-knowledgeable, all-powerful leader to take responsibility. It can be very seductive to be accorded that sort of power, but facilitators must be clear that their role is to be responsible *to* the group for the maintenance of safety and support structures built into the course. Facilitators are not, nor can they be, responsible *for* the group, or for the individuals within it. If responsibility *for* the group is accepted, explicitly or implicitly, then:

- the group will fail to function as a creative unit
- facilitators will be struggling under an impossible burden which will rapidly de-skill them
- ultimately, the would-be saviours will be toppled from the pedestal on which they have allowed themselves to be placed.

More information about facilitators' role and methods of work is included later in this section.

## Learning by co-operating and sharing

In some skills-teaching and training situations (for instance, athletics and other competitive sports), a controlled element of competition between small groups or individuals can be a positive, helpful factor. But overt or covert competition between participants in a group learning how to help others cope with loss and grief is always at least disturbing. At worst, it is cruel, painful and seriously disruptive. The experiential style of training adopted here, with its deliberate encouragement of self-discovery and acknowledgement of emotional involvement, is particularly vulnerable to the negative aspects of a competitive atmosphere. Facilitators often express this explicitly when they record notes before and after a course. Participants also frequently articulate this feeling when they state that they do not want to be tested, assessed or compared with others in the group. In a course of this kind, there is a premium on co-operation, and there are many ways in which this can be fostered by trainers:

- Consult and negotiate with the group at every opportunity.
- Stress the importance of confidentiality. Nothing said within the group should be repeated outside, and nothing which passes between people in a small sub-group should be shared with the main group, unless this is agreed by all of those involved.
- Make it clear that self-assessment and peer assessment are built into exercises in the form of small-group feedback sessions. Participants should be reminded to give negative feedback in a way that will maximize its acceptability, and not to omit positive feedback.
- Encourage and accept negative and positive feedback from the group by structuring time for this into the programme at the end of each day. (These feedback items can be in the form of sentence completion; for example, *'What I enjoyed least today was…'*, *'What I enjoyed most today was…'*.
- A paired support session might be introduced towards the end of each day's work. This is similar to the idea of co-counselling. Pairs of participants, established on day 1, meet each day to share their experience of the day concerned. This should not be a conversation. Participant *A* should listen to *B* during a predetermined interval (15 minutes, say), followed by a complementary reversal of roles.

## Fun and pain in learning

How people feel about learning depends to a large extent on their past experiences of education and training. Many participants arriving at the course may expect it to be a boring chore which has to be undertaken to advance professional skills. It is a fact, however, that the range of feelings that participants have expressed in the past, on completing this course, has never included boredom.

Low energy and a heavy atmosphere in the group are usually the result of tension or pain, or both. As trust builds, as people become more open with each other and lower their defences, so they become more vulnerable. Deepening insight leads to discovery – of strengths and of weaknesses, of joy and of pain. Occasionally a participant may recall a painful memory which has been locked away from consciousness for years. The warmth and support of the group can then help her to express the feelings arising from the discovery. It is unlikely that such an issue will be resolved within the compass of the group's life. But if the individual concerned wants to continue her voyage of self-discovery, then information can be provided about appropriate resources to help make choices. Her right to seek support, if she so chooses, can thus be validated.

When the atmosphere feels heavy and energy is low, it is sometimes useful to introduce a game. Here, too, it is important to be sensitive to varying reactions, and to provide for people to opt out.

The course climate can be influenced by making an effort to establish a relaxed, good humoured environment, where laughter always has a place. Laughter lightens the mood of a group when the going gets tough. Laughter defuses tension. A joker in the pack can be a great asset to the learning environment. But it is important to be alert for the sort of humour that blocks or sabotages learning; the apparently lighthearted but spiteful quip that causes pain to others.

## Creating the learning environment: a summary of the trainers' role

- Use a range of communication skills.
- Explain clearly both the steps and purpose of exercises that are offered to the group.
- Demonstrate qualities of warmth, respect and integrity.
- Respect people's right not to contribute.
- Define and identify ground rules and boundaries clearly. This helps people to function with maximum freedom within the learning structure.
- Negotiate with the group about difficulties that may arise or tension in the group climate.
- Encourage co-operation and sharing.
- Increase your own self-awareness. This includes identification and, when appropriate, articulation of your own needs.
- Be an equal within the group, with responsibility towards participants; but do not accept responsibility for their learning.
- Strive to be open and available. This means being prepared to make mistakes, take risks and get hurt while enjoying close contact with people.
- Learn about groups and their dynamics.

## WORKING WITH GROUPS

The following pages summarize some important aspects of working with groups. They are no substitute for a full discussion of group dynamics, but they provide a concise outline that may be helpful for trainers unfamiliar with the subject. The recommendations for 'Further Reading', in Section 5, includes relevant texts. Trainers are urged at least to browse through some of these and to seek whatever further specialized training they might need.

Group processes have been described as an outward display of the inner lives of its members. When individuals' lives are meshed together in a group that is working towards the achievement of a collective task, that group takes on a life of its own. 'Group life' passes through certain recognizable stages that are described variously in different models. One such model is described below. It is relatively uncomplicated and it has been found helpful by trainers working on courses of the kind described in this manual. The description of the model is followed by consideration of how it may be used to promote a creative approach to difficulties that can occur in the life of a group. This summary of ideas on working with groups then ends with a brief discussion of what is meant by 'group cohesiveness'.

### Tuckman's (1965) model of group life

A group may go through five stages: *forming, storming, norming, performing* and *ending*. Many groups pass through the whole sequence; some might skip a stage. A dramatic incident in a group (for example, someone accessing a memory of a hitherto forgotten trauma) might have the effect of causing group life to take a step back before progressing further. Alternatively, the same event may be the stimulus for moving to the next stage. The five stages are described briefly below, as they might present themselves in a course of this type.

#### FORMING

When people enter a new group, there will be uncertainty and caution. The group is dependent on the trainer for the information that will help it to determine what will be the behavioural norms. At this stage, the presentation of clear guidelines and the provision of concise information, provide an initial 'map' that helps the group members to feel that they know where they are going. Taking time with lighthearted introductory exercises can begin to inform the group of the quality of support and acceptance in the learning environment. This eases the way to familiarity and connection between individuals within the group.

#### STORMING

At the 'storming' stage there may be differences of opinion in the group and a tendency to split into opposing camps. There could be resistance to getting on with learning. This is a testing time for the trainer. If the rebellion and resistance are dealt with creatively and sensitively, the conflict is transformed into co-operation, and the group can progress to the next phase of its life.

### NORMING

At this stage, group norms are becoming established and the group is beginning to cohere. Support and negotiation replace conflict and polarization. Resistance lessens, and individuals become more receptive to the views of others.

### PERFORMING

The group's norms are now established; it is ready and willing to proceed with the learning task. People have sufficient trust and safety to express opinions more freely, and they are accepting that the views of others may differ from their own. The atmosphere is energetic and enthusiastic. Solutions to problems begin to emerge. At this stage, exercises with a higher risk can be offered to the group. Many will accept the challenge.

### ENDING

The approaching end of the group's life results in a mixture of withdrawal and a reluctance to part. There is a nostalgic review of the milestones of the group's experience. Addresses and telephone numbers are exchanged. Dates are suggested for group reunion meals. There is an atmosphere of sadness. That sadness will be particularly poignant in a group completing this particular course, since it has been dealing with loss. It will be important to draw attention to this special feature of the group's dissolution and the link between loss and change. (The point will often be made spontaneously by someone in the group.) The programme should allow sufficient time for exercises to facilitate closure.

## A creative approach to difficulties

Tuckman's model helps one to understand and respond to the learning climate of the course. Linking behaviour to group life is especially valuable in promoting creative responses to difficulties, rather than succumbing to personal insecurities, and feeling attacked and therefore defensive.

### SOME DIFFICULTIES ASSOCIATED WITH GROUP LIFE

The following 'difficult' behaviours may be evident at the 'forming' and 'storming' stages, when group members feel most vulnerable and adrift in uncharted waters:

- *aggression* – unfounded criticism or hostility towards other group members, trainers, or both
- *blocking* – obstructing the progress of the group by raising 'red herrings' or persisting with an issue that has been resolved by group agreement
- *special interest* – issues are raised which are of special concern to just one group member, or on behalf of persons who are not associated with the group
- *status-seeking* – someone draws attention to herself through excessive talking or by introducing extreme ideas
- *dominance* – authority being asserted through the manipulation of group members
- *withdrawal* – passivity or indifference, sometimes demonstrated through an activity such as doodling or ostentatious fiddling with hair
- *pairing* – joining with another or others to criticize the course

- *dependence* – 'setting up' the trainers, or one trainer, as all-knowing experts.

### WHOSE DIFFICULTY IS IT?

These difficulties are expressed through the behaviour of an individual. But because they occur in the context of the group's activity they have to be seen, and resolved, as a part of group life, rather than as irritating or aberrant behaviour of an individual. Viewed in this way, the difficulty may be interpreted as a part of the learning process. Very often, those who appear to be least comfortable within the group are the most supportive and creative – once they have found a way of working in the group that is acceptable to them. This is more likely to happen if the trainers listen and acknowledge that there is a problem. Above all, trainers should try not to feel blamed or to respond defensively. That would be a sure way to de-skill oneself.

### HOW SHOULD THE TRAINER REACT?

It is easy to write, '*try not to feel blamed or to respond defensively*'. The reality is that trainers, too, have sensitivities. If an individual or group unwittingly touches a raw nerve, then a trainer might well react to the challenge or criticism by withdrawing, interrupting, attempting to divert the challenge or becoming authoritarian and controlling – in fact, by any of the manoeuvres listed above as examples of 'difficult' group behaviours. A trainer's 'difficult reaction' may be interpreted by the group as a signal that this is to be part of the group norm. If that happens, then the work of the group will be unproductive until the difficulty is addressed.

A constructive response to such an event is to explore one's reaction to the 'problem' with a co-trainer. Thus one may identify alternative responses that can break the vicious cycle which might otherwise spiral and contaminate group life. *This is one of the most powerful reasons for working with a co-trainer.*

### WHEN A TRAINER REACTS INAPPROPRIATELY

If a trainer has reacted inappropriately it may be tempting to fall into the trap of making excuses, by way of apologies, to the group. When that urge arises a trainer should ask herself, or her co-trainer, whether such an apology is really in the best interests of the group. Perhaps it arises from a desire to satisfy a personal need? This is not to suggest that an apology would be wrong. What needs to be considered is the way that the apology might be interpreted by the group. For example, it could be taken to imply that it is not permissible to make mistakes. This would contradict one of the principles already transmitted to the group in the guidelines: that mistakes are allowable. One way of dealing with the situation which has worked well in practice, is to state that the mistake was creative. Boast about it a little, and share what can be learned from it. But even such an intervention should be brief and non-indulgent.

### IF THE GROUP IS RESPONSIBLE FOR ITS OWN LEARNING, WHY DOES THE TRAINER FEEL THAT SHE IS WADING THROUGH SYRUP?

Another guideline that trainers may easily contradict in practice is that people are responsible for their own learning. It is a simple matter for a trainer to identify when this occurs: she will find herself working harder and harder to resolve a group difficulty. She may even be feeling a little resentful that the group refuses to accept her solutions.

If the group process hits a snag, remember that it is more helpful for the group to be encouraged to think of alternatives than for the trainer to rush to the rescue. Ask the group for suggestions. For example: *'I'm feeling a bit stuck here. I have made some suggestions about how you might want to handle the issue of smoking in the group room, but the group's responses leave me unclear about what your wishes are. Maybe if you have some other suggestions it might help us come to a decision...'*.

Do not be surprised if some members are inclined to leave the issue unresolved. Others may be willing to work towards a solution. If the group consensus is that the matter should be left open, then record this in your notes. Thus, if the issue creates difficulties later, it might be appropriate to make a learning point about the value of facing and resolving difficulties.

## CHALLENGING AND RESPONDING

When questions are posed within the group, or when someone makes a statement that ought to be challenged, trust the resources within the group to respond. If it appears that this will not happen spontaneously, try drawing attention to the question or statement and invite comments. Only as a last resort should the trainer intervene, and then only if it is likely to assist the group's learning process.

## CRITICISMS OF THE COURSE

If one or more of the participants make general criticisms of the course, ask, in an open way, what particular aspect of the course is causing the difficulty or discomfort. Stay positive and confident; avoid becoming defensive.

## KEEP TUNED IN TO THE GROUP PROCESS

Stay tuned in to what is going on in the room. Trust your own feelings: not just emotions, but also physical sensations, such as a knot in the stomach or heaviness in the chest. Draw this to the attention of the group and invite them to comment. (For example: *'I notice that a few people are frowning and that some others are looking drowsy. I am feeling restless and uncomfortable. What do you think is going on?'*.)

## MEETING THE GROUP'S NEEDS

Structure the programme to leave room for negotiation with the group about the specific content of some sessions. Maximize choice by arranging for some parallel sessions offering different options. Use resources from within the group for some sessions. (A spectacularly successful 'looking after yourself' session in one course occurred when a participant led a T'ai Chi lesson.)

## PERSISTENT 'DIFFICULT' BEHAVIOUR BY A GROUP MEMBER

If someone persists with 'difficult' behaviour, beyond what might be expected in the group life, concentrate first on drawing her into activities: ask her opinion; give positive feedback. If this is not effective, challenge the behaviour within the group, being specific and assertive. For example: *'Sandra, I have noticed you playing with your hair, tapping your pencil, and casting your eyes heaven-ward three or four times within the last two days. I have no clear idea from these clues about what is going on for you, but it seems obvious that you are uneasy about something. Will you please tell us if there is some difficulty, and give the group an opportunity to try to resolve it?'*.

As a general rule, all business should take place within the group and should be regarded as part of the group process. The only exception to this rule that may be necessary occurs when a trainer suspects that a person's behaviour is connected with having accessed a major traumatic issue. In such a case, a move to invite disclosure to the group would be inappropriate. The trainer will want to approach the person privately. This does not mean that the individual concerned should be discouraged from revealing her discovery. If she chooses to do this, then there is an opportunity for her to receive valuable support and validation from the group. This can begin a healing process, and could encourage her to seek continuing support, in an individual or group context, so that healing can continue. However, it is essential that trainers do not imply that the group's task includes dealing with deep issues that may emerge for some individuals. This would be unrealistic, raise false expectations in the person concerned and, in a sense, would trivialize the experience. It would also be a frustrating and counter-productive diversion from the aims of the course.

## Group cohesiveness

Cohesiveness describes how close individuals have grown in valuing their membership of a group, and how great is the sense of ownership and security they derive from it. When an individual becomes aware of understanding, of empathy and of acceptance within the group, issues may be raised and feelings may be expressed that previously were guarded closely. Such an alliance between group members indicates the evolution of group cohesiveness in a safe learning environment.

Cherry, Robertson and Meadows (1990) provide a helpful model of group development, structured around the key issues of *confluence, conflict* and *co-operation*.

*Confluence* submerges differences between people in the interest of promoting similarity. This promotes integration – a flowing together into group life, where people feel safe. It is particularly important to encourage confluence in a newly forming group where anxiety is high. 'Getting to know you' exercises have this function. If individuals are to work effectively within the group, then they need at least to feel accepted. They will function even better if they feel they are liked. Lack of confluence in the early stages of a group can paralyse learning.

However, persisting confluence in the group life can become an inhibiting factor. This is because it is precisely peoples' *differences* which enrich the quality of the group's experience, so that *conflict* can be a valuable way for a group to move on.

Given a secure base built on confluence, conflict allows people to assert the ways in which they are different from each other, without denying their similarities. Conflict allows people to interact in the context of their differences; to learn from each other and be open to change. Suppressing conflict is exhausting. It may also reinforce a common dread of conflict, based on life events in which conflict was experienced as dangerous and destructive. However, a group without conflict has limited learning opportunities. Discovering the value of the acknowledgement and constructive challenging of differences can be a liberating learning experience.

*Co-operation* arises from relationships in which people acknowledge and accept their similarities and their differences. Both can then be used creatively to pursue the learning task of the group.

## THE ELEMENTS OF THE COURSE

The five day course described in Section 2 is constructed using four types of material:

1. Information.
2. Skills' development exercises.
3. Self-awareness exercises.
4. Techniques for 'looking after ourselves'.

All four elements may be intertwined in any one segment. For example, if there is a focus on an educational aspect, then the effect of that learning may trigger insights. These in turn can help participants to look after themselves more effectively. It is helpful, nevertheless, to identify each element separately.

## I. Information

Information input is in the form of mini-lectures by trainers and reading assignments for participants. These are then discussed by the group. The mini-lectures last no longer than 15 minutes. Each such lecture is on a limited and specific topic, for example, information about the various models that describe the stages of grieving. Such formal didactic material is an essential, but by no means central, constituent of the course.

Discussion of the information provided by books and mini-lectures draws on the group's collective knowledge, including that absorbed through life experiences before the start of the course. Another simple and effective way to tap the latter valuable resource is by 'brainstorming' (see **LP 1.5** in Section 2). This pooling of existing knowledge helps to build the group's confidence. Information derived from the course itself may validate the existing knowledge, and thus enhance the group's respect for its collective wisdom. Brainstorming may also reduce possible resentment at having had to listen to the delivery of information with which one is already familiar.

## 2. Skills' development exercises

Theoretical information is consolidated by providing opportunities to practise the skills required when responding to someone who is grieving. These exercises may be based on a participant's personal experience or on structured role-play. Sub-groups of two or three participants will work together, perhaps responding to a colleague's personal account of loss, or watching and then responding to a role-play by other participants or by facilitators. Videos of role-play may also be used. All these exercises involve giving and receiving peer feedback, a vital part of helping people to evaluate and improve their skills.

In a course involving people who are relatively new to role-play it is not productive to expect participants to undertake that activity in front of the whole group. Role-play is discussed in greater detail later in this section.

## 3. Self-awareness exercises

Self-awareness exercises are structures within which people can explore a personal experience. They then use that exploration to discover the extent to which theoretical information applies to their experience. For example, after 'brainstorming' different types of loss and hearing a mini-lecture about models of grieving, participants could be asked to think of a personal loss and to re-experience it, as if it were happening 'now'. They would then be asked to record their physical, emotional, intellectual and spiritual response to that experience. This information would be shared with a partner.

Structures like these look deceptively simple on paper. In practice they can have a very powerful effect on individuals. It is always advisable for facilitators to work through such exercises in advance of the course, so that they fully appreciate the kinds of response that may be evoked.

## 4. 'Looking after ourselves'

### SAFETY

When using self-awareness exercises, participants should always be cautioned to choose an event that feels safe for them to explore and to share. This is one aspect of encouraging them to look after themselves. Even so, some people will be surprised by the strength of feeling which they experience.

### PROCESSING

This is an important part of every experiential exercise. It helps people to look after themselves, to understand and learn from their experiences, and to recognize and respect their emotional boundaries. Participants could be encouraged to ask themselves the following sorts of question:

- Is what I am feeling an example of unfinished grieving?
- What, if anything, do I need to do to complete this grieving?
- Will this unfinished grieving cause me distress when I am working on bereavement issues with others?
- Might it have already been the unrecognized cause of distress?
- Did I really choose a 'safe' loss to examine or did I challenge myself to look at a sensitive issue, although I felt vulnerable?
- If I did this, was it because the issue was clamouring for my attention or was it because I thought that, as a competent professional, I 'ought' to take the risk?
- If the latter is true, is this part of my pattern, that I push myself to do things, ignoring my 'gut reaction' and causing myself stress?
- What would I lose and what would I gain if I stopped doing this?

Processing continues in people's minds after the formal session has ended. Often people need time to get the events of the day and their effects into focus. A brief closing round can invite people to dump any unfinished business from the day and to affirm something positive about themselves and their experiences. In addition, half an hour at the beginning of each day should be spent on collecting reflections that may have emerged overnight. This session is called the 'Learning review'.

### CENTRING

Another aspect of looking after ourselves is the *mini-meditation* or *centring* which follows the learning review (**LP 1.2** in Section 2). This provides an opportunity to end reflections on the events of the previous day, and to focus energy and attention on the day ahead. The centring is brief, lasting five to eight minutes, and often ends with a poem that has some relevance to the topic of the day.

### RELAXATION

The last exercise of the day is always some form of relaxation or massage. When time is squeezed, often due to reluctance to break off fascinating discussions, there is sometimes a temptation to encroach on relaxation time. Resist this. It is difficult enough to persuade people in the caring professions to take 'looking after themselves' seriously. It seems imperative that, in the context of this course, relaxation time is treated as sacrosanct.

## SUPPORT STRUCTURES

The principle of 'looking after ourselves' has been described as a constituent element in this experiential learning course, one of the essential building blocks. If it is to become a reality, that block requires adequate support networks to be built into the structure of the course. Support is an aspect of looking after ourselves that might be acknowledged in theory but that may be difficult to accept in practice. It is not uncommon for trainers, participants or both, to have absorbed the message, *stand on your own two feet*, and to have lived their lives accordingly. To ask for support, or to accept an offer of support, may then be experienced as failure. But all involved in this kind of course must be prepared to accept support.

### Support for trainers

It is strongly recommended that at least two trainers are involved with any one experiential course group. By arranging for peer support, trainers maximize their safety, and therefore also their learning and development of skills. Trainers with peer support are in a stronger position to be supportive of others and to foster a learning climate that will enhance the quality of group life.

### Structures that help participants to support themselves

Early in the course, trainers should introduce ways in which participants can support themselves. Here are some suggestions:

1. Encourage people to keep a course journal. This is a place where participants can confide those things which they are not yet ready to confide to others. The act of recording insights about ourselves, our feelings, our lives and our relationships is not only an important record of that discovery; it is also a witnessing and valuing of ourselves. If we neglect to record such information, we are in danger of dismissing ourselves and our importance – as others may have dismissed us previously.

2. Introduce the idea of paired support, to take place each day.

3. Support can be offered as an optional session. Several suitable exercises are included in Sections 3 and 4 of this manual. If people talk of having been very unsupported in their lives, they can be offered the experience of physical support from the group (see **FM 12** in Section 3).

4. Suggestions for setting up support groups are included in Section 4 (**PM 32, 33** and **34**).

5. In the closing stages of the group it is useful to have available a list of local resources for people to continue to support and develop their skills. These may include:

- names of organizations which provide individual counselling and counselling training
- sources of information about complementary health practitioners and training courses
- names of therapeutic communities where people can go for retreat, counselling or both
- personal development holidays.

6. Paired support and working in triads can also continue to be a support beyond the life of the group.

## Trainers' support for participants

In addition to facilitating support exercises and strategies, a trainer should also demonstrate a supportive way of being with individuals within the group who are experiencing powerful feelings. These feelings may be painful, distasteful or distressing. On the other hand, they could be triumphant, joyous and exuberant. In any case, the support from trainers should aim to:

- validate the experience and confirm that such feelings belong in the group
- encourage participants to recognize and accept those feelings
- encourage them to stay with the feelings in an effort to identify their origin.

In practice, trainers may:

- *Encourage effective breathing.* People's breathing almost invariably becomes shallow and erratic when they are distressed, depriving their brain of oxygen and thus reducing their capacity to process what they are experiencing.

- *Encourage 'grounding'.* When people experience extreme emotion, their feet often lose firm contact with the ground. 'Grounding' is a conscious effort to place both feet firmly on the ground and to release tension in the thighs, thus allowing the feet to provide firm support.

- *Offer physical contact.* Physical contact can be a way of reminding people of the safety of their present surroundings. This support may allow them to acknowledge a lack of safety, and possibly even terror, in their past environment. If an offer of contact is accepted, then a firm hand in the center of the back is most effective. An arm around the shoulders might be appropriate and comforting at the end of such work. Bear in mind, however, that when people are confronting their emotions, consoling can have the effect of curtailing the process, rather than supporting it.

Trainers should never give the impression that they endorse the familiar cultural norm, that 'showing feelings is a weakness and an embarrassment to others'. Therefore, try to stay in the same room with the group when offering support. This allows the participant to experience the power available from the group's support, and it gives the group an opportunity to experience the effect on them of providing that support. *Always acknowledge people's courage when they face up to powerful feelings and dare to explore them.*

## STAGES IN EXPERIENTIAL LEARNING

Application of the teaching approach outlined above is guided by the idea of seven stages in experiential learning (Jacobsen and Mackinnon 1989):

1. A general introduction to the learning process.
2. An explanation of the specific learning task on the agenda.
3. Performance of the task.
4. 'Processing' or reflecting on what has been learned.
5. Linking the learning to life outside the learning environment.
6. Applying the learning to life outside the learning environment.
7. Evaluating the learning.

These stages may refer to any one exercise, a group of exercises, to one day in the course or to the course as a whole, as illustrated in the following examples:

### Stage 1. Introduction to a session

Explain briefly what the session is expected to achieve, and outline its structure and relevance to the other sessions. Follow this with a mini-lecture that may be supported by audio-visual aids and handouts, as appropriate.

### Stage 2. Explanation of an exercise in a session

Describe the steps of the exercise briefly and precisely. Use a flip-chart if appropriate. A short demonstration by the trainers can sometimes be useful. Make it clear that the exercise is available for those who want to participate, but that no one is *obliged* to take part. This might be an appropriate time to remind people about other relevant ground rules.

### Stage 3. Performing an exercise

Experiential exercises are usually carried out in pairs, triads or larger groups of participants.

### Stage 4. Processing, reflecting on and sharing an experience

Some sharing will have occurred within the pair or small group where the experience was manifested. This helps people to learn how disparate their experiences of the same events can be. Participants should be reminded to respect the confidentiality of the small group.

Processing is a part of learning; it lays the foundation for increased sensitivity to others, and there may be comfort in learning that others' feelings are similar to one's own.

Processing of an exercise, or of impressions from a whole session, will continue in plenary discussion. The earliest feedback is often from those who are excited and enthusiastic about their experiences. This can have the effect of silencing those who had a different response, because traditional educational methods imply that there is a 'correct answer' to most questions. The more silent participants, who may have had a different experience, might feel, '*I have made a mistake*'. It is helpful, therefore, having acknowledged and welcomed initial responses, to explain that others' experiences might have been quite different. It should be pointed out that these feelings and their articulation are equally valid and valuable contributions to the learning process. The more open and accepting the collective sharing, including negative responses, the more safe and profitable the group learning climate will become.

## Stage 5. Linking new learning to professional practice and personal life

Help people to see the relevance of new experiences and learning to their professional and personal lives. Encourage them to reflect on how this can enhance their existing skills and empower them. Such encouragement promotes integration of learning.

## Stage 6. Applying learning in professional practice or personal life

Most courses of this kind are not residential. Participants will go home at the end of a day and interact with family and friends. At the end of five days they return to their usual domestic and work environment. Offer a framework to help participants apply and practise their newly learned skills when away from the course environment. Suggest the use of a diary to help them monitor and acknowledge progress. This will be a useful record when they later share and compare notes with co-participants on the follow-up day, six months after the course has been completed.

Certain exercises (for example, 'setting goals' on day 5 of the course) may be used as the basis of 'contracts' between participants, on how they plan to use the knowledge they have gained in practice. Progress may be monitored by personal arrangements to meet periodically or to talk occasionally on the telephone. Again, notes may be compared on follow-up day.

## Stage 7. Evaluation of learning

Processing and reflection (stage 4) may include an element of informal evaluation – of an exercise, an interaction, an experience, a session or a day. Encourage such ongoing evaluation during the course by explaining, on day 1, that participants will be asked at the end of the course to complete evaluation forms. Completion of these personal evaluations is preceded, on the last day, by collective evaluations within sub-groups, of the extent to which goals and expectations recorded on day 1 have been met.

Allow ample time for thoughtful completion of the personal evaluation forms on day 5. Ask that the form be signed, as an indication that participants are accepting responsibility for their feedback to facilitators. Most course-groups value seeing a collation of these evaluations. If this is requested and agreed by the group, anonymity can be secured by using code letters, and the collated evaluations can be circulated to participants soon (say one month) after the course.

Private evaluations will continue after the course, as skills acquired are applied in practice (stage 6). If participants are encouraged to make notes of these personal feelings as they are experienced, then these too will provide valuable raw material for the collective evaluation on follow-up day.

Send a retrospective evaluation questionnaire to arrive two weeks before the date arranged for the follow-up day. This provides an opportunity for reflection and preparation that will enhance the value of the day. These questionnaires also provide trainers with thoughtful and instructive written feedback regarding the effectiveness of the course as viewed from a distance of six months. The completed questionnaires can be collated similarly and then circulated to the group. Dealing with evaluations in this way is an important part of the process of closure for the group.

## BALANCING CHALLENGE AND SUPPORT

The basic elements of the course, particularly the parts involving skills' development and self-awareness, challenge participants. As indicated previously, the challenges that arise in experiential learning may stir up feelings and memories that can be painful. The structure of the course places great emphasis on adequate support, to help people look after themselves in these circumstances. A major challenge to trainers is to monitor the changing balance between challenge and support in group life as the work progresses, and to try to steer it in the most fruitful direction. Figure 1.1 symbolizes some characteristic patterns of participants' behaviour in response to extreme variations in the balance.

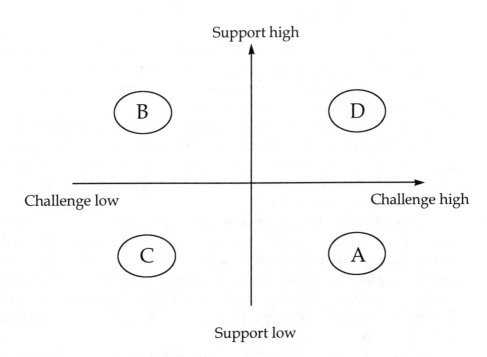

*Figure 1.1 Challenge and support*

In Position A, the challenge is high and support is low. People may become anxious, defensive, perhaps even hostile, showing signs of 'flight or fight'. Alert facilitators will take measures to increase support.

In Position B, the challenge is low; support is high. This represents a cosy atmosphere, but with not much going on. This may well appear to be the situation during the first session, since the early exercises present a relatively low level of challenge. However, the novelty of the situation, and the uncertainty about what is to follow, will be challenging to a degree.

In Position C, challenge and support are both low. Here people may be bored and apathetic; seem 'switched off', opting out and creating their own stimulation. If this occurs, something has gone seriously wrong.

In Position D, challenge and support are both high. People are taking risks, learning new things, profiting from each other's mistakes and being mutually helpful. There is a vigourous atmosphere in the group, supporting adventurous learning.

In practice, the group and sub-groups, will move through various points on the plane depicted in Figure 1.1 as the course proceeds. When the going gets tough, facilitators may want to ask themselves, '*Where are we now in the diagram? How should we adjust elements and structure so that the group will move forward?*'.

A group is a sensitive, responsive, living entity. Responding to group needs is a vital part of being a group facilitator. The quality and effectiveness of that response depends on maintaining a balance between challenging and supporting which is appropriate to the particular stage that the group has reached.

## ROLE-PLAY AS A TOOL IN EXPERIENTIAL LEARNING

The course described in this package is designed for persons who already have some basic counselling skills. This restriction is necessary because participants are expected to work, during the course, with colleagues who are exploring painful memories. A certain level of professional skill and sensitivity has to be assumed if this kind of interaction is to occur safely and ethically. It is assumed also that applicants for the course have already developed self-awareness to a level consistent with an informed decision that they want to take part in this kind of training (see 'Voluntary and Active Participation').

Many of the exercises involve skilled listening and responding. The programme includes two longer opportunities for participants to role-play. These enable participants to practise and evaluate their ability to cope with emotionally challenging material in a safe and supportive environment. A text by Van Ments (1983) includes a helpful chapter on role-play.

Trainers should be prepared to role-play in front of the group by way of example. This enables participants new to the technique to see what is required when adopting the 'counsellor', 'client' and 'observer' roles. Trainers can use this opportunity also to demonstrate how to give and receive feedback, and the importance of 'de-roling'. Details are included in **LP 3.5** (Section 2). The handout **PM 16: Guidelines for counselling practice** (Section 4) will help participants to practise these skills later.

Section 4 of the manual includes some examples of role-play scenarios. But the most effective are those devised by participants, based on their own experiences. A session is included for this on day 2. The relevant lesson plan (**LP 2.5**) is detailed, because this session presents a formidable organizational challenge. Alternatively, participants can be invited to undertake a homework assignment at the end of day 2 with the help of **PM 10: How to write a role-play**. People can choose to not role-play their own scenarios, but nevertheless place them into a common pool for others to use.

Even when people have chosen to work on issues that are not their own, elements of the emotional spectrum aroused can touch on personal pain and sensitivities. Trainers need to be alert to this and be ready to offer support if, *but only if*, it appears that a person needs it.

At the end of the first session of extended role-play (**LP 3.6**), feedback often includes some painful acknowledgement of inadequately developed skills, as participants compare their efforts with those of more practiced colleagues. This is a good time to introduce and distribute **PM 17: Experiential learning progression**.

## TRAINERS HAVE NEEDS, TOO

Part of looking after oneself is to identify needs and take appropriate steps to meet them. Trainers need skills learned in counselling and in working with groups. If they are to be effective, these skills have to be developed continuously. Their use challenges every aspect of our humanity. Trainers' needs are many; and they vary depending on the individual's experiences.

If one is planning to facilitate a course, the first step must be to negotiate the time and resources that will be needed. Time will be required for reading and for exploring audio-visual resources. Those with limited experience in using experiential methods, or with group work, may want to:

- participate in appropriate training
- arrange to be a co-trainer on another course
- invite a more experienced colleague to co-train with them.

What follows are suggestions on how facilitators may maintain and improve skills before, during and between courses.

### Maintaining and improving skills

1.  Negotiate with one or two colleagues who have counselling skills to spend a specified amount of time each month co-counselling. The time might be divided so that each person has, for example, half an hour to talk about issues concerning them, while the other (or others) supports and responds. A final ten minutes could be reserved for discussion and feedback to 'listeners' and 'counsellors' about the effectiveness (or otherwise) of their techniques. This structure helps to keep skills well honed; it is supportive because it relieves stress.

2.  Attend an occasional weekend workshop on massage, aromatherapy, meditation – or any of the other nurturing skills which interest you. If you decide later, as a facilitator, to offer these skills to a training group, it should be in the spirit of sharing an interest, rather than as an expert practitioner.

3.  Complete the **Group skills checklist (FM 1)** before the course. Select one or two aspects that you need to develop and concentrate on these during the course. At the end of the course, re-evaluate yourself on all items, with particular attention to those that you identified before the course.

4.  Seek the group's consent to tape a session and from the recording evaluate your skills. Listening to the recording is likely to reveal unexpected strengths and weaknesses in your facilitation skills. Be sure to identify both.

5.  At the end of each course-day, complete the **Daily record form (FM 2)** together with your co-trainer(s). Then spend 15–20 minutes comparing and discussing your different perceptions. This allows facilitators to:

    - summarize the day's events
    - clear up differing perceptions of events on a daily basis, as they occur
    - provide supportive and constructive feedback, thus generating trust between trainers

- make adjustments to the programme for the following day.

6. Invite other trainers to join you in a trainers' support group. The group will need to define its aims and functions. Someone with advanced skills might be invited to lead a weekend workshop.

### The 'Alter Ego Game'

Brandes and Ginnes (1986) have several helpful suggestions for trainers. Here is one which you might find useful:

| | |
|---|---|
| **Aims** | • To evaluate a trainer's work. |
| | • To enhance self-awareness. |
| **What you need** | A trusted co-trainer with a paper and pencil. |
| **What you do** | 1. Choose a suitable session in which your colleague is free to observe. |
| | 2. Your colleague observes the session, or a part of it, and writes down what she thinks your unspoken thoughts are. |
| | 3. At the end of the session or day, your colleague shows you her notes and you discuss these. |

## PRACTICAL STEPS IN COURSE PLANNING

### Sharing the planning

Having at least two trainers makes trainers feel more secure, and thus enhances the learning experiences of both participants and trainers. It is important, however, that the trainers discuss their possibly varying approaches to teaching before the course, to accommodate differences. An exercise (**FM 3: Co-trainer dialogue**) might help.

### Choosing a venue

The course should not be close to participants' work places. This avoids the temptation to 'pop in' to the ward or office to help over-stretched colleagues. Such extra-curricula activity can distress participants and distract them from the business of the course.

Minimum requirements for the venue are:

- available public transport, adequate parking facilities and wheelchair accessibility
- a well-heated and ventilated room, away from unscreened windows overlooking busy corridors
- enough space in the room to accommodate a circle of chairs to seat the expected participants and to ensure aural privacy during small-group, paired and triad activities
- comfortable chairs, since people will spend much of the time sitting
- carpeted floors, for warmth during relaxation
- adequate and accessible toilet facilities

- on-site catering facilities for refreshment in breaks
- access to a telephone
- an ambience that takes account of the need for privacy and the absence of noise
- sufficient small rooms for the afternoons of days 3 and 4. You might need to negotiate for their use more often if groups are divided for separate sessions on other days.

If possible, there should also be:

- access to a garden or nearby park
- photocopying facilities
- on-site, or nearby, catering facilities with provision for meals and special diets.

## Publicizing the course

Advertisements should be placed in appropriate journals. Ewles and Simnet (1985), in their chapter on 'Using and producing health education materials', provide a useful guide on how to produce effective 'flyers'.

Information in pre-course handouts should include:

- name and dates of the course*
- the type of course, teaching and learning methods, and its aims
- venue address and telephone number
- name, address, telephone number and designation of the organizer(s)*
- name, address and telephone number for further information, if different from the above*
- costs
- pre-requisite training for applicants
- for whom the course is designed*
- the importance to participants of themselves choosing to attend
- who will be the trainers.*

Information marked * could form the basis of flyers. These can be distributed to appropriate contact persons, together with the handout and application form.

## Application forms

Application forms should be kept simple.

Information on the form about the course should include:

- name, dates and venue of the course
- number of places available
- name, address and telephone/fax numbers of organizer(s)
- a reminder to the applicant to read the accompanying pre-course information before completing and submitting the application form
- closing date for applications.

27

Information required from applicants should include:

- name, address and telephone number
- nature of work, where employed, position, work place address and telephone number
- summary of counselling training and experience, and any previous group-work learning
- areas of special interest to the applicant
- date of application.

One could also include a short declaration, requiring a signature, which states that participants have read the pre-course information before completing the application form. This is intended as a stimulus and support for applicants, to help them ensure that they receive all the information they need.

## Timing and circulation of advertising materials

Send several copies of publicity material to training officers or other appropriate persons in organizations where your potential participants will be found. Ideally, this material should arrive approximately six weeks before the course date, with a closing date for applications set for three weeks before the course date.

## Constructing the programme

The following framework is intended to help you to construct the programme.
Based on the broad aims of the course (see p.2) define specific objectives:

- arrange the specific objectives in a logical sequence
- choose a learning strategy or strategies by which you will achieve each aim
- produce a skeleton programme, indicating starting, finishing, meal and break times.

Elaborate the skeleton programme, taking account of:

- stages in building the learning environment (pp.62–68)
- the elements of the course (pp.50–56)
- looking after ourselves (pp.54–56)
- the need for variety, and for extra stimulation following lunch.

Leave some unprogrammed sessions to accommodate participants' choices.

## Selecting and notifying participants

Soon after the closing date, meet with your colleague(s) to review the applications. It seems fair to accept people on a 'first come first served' basis, but you have to exclude people who do not provide evidence of existing counselling skills.

Send a letter to all successful applicants, to arrive two weeks before the start of the course. Try to make it as warm and welcoming as possible. This reflects the learning climate which you aim to build. It must also include the following essential information:

- A brief description of the venue, with details of available transport routes. A map will be helpful. This information is often included in the venue's own publicity leaflet.

- If there are special facilities, for example an on-site swimming pool, encourage those who might be interested to come prepared.

- If you wish, enclose a reading list for general interest. Stress that there is no required pre-course reading.

Draw attention to the starting time, and point out that the programme is flexible, with some scope for changes. Enclose a further copy of the pre-course information, and ask participants to re-read this before the course.

Do *not* provide a list of participants at this stage (see p.9).

Training officers or managers appreciate it if a course package is sent to them, for information. Send one also to the administrator of the venue.

Applicants who have not been offered places can be offered a place on your waiting list for future courses. If refusal was because of inadequate counselling training, it is helpful to offer appropriate suggestions.

## Equipment and materials

You may decide to take some items with you. Others may be available at the venue, either included in the cost of hiring or for an extra charge.

Arrange ahead of time that any unwanted furniture is removed from the room. Two or three long tables are useful, to hold equipment, books and handouts. In addition you will need:

- at least one, preferably two, flip-chart stands with pads
- a notice board for newspaper cuttings and journal articles
- poster-pens, in various colours
- clip boards (or ask participants to bring their own)
- extra paper and pens
- 'blutac' or poster putty, and drawing pins
- scissors and 'Sellotape'
- an overhead projector and transparencies (optional)
- a portable audio cassette player
- a video recorder/player
- audio and video cassettes
- art materials (a generous supply of coloured pencils and any other aids with which you are familiar and comfortable, and which are suited to your plans)
- name badges or labels.

It is usually more economical and convenient to photocopy learning and other materials in advance. They will include:

- handouts for individual study
- handouts of exercises
- the list of participants.

Arrange for a selection of books, and a folder containing photocopies of relevant journal articles, to be available. (Keep a record of who is borrowing the books.) If there is an on-site library, librarians are usually co-operative in producing at least lists, and sometimes displays, of relevant books. However, they need to be notified well in advance. Relevant audio and video material also adds to the variety of choices available to people who decide to opt out of a particular session.

## Final planning

A few days before the course, check with your co-trainer(s) on the following points:

- You should be clear on who is making arrangements to prepare the main room. If staff at the venue are not available to do this, then it is worthwhile going in the evening before to do it yourself. It is difficult to begin to create a supportive learning environment if the arrangement of the room is inappropriate and unwelcoming.

- All the learning materials should have been photocopied and assembled, with the handouts for the first day readily available.

- You have agreed which of you will welcome the participants, and how.

- You are confident that the venue will be welcoming, with flowers or plants to cheer up the room, if necessary.

- If you plan to collate participants' evaluations after the course, decide which of you will do this, and by when.

- You need to arrange a date for a meeting to review the course, after participants' evaluations have been processed.

## Reviewing the course

Allow two weeks to elapse before this meeting with co-facilitators. The evaluations will help recall of events, and the time gap may increase objectivity. You may want to make decisions on:

- What action, if any, is required to meet the additional learning needs expressed by participants.

- What adjustments may be necessary to the existing course.

- Who will get copies of the evaluations: participants only or also training officers? (The latter only with prior agreement of participants.)

- What thank-you letters need to be written, and who will write them.

# PART 2

# Course Programme and Lesson Plans

This section is arranged in seven parts. The first five provide some introductory remarks and programmes, and a series of lesson plans for each of the five days of the course. The sixth part contains corresponding material for the follow-up day. Part seven consists of nine additional lesson plans that facilitators may wish to use. The lesson plans are identified by a simple notation. (For example, LP 4.2 is the second lesson plan for day 4; LP F.3 the third for the follow-up day; and ALP.1 is the first of the additional lesson plans.)

The first lesson plan on each day provides material for introducing the day's work. The second lesson plan for any one day describes a centring exercise. The last is always concerned with 'looking after ourselves', involving some sort of relaxation or massage.

The lesson plans presented here were all developed in response to points raised by participants in previous courses. One issue that was mentioned occasionally, but which is not included in this manual, is suicide. We felt that the standardized structure for lesson plans, as used here, would not provide helpful support for trainers who might want to include this topic specifically as part of a course. However, trainers who expect to be asked to deal with the problem should ensure that they are familiar with, and have available, the British Association for Counselling's *Code of Ethics and Practice for Counsellors* (British Association for Counselling 1993). Participants who raise the issue may be referred to the section on suicide in Bond (1995).

# DAY I

On the first day of the course, feelings of excitement, anticipation and anxiety are likely to be high. Be ready and centred, so that you can welcome people on their arrival without feeling disempowered by any anxieties which your own feelings may cause you. Some fresh flowers or plants and relaxed music can help to create a welcoming atmosphere.

As participants are likely to be emotionally charged, it is important to start with a low level of challenge and to balance this with adequate support (see Figure 1.1). Sessions are relatively short, and there is a variety of learning methods. The 'Getting to know each other' exercise (**LP 1.3**) may be quite challenging for some, but it moves quickly and this helps to limit the depth at which it is experienced. It also serves as a preparation for the theme of the second day. The most challenging exercise is 'The grieving process' (**LP 1.6**). This, too, is kept short, to limit the emotional depth at which people experience it. The day ends gently with 'paired support' (**LP 1.8**) and a simple massage (**LP 1.9**).

## Programme for day I

| | |
|---|---|
| 9.30 a.m. | Welcome and introductions |
| 10.15 a.m. | COFFEE |
| 10.45 a.m. | Centring |
| 10.55 a.m. | Getting to know each other |
| 11.30 a.m. | Sharing expectations (work-sheet) |
| 12.30 p.m. | LUNCH |
| 1.30 p.m. | What do we mean by loss? (brainstorm) |
| 1.45 p.m. | The grieving process |
| 2.15 p.m. | Responses to loss – feelings and self-awareness |
| 2.50 p.m. | TEA |
| 3.10 p.m. | Responses to loss (continued) |
| 3.30 p.m. | Paired support |
| 4.00 p.m. | Looking after ourselves and summarizing the day |
| 4.30 p.m. | FINISH |

**Lesson plans for day I**

## LIVING THROUGH LOSS LESSON PLAN     LP 1.1

| | |
|---|---|
| **Title** | Welcome and introductions |
| **Time** | 9.30 a.m. |
| **Timing** | 45 minutes |

**Aims**

- Welcome people to the course.
- Begin the process of getting to know each other.
- Share information about the structure, content, methods and philosophy of the course.
- Clarify practical arrangements.

**What you need**  Name badges and marker pens.

- Spare copies of course information and programmes.
- A list of participants.
- Participants' materials (see Section 4): **PM 1: Professional and ethical Guidelines**.

**What you do**

1. Greet people on arrival and invite them to:

    (a) write a name badge for themselves

    (b) tick off their name on the list of participants.

2. If you decide to wait a few minutes for late comers, let the group know of this decision. (A delay of more than five minutes can cause problems.) As late comers arrive, take time to acknowledge and welcome them, and ask for a volunteer in the group to take responsibility for supplying them, during the coffee break, with information which they have missed.

3. Introduce a 'name round', for example: *'My name and why I was given it'* or *'My name and how I am feeling right now'*. Rounds involving occupation or professional status are avoided. It is helpful for people to be aware of how they, as individuals, respond to and feel about issues and situations, rather than how they, as professionals, 'should' feel or respond.

4. You may now wish to give information on:

    (a) *Practical arrangements*. For example: eating arrangements, refreshment breaks, starting and finishing times, telephone number of the venue, site of public call boxes and toilets and the importance of individuals letting the group know if they are delayed or unable to attend. Draw attention to any special features of the venue such as gardens, swimming pool or library. Remind people to bring a blanket and pillow for relaxation.

(b) *An outline of the course.* For example: learning methods, provision of handouts, expectations regarding home reading, course evaluation. Programmes and course information may be distributed to those who have not received them.

(c) *Ground rules.* For example: confidentiality, accepting mistakes for their learning value; balancing taking risks with taking care of oneself; the right to opt out of activities; taking responsibility for one's own learning; progressing at one's own pace and respecting the right of others to do likewise; time and personal boundaries, for example, trainers may not wish to be available over lunch time.

Distribute and discuss **PM 1**. Emphasize that this key handout should be kept available and referred to throughout the course.

(d) *What to wear.* People are free to wear whatever is comfortable for them, bearing in mind the nature of some of the activities (for example, relaxation, exercise, massage).

Trainers take turns to introduce various sections, inviting suggestions, responses and questions as they proceed. Encourage and accept expressions of anxiety about the course or resentment from those who have been 'sent', as opposed to choosing to come. Time for further discussion on issues raised will be available later (**LP 1.4**). Try to keep all discussion of issues within the group. This encourages the group to take responsibility, and individuals to feel responsibility to the group.

(Adapted from Jacobsen and Mackinnon 1989)

# LIVING THROUGH LOSS LESSON PLAN          LP 1.2

| | |
|---|---|
| **Title** | Centring |
| **Time** | 10.45 a.m. |
| **Timing** | 8 to 10 minutes |
| **Aims** | • Provide participants with a simple way to look after themselves. |
| | • Introduce them to a way of learning from themselves, about themselves. |
| | • Help participants to prepare to give their full attention to each other, by clearing their minds of the various other competing demands for attention. |
| **What you need** | A centring script (see example below or one of your own choice). |
| **What you do** | 1. Briefly introduce the concept of centring as a mini-meditation; outline the aims, as above. Acknowledge that there is likely to be a certain amount of reservation and anxious anticipation on the first morning. This activity might be new to some people, and some will be resistant to committing themselves to it. Remind people that they should only do what feels comfortable for them, but also encourage them to take risks within their own boundaries. Check that everybody can put their feet on the ground. Short people may need one or two books under their feet so that they can ground themselves. |
| | 2. Read out the script below, speaking fairly slowly and allowing pauses in the appropriate places. Try to keep a reasonable amount of variation in the range and rhythm of your voice. (Monotones can be very soporific.) |

CENTRING SCRIPT

Note: the numbers in brackets, for example (4), are guides to the number of seconds' pause.

*Sit comfortably with your seat to the back of your chair and your back well supported; feet flat on the floor. It is a good idea to take off your shoes if you are wearing high heels.*

*Place your hands on your knees, palms up or down, whichever is the most comfortable. If your chair has arms, you might want to rest your hands and arms there.*

*Now, only if it feels comfortable for you, close your eyes. Don't force yourself, it is quite alright to leave them open and let them go out of focus.*

*Let your head tilt forward a little, and breathe easily and regularly. (8) Take your mind to this morning as you got up. How did you feel? (4) Excited? Anxious? Resentful? Curious? What were those feelings connected with: (3) home? work? this course? Concentrate on the negative feelings for a few seconds and confirm that was the way you felt. (10)*

*If the feelings were not connected with this course, push them aside for the time being. You might want to keep open an option to talk with someone about them, while you are on the course. The choice is yours. (6)*

*If they were connected with the course, note your negative feelings and see if you can find some time to share them with someone today. Meanwhile, push them aside so that they don't get in your way. (6)*

*Think of the positive feelings that you had and try to recreate these for yourself. Savour them for a few seconds, like good food, (4) hold on to those feelings. Look on them as nourishment.(6)*

*Think of your journey here. How was it? Was it through stressful, rush hour traffic? Did you have trouble finding the venue? Were you anxious about being late? (4)*

*Acknowledge those feelings (4) and let them go.*

*You may have had a brisk walk through pleasant surroundings, in the sunshine. Recreate the good sensations that went with that (4) and keep them with you.*

*How about when you arrived here? (4) What did it feel like, meeting new people, old colleagues? Allow yourself those feelings, the comfortable and the uncomfortable ones. You may be able to make use of them more creatively if you acknowledge them than if you try to suppress them.(6)*

*Concentrate on this room now,(4) on the sounds around you,(4) and the fragments of thoughts going through your mind.(8)*

*How easy has it been to stay with the exercise so far? Are you aware of interrupting or blocking the process of the exercise? How are you doing this? Is it by dismissing it? Labelling it? Ridiculing it? (6) What else?*

*Be aware of these blocking techniques you use. You might find it useful to list them for yourself, later. It is likely that you also use these to block contact with others in some other situations. This is valuable information for you to have about yourself if you are working in counselling-type relationships. (10)*

*Now take your attention to yourself. Be aware of your breathing, of any squeaks or gurgles your tummy is making. (4) Can you feel your heart beating or pulsation in some part of your body? Are you aware of areas of tension in your body? (10) Stay with yourself a few moments.(30)*

*How easy was it for you to do that? Did you notice any of the blocking techniques we spoke of just now, keeping you from staying in contact with yourself? Take a little longer.(20–30)*

*Now, taking your time (4) deepen your breathing, (4) open your eyes and, if you wish, have a stretch and a yawn.*

(Adapted from Jacobsen and Mackinnon 1989)

# LIVING THROUGH LOSS LESSON PLAN     LP 1.3

**Title**            Getting to know each other

**Time**             10.55 a.m.

**Timing**           35 minutes

**Aims**
- To help people identify themselves with their origins.
- To share this view of themselves with other group members.
- Active listening.

**What you need**
- Plain paper.
- Coloured pencils or pastels. (You may have asked people to provide their own.)
- Plenty of floor space.

**What you do**

1. Ask participants to draw a picture of themselves and their family when they were five years old or at the earliest age they can remember. This can be a representation of a family photograph or of a memorable event. Emphasize that this is not a test of drawing ability and that stick figures are acceptable. Time: 15 minutes.

2. When the pictures are finished, each person looks around for another and they share their pictures with each other.

3. When a pair have finished sharing, they join another pair. We will call the first pair *A* and *B* and the second pair *C* and *D*. *A* introduces *B's* picture, indicating *C* as the person of the new pair who will pay special attention, so that she will be able to reproduce the story in the next stage of the exercise. *B* introduces *A's* story, indicating *D* to reproduce it similarly. *C* and *D* repeat this process with *A* and *B*.

4. When the fours are ready to move on, they join another four. Each person briefly introduces the story of one of their group of four to the larger group. Time for stages 2 to 4: 20 minutes.

5. Ask the large group to re-assemble and invite feedback on the experience of the activity. What similarities? What differences? What surprises?

(Adapted from Williams and Lockley 1989)

# LIVING THROUGH LOSS LESSON PLAN       LP 1.4

| | |
|---|---|
| **Title** | Sharing expectations |
| **Time** | 11.30 a.m. |
| **Timing** | 1 hour |

**Aims**

- For people to acknowledge to themselves their wants, hopes and fears about the course.
- For people to share what they choose of these feelings with a small group.
- For the groups to record their responses.
- For course facilitators to reply, clarifying the extent to which it will be realistic for the course to meet the expectations.
- For people to have a reference point, or 'course contract', for subsequent evaluation of the week's activities.

**What you need  PM 2: Sharing expectations worksheet.**

- Flip-chart paper and marker pens.
- 'Blutack' or poster putty.

**What you do**

1. Outline the aims of the activity.

2. Ask people to get into four groups. Offer to help. At this stage your offer will most likely be accepted.

   *Getting people into groups*

   For a group of 18 people, go around the circle giving each person a number (1,2,3,4) or a colour (violet, indigo, blue, green) or a name (tinker, tailor, soldier, sailor). Then ask people to get into groups with those of the same number (1s, 2s, and so on) or the same colour (violets, indigos, and so on) or the same names (tinkers, tailors, and so on) You should find that you have four groups: two of four people and two of five people. (If you want more or fewer groups, increase or restrict the numbers/colours/names. For example, six numbers for six groups or three names for three groups.) Facilitators form a group of their own.

3. Ask people to spend five minutes filling in the worksheet individually. Make it clear that this is private and that they need only share what they choose with the group.

4. Ask people to pool their ideas with others in their group, with a view to making a group poster under the headings:

    - what we want
    - what we don't want
    - resources we bring

    If you are planning to fill in some sessions with subjects requested by participants, ask them to include their suggestions under the 'what we want' heading.

    *Remind them to write their names on the bottom of their poster. They will review this collectively before evaluating the course on day 5.*

    Go from group to group reminding people that they have 15 minutes for this. Time for steps one to four: 35 minutes.

5. Ask people to display their posters and for a volunteer from each group to give a two minute summary of the most important aspects of their discussion.

6. What follows is important, first because it encourages facilitators to look after themselves, and second because it serves as an example to participants of how not to endorse clients' unrealistic expectations. If requests have been made that cannot be fulfilled within the scope of the course, then this should be stated clearly at this stage. For example: an expectation that, as a result of the course, people want '*to feel secure when working with clients who are suicidal*'. Such security comes from self-awareness, development of skills, and experience over time. There is no short cut, and it would be grandiose of trainers to suggest that they can provide one.

    Frequently, people's 'don't wants' include not wanting to feel vulnerable, distressed or exposed. It is important to make clear that this cannot be guaranteed by the facilitators. This is because:

    (a) People bring to the course pain and grief, of which they may or may not be consciously aware. No one can predict how or when this might be triggered.

    (b) Participants themselves have the responsibility to stay aware of, and to set, their own safety boundaries. If a memory is triggered for them, it is supportive to encourage them to trust the wisdom of their subconscious 'gut reaction', that this is, or is not, the right time for them to deal with it. It is up to individuals to decide if this is the right place.

    (c) If pain is triggered for some people, the aim should be to make the group a safe and supportive environment in which to learn how to begin to work through the pain.

    (d) This experience can be valuable learning, and help participants to feel less vulnerable when they are alongside others who are grieving.

7.    Refer again to **PM 1**, where many of the above points are discussed.

8.    If further suggestions have been made for course safety guidelines, these should be collected on a flip-chart paper and displayed in a prominent place for the duration of the course.

9.    When subjects have been suggested for sessions, ask if someone in the group has a special interest or knowledge of this; invite the person concerned to co-facilitate the session. Subjects which are outside the experience of the facilitators can be offered as discussion sessions. Pooling the group's knowledge in this way can be very satisfying.

10.  Tell the group that you will work on incorporating their suggestions into the programme and present your suggestions the next day.

11.  Invite people to take a quick stretch and move about a little before the next exercise.

# LIVING THROUGH LOSS LESSON PLAN LP 1.5

| | |
|---|---|
| **Title** | What do we mean by loss? |
| **Time** | 1.30 p.m. |
| **Timing** | 15 minutes |
| **Aims** | • For people to share their perception of loss and grieving. |
| | • Energizing |
| | • To generate as many ideas as possible in a short time. |
| **What you need** | Flip-chart and marker pens. |

**What you do**

1.   Outline the aims of the activity.

2.   Outline the rules of brainstorming.

*Brainstorming rules*

Invite ideas, from the group, in the form of short phrases or single words.

These are written down verbatim on the flip-chart. Every contribution is accepted and no one comments on them. Lateral thinking is welcome and often stimulates a burst of new ideas. The collaborative nature of this activity helps in the process of forming the group.

3.   You may wish to invite a volunteer to scribe for the group.

4.   When no further ideas are offered, invite comments and observations on the scope of the ideas generated.

## LIVING THROUGH LOSS LESSON PLAN    LP 1.6

| | |
|---|---|
| **Title** | The grieving process |
| **Time** | 1.45 p.m. |
| **Timing** | 30 minutes |

**Aims**

- To provide an opportunity for people to focus on a loss of their choice, and to identify the thoughts, feelings and physical sensations which accompanied that experience.

**What you need**

- Each person needs a notebook or paper and pencil or pen.
- Enough space for people to feel private, while remaining together in the same room.

**What you do**

1. Outline the aim of the activity. Tell people that it is in several parts, and that you will guide them through it. The following example might be used to illustrate re-experiencing a loss in the present:

   *'I am in John Lewis' and I am choosing a new coat. I really like this one. It is scarlet with fur trimmings, and I look very elegant in it. Now I am accompanying the sales assistant to the cash desk. I will have to pay by credit card, as this coat is expensive. I am reaching for my bag and I am surprised to find it open....'*

2. Ask people to choose a partner, and make it clear that they will not work with their partner until the end of the exercise.

3. Invite people to find a space and sit comfortably as for centring.

4. Briefly centre the group and read the following script.

   *Centring script – experiencing loss*

   Note: The numbers in brackets, for example (4), are a guide to the length of the pauses, in seconds.

   *If you are willing, close your eyes, or otherwise let your eyes go out of focus. Make sure that your feet are firmly on the ground. Slow down your breathing and breathe so that as you breathe in your belly expands, and as you breathe out, it falls. You do not need to inhale any deeper than normal.*

*Repeat this breathing for five or six breaths, concentrating fully on your inhalation and exhalation. (20)*

*Allow a loss that you have experienced to come into your awareness. Try not to censor yourself. If you are willing, risk working with the first thing that comes into your mind. You will not be expected to share this, although you may choose to do so.*

*Maintain your breathing, and spend a few minutes reliving that loss as if it is happening to you now. I will indicate to you when we will move on. (20) Now, focus on what your thoughts are as you re-experience this event. (60)*

*Hold on to the thoughts which you identified, while we move on to next stage of the exercise. Make sure that your breathing is still rhythmic and relaxed, and that your feet are firmly on the ground.*

*Staying with your loss experience, or recreating it if it has faded, (10) this time focus on the feelings you are having associated with the experience. (60)*

*Hold on to the feelings which you have identified. Check your breathing and make sure your feet are still well grounded, stay with your loss (10) and this time focus on the physical sensations which accompany that loss. (60)*

*Allow yourself to let go of the scene of your loss and be aware of your present surroundings in this room, (10) open your eyes (10) and, without making eye contact with anyone, take time to note down the thoughts, feelings and physical sensations that you became aware of during that exercise.*

*(Pause for five minutes).*

5.  Ask people to join their partners and to share with them:

    (a)  how easy it was for them to think of an example

    (b)  what were their thoughts, feelings and physical sensations

    (c)  how easy did they find the exercise (five minutes).

    Make it clear that people are not expected to share their story, although some may choose to do so.

6.  Ask people to 'de-role' each other by each stating to the other something like: *'That experience happened...years ago. I lived through it, and now it is 199...it is behind me. Something which I have achieved since, about which I feel really proud (happy, excited) is...'.*

7.  Invite large-group feedback.

(Adapted from Fisher and Warman 1990)

Note: This activity has been adapted to be conducted as a group centring exercise. The advantage of this is that facilitators can observe participants and offer support if people become distressed. Trainers use it as a supportive tool, to help people to monitor their breathing and grounding, and to learn that this is a way of supporting themselves when in distress.

In its original form, the exercise gives all the instructions to individuals; they can then do the exercise alone, in private. This is an alternative that you may want to try.

# LIVING THROUGH LOSS LESSON PLAN    LP 1.7

**Title**    Responses to loss – feelings and self-awareness

**Time**    2.15 p.m.

**Timing**    35 minutes; 20 minute break; further 20 minutes

**Aims**
- To enable people to identify aspects of self-awareness.
- To enable people to appreciate the relevance of self-care when working with the bereaved.
- To help people to identify emotions and appreciate their effect.

**What you need**
- **PM 3: Johari window** and **PM 4: Feelings: their purpose and distortions.**
- **FM 4: Johari window trainers' guide** and **FM 5: Feelings: their purpose and distortions.**
- Prepared flip-chart or overhead projector transparencies of the above. Individuals will need a notebook and pen or pencil.
- Flip-chart or overhead projector or both, and appropriate pens.

**What you do**
1. Using the prepared flip-chart diagram or transparency, introduce or remind people of the concepts represented by the Johari window (five minutes).

2. Ask participants to talk informally ('buzz') in groups of two or three, about the sort of feelings which were considered to be 'bad', 'unacceptable' or 'shameful' in their families (five minutes).

3. Ask groups to give one example each and note these on the flip-chart until all examples are exhausted. For each example, ask if other groups also had that, and tick the example an appropriate number of times (five minutes).

4. Using a prepared flip-chart, or transparency of the 'Feelings' handout (**PM 4**), give a mini-lecture on this material. Take care to reveal sections one at a time. The group can be distracted and lose focus if too much material is revealed at once (ten minutes).

5. Ask for people's response to the idea that feelings, even the ones which we may have been accustomed to think of as 'bad', might have a positive function. Where might they reside in the Johari window?

   If any of the following points do not arise from group discussion, then they can be made by the trainers:

(a) by labelling feelings as 'bad', one is likely to deny or suppress them

(b) the feelings labelled 'bad' may be concealed in our 'hidden self' or buried in our 'unconscious self'

(c) there they are liable to be triggered by issues and emotions expressed by clients

(d) this is the hidden or suppressed knowledge which causes us to feel vulnerable and fearful when we know that we are likely to be in the presence of strong emotion

(e) if we remain in this state of fear we are likely: i) to be ineffective with clients, because we will avoid using skills which will release strong emotions (and it is from emotional release that our clients gain most benefit); and ii) to suffer severe stress with all its consequences.

An important point to make, and to repeat whenever relevant, is that there is nothing wrong with feeling vulnerable. On the whole, people seem to see this as a weakness. But vulnerability is an aspect and expression of our humanity; our capacity to feel. As such, it is a major asset when working with people in pain (five to ten minutes).

*Take a 20 minute break before proceeding.*

The following two activities, numbered a) and b), are alternatives; only one is feasible in the time available for the remainder of this exercise. Choose which (if either) you wish to use. Alternatively, you can offer both and let pairs or triads of participants choose.

6. Introduction to activity

People sometimes choose their occupation so as to meet unfulfilled needs. Paradoxically, some people choose occupations to *avoid* recognizing unfulfilled needs. For example, often we do for others what we would dearly like someone to do for us; but somehow nobody ever does it. One may or may not be conscious of this.

(a) Working with a partner, share your ideas about why it is important to look at yourself and your responses to your own losses. Make notes of the points raised between you.

(b) Take a little time, alone or together, reflecting on your professional role:

(i) What do you get out of it?

(ii) What needs of yours does it meet that are not met adequately elsewhere in your life?

(iii) How does it help you to continue avoiding or ignoring you own needs?

Jot down your answers. These are private (15 minutes).

(Adapted from Fisher and Warman 1990)

## LIVING THROUGH LOSS LESSON PLAN   LP 1.8

| | |
|---|---|
| **Title** | Paired support |
| **Time** | 3.30 p.m. |
| **Timing** | 30 minutes |

**Aims**

- To provide an opportunity for participants to experience receiving and giving support with one other person.
- To provide a forum to process the day's experiences and 'dump unfinished business'.

**What you need**

- A room or rooms to enable people to talk in privacy. If the weather is fine, one could take a walk in a garden or park.

**What you do**

1. Outline the aims of the exercise. Explain that this is a very simple version of co-counselling, something that might be pursued after the course. (See subsection on counselling in 'Further reading', Section 5.)

2. Ask everyone to choose a partner with whom they would like to share support for the duration of the course. For some, a preference might be for someone previously unknown to them. Others might want to work with a known colleague, with whom they might choose to continue sharing after the course.

3. Remind people that an important part of the contract between them is that each takes an equal share of the time.

4. Suggest that person *A* takes 10–12 minutes to 'share', while person *B* uses active listening skills. At the end of this time, *A* gives three to five minutes' feedback to *B* on the skills which she found supportive and the interventions that were not supportive. The process is then reversed, with *B* sharing and *A* listening.

5. Ask participants to be back in the room by 4.00 p.m.

# LIVING THROUGH LOSS LESSON PLAN    LP 1.9

**Title**        Looking after ourselves and summarizing the day

**Time**        4.00 p.m.

**Timing**     30 minutes

**Aims**
- To provide an opportunity for people to accept a nurturing touch from a colleague.
- To provide an opportunity for a quick evaluation of the day.

**What you need**
- Space for a circle of chairs for half the group.
- Some soothing music (optional).
- **PM 5: Constructive use of feedback** and **PM 6: Looking after ourselves.**

**What you do**
1. Outline the aims of the exercise.
2. Ask everyone to take a partner; a good choice might be their 'paired support'.
3. One partner sits in a chair and the other stands behind the chair. Both should make sure that they can see the demonstrator. Pairs change over half way through, so that each has a turn at giving and receiving.
4. Remind people that they should keep their feet grounded and concentrate on regular 'belly breathing'. This applies to givers and receivers. Those standing should keep their knees softly unlocked. Continue using the following instructions for 'Simple Massage':

    *Snowflakes*

    *Using all your fingers, tap across your partner's shoulders very lightly, like falling snowflakes. You might start at one side and tap across to the other, or you might start at each shoulder tip and move towards the middle and out again. You can try both, or tap randomly, letting your hands roam where they will, in a six inch strip from the top of the shoulders down. Check with your partner what feels best for her/him (one minute).*

    *Raindrops*

    *Again using all fingers, tap harder, like rain falling. Your partner can tell you whether she prefers a gentle shower or monsoon rain. Remind about breathing (one minute).*

*Galloping Hooves*

*Cup your hands slightly and use them in this position to patter or gallop across your partner's shoulders (one minute).*

*Brush strokes*

*Using the flat of your hands, brush them over your partner's shoulders. Partners, give guidance as to how firmly you want this done (one minute).*

*Miss Jenkin's chop*

*Using the side of your hands and using a chopping action, move across your partner's shoulders. Vary your speed and pressure as your partner asks you. A favourite place to concentrate your attention is at the base of the neck. Make sure your partner keeps you right (one minute).*

*Invite partners to discuss how each of these methods felt. The 'giver' then provides an extra two minutes of the 'receiver's' favourite stroke.*

*This cycle takes about ten minutes, after which time the partners change places and the exercise is repeated.*

5. Invite participants to evaluate the day briefly, using the following two sentence-completion rounds. Remind them that they have the right to pass.

   *'The thing that I resented most today was…'.*

   *'The thing that I appreciated most today was…'.*

6. Distribute **PM 5: Constructive use of feedback** and **PM 6: Looking after ourselves**. Ask that these be read before the next day. Close the day.

# DAY 2

By day 2, people begin to respond to the level of support that they experienced on day 1. Trust is beginning to build, so that challenge can now be increased.

The morning's activities focus on the origins, in childhood, of much emotional pain, and on the coping mechanisms. The reading exercise (**PM 7: The hidden child**) can make powerful connections for some, but because it is presented as a reading exercise, and is therefore processed at an intellectual level, the emotional depth at which it is experienced is limited. Sad or happy memories might affect some people deeply; they may be encouraged to stay with memories, rather than move on to the next exercise ('What is child abuse?').

Writing role-plays also draws on personal experiences, but people can choose the depth to which they wish to commit themselves to this.

The day winds down with paired support and the giving and receiving of a more complex massage. This sustains the level of nurturing.

Remember that anyone who opts out can be offered books, journal articles or relevant videos as alternatives.

## Programme for day 2

| | |
|---|---|
| 9.30 a.m. | Introduction to the day<br>Learning review |
| 9.45 a.m. | Centring |
| 9.50 a.m. | The hidden child (reading)* |
| 10.30 a.m. | COFFEE |
| 11.00 a.m. | Recalling our 'hidden child'* |
| 12.15 a.m. | Large-group feedback |
| 12.30 p.m. | LUNCH |
| 1.30 p.m. | Writing role-plays in threes |
| 2.45 p.m. | TEA |
| 3.00 p.m. | Paired support |
| 3.30 p.m. | Looking after ourselves (head and neck massage)*<br>Summarizing the day |
| 4.30 p.m. | FINISH |

Note: Sessions marked * are alternatives, to be negotiated with participants.

## Lesson plans for day 2

# LIVING THROUGH LOSS LESSON PLAN    LP 2.1

| | |
|---|---|
| **Title** | Introduction to the day: learning review |
| **Time** | 9.30 a.m. |
| **Timing** | 15 minutes |
| **Aims** | • To exchange greetings and open the day. |
| | • To present the revised programme. |
| | • To recall and acknowledge individual learning of the previous day. |
| | • To provide an opportunity for comments or questions that might have occurred to participants overnight. |
| **What you need** | • Flip-chart and pens. |

**What you do**

1. Welcome people to day 2 of the course. Suggest how their requests from the previous day might be fitted into the programme for the day. The week's programme can be displayed on the wall for everyone to look at later. Make final adjustments to the programme in the light of proposals.

2. Ask participants to form pairs, as follows. Each alternate person raises their hand. They are then asked to work with the person on their left. (This rather formal, structured approach is helpful when working with groups that are relatively new to group work. If you say, '*Work with the person on your left*', everyone may turn their back on everyone else!)

3. Ask pairs to 'buzz' for a few minutes about what they learned for themselves from yesterday's work. (It might be useful to give an example: '*I learned that loss is a lot wider than I had previously thought*', or, '*I learned how frightening it is to stay with my feelings*'.) Ask each pair to decide which one of the items noted they would like to feedback to the big group. Allow about four minutes' 'buzzing'.

4. After three-and-a-half minutes ask people to begin to close their conversations, and then ask each pair for one of the things that they learned. Record each item exactly as it is said, or, if summarizing is necessary, check with the originators that your summary is acceptable. When you have taken an example from each pair, invite additional comments that were not recorded.

5.  Date the learning review and remove it from the flip-chart. Display similar reviews on subsequent days of the course.

# LIVING THROUGH LOSS LESSON PLAN    LP 2.2

| | |
|---|---|
| **Title** | Centring |
| **Time** | 9.45 a.m. |
| **Timing** | 5 to 7 minutes |

**Aims**

- To provide a way of closing the previous day's business and focus on the present day's work.
- To help participants to acknowledge the range of feelings possible in the group.
- To help individuals realize that they are neither alone nor unusual in having such feelings.
- To help them accept that the trainers are aware that some may feel in turmoil, even a little fragile, and that you are 'taking care'.

**What you need**

- The centring script provided below, or one of your own choice.

**What you do**

1. Suggest positioning as you did for day 1.
2. Read out the centring script.

*Centring Script*

*Numbers in brackets, for example (4), are a guide to number of seconds' pause.*

*What are you feeling this morning? (4) Perhaps you are still feeling newly arrived in this group. A bit cautious and apprehensive? (4)*

*How was yesterday for you? Did it touch you in some sensitive areas and challenge you with some uncomfortable ideas? Or did you go away last evening buzzing with excitement and interest, and now feel ready to take on anything you will encounter today? (6)*

*People in the group may feel very differently about their experiences of the course. It is important to hang on to the fact that what you feel is what you feel. (4) There are no 'right feelings' or 'wrong feelings' here, just feelings. Perhaps we can learn to let go of some which are dysfunctional for us, and encourage the growth of those which support us, but first we must accept the feelings we have. Whatever they are, take time now to get in touch with your feelings. (8) If they are shaky ones, try to let yourself feel, rather than suppress them. (6) You might want to take some time here today, in a suitable setting which feels safe for you, to share your*

*feelings with one or more people in the group. You may find
that you are not alone. However, don't feel obliged to do this.
(6)*

*Try to acknowledge your positive feelings: something good
that happened to you, here or elsewhere. It may be something
very obvious or something quite subtle, like the smell of a
newly cut lawn or freshly baked bread. (6)*

*Breathe into your belly and continue inhaling, letting your
chest expand right up to the top. (4) Now, let your breath go
in a slow sigh and feel that you are breathing out all your
tension with that sigh. Repeat this if you wish. (8)*

*Now, breathe normally, but try to continue letting your belly
move out with your 'in' breath and fall back with your 'out'
breath. (6) Be aware of a pulse or your heart beat, and stay
with yourself for a while. (30–45)*

*How easy do you find this, giving yourself your full
attention for 30 to 45 seconds? Can you learn something
from that to help you look after yourself? Stay with yourself
a little longer. (30)*

*Deepen your breathing (5) and, taking your time, open your
eyes (5) and if you wish to, have a stretch and a yawn.*

(Adapted from Jacobsen and Mackinnon 1989)

# LIVING THROUGH LOSS LESSON PLAN     LP 2.3

| | |
|---|---|
| **Title** | The hidden child |
| **Time** | 9.50 a.m. |
| **Timing** | 40 minutes |

**Aims**

- Participants are introduced to the concept of the 'hidden child', and to her relevance as a repository of adult insecurities and coping mechanisms.

**What you need**

- Space to read and quietly discuss **PM 7: The hidden child**.

**What you do**

1. Outline the aims of the session.

2. Distribute **PM 7** and ask people to read it. When finished, ask them to look for someone else who is ready, and spend some time discussing any ideas that are new, difficult or challenging.

3. Allow ten minutes for questions in the large group.

# LIVING THROUGH LOSS LESSON PLAN     LP 2.4

| | |
|---|---|
| **Title** | Recalling our 'hidden child' |
| **Time** | 11.00 a.m. |
| **Timing** | 1 hour 15 minutes |

**Aims**
- For participants to recognize the relevance of their own 'inner child'.
- To appreciate the scope of the term 'child abuse' and its possible relevance to participants' experiences.

**What you need**
- Extra rooms, so that the group can divide into two or three sub-groups.
- Coloured pencils, paints, paper and notebooks.
- **PMs 8 and 9: What is child abuse?**

**What you do**
1. Outline the aims of the session.
2. Divide into smaller groups, with a trainer to each group. Outline the following activity:

   *Activity script*

   *Recall and record at least one happy and one sad memory from your childhood. You may record more if you wish, but keep a balance between the happy and the sad. You can record your memories in any way you please. You may want to recall a photograph connected with the memory and draw or paint a picture to illustrate it. For some, poetry or a dialogue is a good way of recording powerful memories. You have 30 minutes for this.*

3. Invite people to share some of their sad memories in the small group. Take a little time, using reflection and open questions to help them explore different aspects. Before leaving each person, ask them to reflect on whether they can recall a time, in adult life, when they felt the same way as the recalled feeling in the childhood memory. There might be an opportunity to share this later. If not, the general point can be made about the way lessons learned from childhood traumas can persist into adult life, continuing to influence relationships.

   Some may not want to share, and this must be respected. Look carefully for signs of distress and acknowledge that this might be a very painful exercise for some. If individuals become distressed, try to encourage them to stay in the group. This gives them the opportunity to hear of similar experiences which are triggered in others, and of experiencing group support, rather than the rejection that they might have anticipated. *Leave time before the session finishes for there to be a round of happy memories.* Remember that this too can be a painful experience for those who recognize a deficiency in their childhood relationships (30–45 minutes). If the feedback session from this exercise merits extra time, take it by postponing the following exercise (step 4).

4. Ask participants to form pairs and work together on the 'What is child abuse?' handouts (**PMs 8** and **9**) (20 minutes).

5. Re-assemble and invite brief feedback from the large group.

# LIVING THROUGH LOSS LESSON PLAN    LP 2.5

**Title**         Writing role-plays in threes

**Time**         1.30 p.m.

**Timing**         1 hour 15 minutes

**Aims**

- To enable participants to identify some difficult experiences which they have encountered, and to share these with colleagues.

- To write these experiences as role-plays that can be offered for use by the larger group, as well as by triad sub-groups.

- To ensure that the material is relevant to participants' needs and experiences.

**What you need**

- Space for groups to work with reasonable privacy.

- **FM 6: Example of a role-play in three parts** displayed on a flip-chart.

- **PM 10: How to write a role-play scenario.**

**What you do**

1. Ask people to think carefully about who they want to work with in triads. (These will be the triads with whom they will work in the skills' practice on day 3.)

2. Ask them to work individually, as follows. Each person notes down two or three examples of situations which they experienced as difficult when trying to counsel a grieving person; or each person notes examples when they were being counselled, and felt that this was handled inappropriately; or each person notes examples of counselling that they witnessed and which seemed to them to be ineffective. (All this refers to counselling in its broadest sense, even if it was not thus identified at the time. In retrospect, participants may nevertheless recognize that counselling skills would have been appropriate in the situation. Allow 15–20 minutes.)

3. Ask the triad groups to discuss the examples, and then to decide which three would be the best to offer as role-plays.

4. Each role-play should be written in *two* parts, on *one* side of a single piece of paper and *in ink*, as follows:

   *Part (1): Client*

   The client profile should include information about name, age and relevant relationships; what is happening in their life at present that is causing them

59

difficulty; how they feel about this; and what has precipitated the immediate problem or crisis.

*Part (2): Counsellor*

The counsellor will need to know the name, age and some (but not all) of the background details. The amount of information supplied will depend on the situation. For example, a community nurse who has visited a family over a long period, is likely to have more background knowledge than a staff nurse in an outpatients department. The important thing is that some of the information known to the client should not be supplied to the counsellor initially. The counsellor should be able to discover such information, if it is relevant, during the course of the counselling.

5. Groups are asked to write a brief, two-line summary of each role-play. This should be written on a separate piece of paper in large, clear writing. For example: *Mandy, 26-year-old single parent whose four-year-old child is in a coma after an accident.*

6. Individuals within triads check each others' role-plays, and make adjustments if necessary. Trainers help where necessary, and at the end of the session two photocopies are made of each role-play.

# LIVING THROUGH LOSS LESSON PLAN    LP 2.6

| | |
|---|---|
| **Title** | Paired support |
| **Time** | 3.00 p.m. |
| **Timing** | 30 minutes |

**Aims**
- To provide an opportunity for participants to give and receive support from a peer.
- To provide a place to dump unfinished business.

**What you need**
- A room or rooms to enable discussions in privacy. (Alternatively, participants could talk while walking in a garden or park.)

**What you do**

1. Form pairs, in the same way as on the previous day. Announce that this activity is likely to be most effective if it is conducted using active listening and exploring skills, rather than as a conversation.

2. Remind individuals in pairs to share the time equally, and to notice if they are tempted to take or give more or less of the available time.

3. Everyone should return to the group room by 3.30 p.m.

# LIVING THROUGH LOSS LESSON PLAN        LP 2.7

| | |
|---|---|
| **Title** | Looking after ourselves and summarizing the day |
| **Time** | 3.30 p.m. |
| **Timing** | 1 hour |

**Aims**

- To provide an opportunity for participants to experience a further nurturing technique.
- To validate the concept of self-care.
- To provide an opportunity for a quick evaluation of the day.

**What you need**

- A large carpeted room. Furniture should be moved away from the walls, so that those giving massage can use the walls to support their backs.
- Comfortable, but not low, chairs for those who wish to sit up while being massaged.
- **PM 11: Head and neck massage.**

**What you do**

1. Check who wishes to participate in this activity. For those who want to opt out, books, journal articles and videos should be available.

2. Ask everyone to find a partner. Partner *A* sits with her back supported against the wall, legs straight out and apart. *B* lies down on her back, head between the thighs of *A*. For those choosing to sit in a chair, *A* will stand behind the chair.

3. Trainer *X* demonstrates on the first occasion, and trainer *Y* on the second. Trainers should sit where they can be seen by all.

4. Proceed, using the instructions in **PM 11**, talking people through the steps.

5. On completion, tell the *Bs* to take a little time to give feedback to their partners, before changing places with the *As*. Timing for steps 1 to 5: 20 minutes.

6. Repeat steps 1 to 5, with *Bs* massaging and *As* receiving. Allow feedback within pairs and to the plenary group.

7. Introduce a closing round, in the form of completing the following two sentences:

    (a) *'The most painful thing for me today was…'*.

    (b) *'The most enjoyable thing for me today was…'*.

8. Warn participants that they may be in a very relaxed and preoccupied state as a result of the massage. Special care is needed if they are driving.

# DAY 3

Group safety is building to its peak on day 3. Therefore there is a high level of challenge both for participants and facilitators. The exercise on helping children grieve, earlier in the course, may have generated 15 minutes' discussion. By day 3, people may well risk going deeper into their feelings about this. The same applies to the exercise on responses to loss.

The demonstration role-play is an opportunity for trainers to put themselves 'at risk' in front of the group. This invariably helps participants to do the same. It also demonstrates the supportive framework within which the participants' skills' practice will take place.

By the end of skills' practice, people will be exhausted. The paired support and relaxation exercise is likely to be received enthusiastically.

Remember that anyone who opts out can be offered books, journal articles or relevant videos as alternatives.

## Programme for day 3

| | |
|---|---|
| 9.30 a.m. | Introduction to the day and review of learning |
| 9.45 a.m. | Centring |
| 9.55 a.m. | Helping children grieve[*] |
| 10.40 a.m. | COFFEE |
| 11.10 a.m. | Responses to loss – drama triangle |
| 11.40 a.m. | Demonstration role-play |
| 12.30 p.m. | LUNCH |
| 1.30 p.m. | Practising skills learnt |
| 3.00 p.m. | TEA |
| 3.15 p.m. | Group feedback from skills' practice |
| 3.30 p.m. | Paired support |
| 4.00 p.m. | Looking after ourselves (relaxation)[*] Summarizing the day |
| 4.30 p.m. | FINISH |

Note: Sessions marked [*] represent possible choices, negotiated with participants. A split group and two options is possible.

## Lesson plans for day 3

# LIVING THROUGH LOSS LESSON PLAN    LP 3.1

| | |
|---|---|
| **Title** | Introduction to the day and review of learning |
| **Time** | 9.30 a.m. |
| **Timing** | 15 minutes |

**Aims**

- To exchange greetings and open the day.
- To recall and acknowledge individual learning of the previous day.
- To provide an opportunity for comments or questions on the experience of the previous day.

**What you need**

- Flip-chart and pens; pieces of paper, approximately 6" x 3"; paste.

**What you do**

1. Welcome participants to day 3 of the course.
2. Ask people to form pairs.
3. Ask individuals to write down briefly, on *one side only* of a piece of paper, what they learned from the previous day's work. (This will be shared with the group later.) Allow four minutes.
4. Ask the pairs to spend a few minutes sharing their thoughts; allow three minutes.
5. Ask each person to share with the group, briefly, one item that they have noted on paper.
6. Collect the pieces of paper and paste them on to a flip-chart sheet, headed with the day's date. Display this next to the record from the previous day. (These methods can be used during the remainder of the course.)

---

## LIVING THROUGH LOSS LESSON PLAN     LP 3.2

| | |
|---|---|
| **Title** | Centring |
| **Time** | 9.45 a.m. |
| **Timing** | 7 to 10 minutes |

**Aims**

- To provide people with a way of closing the previous day's business and focusing on the present day's work.
- To help people to acknowledge the range of feelings possible in the group.
- To help individuals realize that they are neither alone nor unusual in having these feelings.
- To help people to accept that the trainers are aware that some may feel in turmoil, even fragile, and that you are taking care.
- To help people to focus on the importance of their 'counselling skills'.

**What you need**

- **PM 12: listen (poem)**

**What you do**

1. Ground people and encourage them to begin 'belly breathing', as previously. Leave them concentrating on their breathing for about six breaths.
2. Ask them to continue their breathing in the same way, while you read them a poem. Slowly read the poem out loud to the group.
3. Make sure that feet are still firmly grounded and that belly breathing is continuing. Ask the group to concentrate on a pulse, or heart beat, for a short while. Allow three minutes.
4. Ask people to deepen their breathing and, when they are ready, to open their eyes and have a stretch.
5. Distribute copies of the poem.

## LIVING THROUGH LOSS LESSON PLAN    LP 3.3

| | |
|---|---|
| **Title** | Helping children grieve |
| **Time** | 9.55 a.m. |
| **Timing** | 45 minutes |

**Aims**

- To help people recognize the effect of poorly managed grief in children.
- To share any personal issues which this raises.
- To share professional experiences of working with children.
- To identify ways of helping children grieve.

**What you need**

- **PM 13: An adult remembers a childhood experience of hospital** and **PM 14: Talking to bereaved children.**
- Flip-chart and pens.

**What you do**

1. Distribute **PM 13** and ask participants to read and make notes, first with regard to personal issues, and then in terms of professional experiences. When they are ready suggest that they form groups of five or six and share responses (20 minutes). If the discussion groups are still very active at the end of this time, ask if they want longer together. If necessary, omit step 3 of this exercise.

2. In the plenary group, invite any information which the sub-groups are willing to share.

3. Ask for ideas about ways of working with children who are themselves ill, or children who are grieving for a lost relative, friend or pet. Note the ideas on the flip-chart. Distribute **PM 14**.

   (In fact, any of the structures used in this course to explore grief can be adapted for use with children. Ward and Associates (1993) include much relevant material.)

# LIVING THROUGH LOSS LESSON PLAN     LP 3.4

| | |
|---|---|
| **Title** | Responses to loss – drama triangle |
| **Time** | 11.10 a.m. |
| **Timing** | 30 minutes |

**Aims**

- To introduce participants to (or remind them of) ideas demonstrated in the 'drama triangle'.
- To help individuals to begin to identify the 'drama roles' in practice.

**What you need**

- **FM 7** and **8** and **PM 15: The Karpman (or drama) triangle.**
- Individuals need a notebook and pencil or pen.
- Prepared flip-chart or overhead projector diagram of the drama triangle.

**What you do**

1. Using the flip-chart, present the ideas in **PM 15** (ten minutes).
2. Introduce the following activity:

   (a) Think of an occasion when, as a helper, in your domestic or professional life, you have felt angry, frustrated, punishing or helpless.

   (b) What was happening between you and the other person? Think back and see if you can identify what aroused those feelings in you.

   Did you have expectations or goals for the other person? Might this have included wanting them to like you, wanting them to show their feelings, stop feeling sorry for themselves, put their bereavement behind them?

   (c) Does the drama triangle contribute anything new to your understanding of the recalled event?

   Note down your thoughts (15 minutes).

   (d) Share as much of this as you choose with a partner.

   (e) Invite brief comments from the large group.

   (Adapted from Fisher and Warman 1990)

## LIVING THROUGH LOSS LESSON PLAN    LP 3.5

**Title**          Demonstration role-play

**Time**          11.40 a.m.

**Timing**        50 minutes

**Aims**
- To enable participants to:
- witness the use of counselling skills
- identify micro-skills
- raise questions about the appropriateness of the strategy they use, and to consider possible alternatives
- question the 'client' about her feelings during the session
- see an example of the triad structure which they will later experience; and (possibly, see 'Additional notes')
- to provide a model in which the 'client' is supported to express emotion freely.

**What you need**
- A room where seating can be arranged so that the 'client' and 'counsellor' can be separate from the group, yet still be seen by everyone.
- Notebook and pens or pencils for participants.
- If possible, a trainer, or specially briefed participant volunteer, to model the 'observer' role.
- **PM 16: Guidelines for counselling practice.**

**What you do**
1. Outline all the aims except the last; the latter is more effective if left implicit.

2. Identify which trainer is taking which of the three roles ('counsellor', 'client', 'observer'). Outline the function of each of the roles. Explain that the role-play counselling will take place in front of the large group only for this demonstration. Triads will be unobserved, unless they request the presence of a trainer.

3. The observer acts as a chairperson in this situation. This draws attention to the very active and responsible nature of the observer role. Participants are asked to concentrate on the counsellor's use of skills, and to take notes on examples of the micro-skills that they identify. They may want to note things that they would have handled differently, or things that they did not understand. (Timing for stages 1 to 3: ten minutes).

4. It is particularly important to offer and to support 15 to 20 minutes' feedback at the end of the allotted time for the role-play. The observer reminds people about the rules of feedback (**PM 5**) which should have been distributed as priority reading on day 1. First, the counsellor is invited to comment. Comments are then invited from the client; and if the counsellor can cope with more feedback, then additional comments are invited from the group.

It is sometimes supportive for the counsellor to be encouraged to see the observer as a consultant. If the counsellor feels stuck or confused, she can turn to the observer for ideas and suggestions on how to proceed.

ADDITIONAL NOTES

A counselling session can be demonstrated at different levels, depending on the confidence and level of skill applied:

1. Most effective, if you feel able to do it, is for the client to work on a real 'loss' issue about which the counsellor has no prior knowledge. The effectiveness of this lies in the degree of risk which the trainers then take. This helps to achieve the last (implicit) aim, listed above.

2. The client might choose a real issue, but may discuss it with the counsellor first. This allows the counsellor to confirm, or otherwise, that she feels she has the skills to deal with the issue.

3. Another possibility is to role-play a fictitious situation.

4. The facilitators may pre-record a video of themselves counselling. An advantage to this approach is that their attention can be fully with the group while the video is showing.

5. Finally, an appropriate commercially made video can also be very effective if it is used skilfully.

# LIVING THROUGH LOSS LESSON PLAN     LP 3.6

**Title**        Practising skills learnt; group feedback from skills' practice

**Time**        1.30 p.m.

**Timing**      1 hour 45 minutes

**Aims**
- To provide opportunities for participants to:
- practise counselling skills
- experience being counselled
- practise observer, support and feedback skills.

**What you need**
- **PM 17: Experiential learning progression.**
- **FM 9: Experiential learning progression trainers' guide.**
- Role-plays written during the previous day.
- Three copies of each of four extra role-plays (in case some participants decide not to work with their own).
- Summaries of extra role-plays on a flip-chart.
- Small rooms to allow triads privacy to work unobserved and unheard. If more than one group has to be in a room, it should be large enough for them not to intrude on each other. If possible put some screening between them.

**What you do**
1. Before the session begins, write brief summaries of the extra role-plays on the flip-chart.

2. Remind participants that they will be working in the way demonstrated in the morning. Once they are settled in their rooms, they should try to begin with a minimum of discussion, to allow the fullest possible practice. Each successive observer has the responsibility of making sure that the time is divided equally between them.

3. Ask people to decide if they want to work with their prepared scenarios or on one of the role-plays provided. If the latter, then they should look at the summaries on the flip-chart and decide which one they want to role-play as 'client'. They then take a copy of the relevant role-play which will contain both 'client' and 'counsellor' parts. When participants are assembled in their separate rooms, they need to decide who will be the 'counsellor'. The 'counsellor' part of the role-play will have to be detached from the role-play sheet and given to the person selected. If the sub-group decides to work with its own material based on one member's

experience, then the individual concerned could volunteer to play the alternative role to that experienced originally (that is, if the original experience occurred while counselling a client, then that counsellor would now take the role of the client). Another alternative is to ask the other two in the triad to take both roles, so that the individual concerned can re-experience the situation as observer.

4.    Confirm the right to opt out for any participants who feel uneasy about role-play, but suggest that they may want to negotiate with their partners in the triad to be observer for the first round, or possibly even for two rounds. For the third round they can then choose either to 'have a go' or to talk through the issues raised by the role-play.

5.    Remind people that they should take their tea break at 3.00 p.m. and return to the group room for feedback at 3.15 p.m.

6.    Before inviting feedback, re-emphasize small-group confidentiality. It helps to say explicitly that anyone should feel free to 'blow the whistle' if they feel that confidentiality is being broken.

7.    Quite often, feedback includes some painful recognition of inadequately developed skills. This is a good time to acknowledge that pain, and to talk people through **FM 9**. (A slightly abbreviated form is available for participants as **PM 17**.)

# LIVING THROUGH LOSS LESSON PLAN    LP 3.7

| | |
|---|---|
| **Title** | Paired support |
| **Time** | 3.30 p.m. |
| **Timing** | 30 minutes |

**Aims**

- To provide opportunities for everyone to experience receiving and giving support with one other person.
- To provide a forum for people to process the day's experiences and 'dump unfinished business'.

**What you need**

- A room or rooms to enable people to talk in privacy. (In fine weather, one can walk in a garden or park, if available.)

**What you do**

1. Re-iterate the aims of the exercise.
2. Individuals will continue working with the partner chosen on day 1, unless they have chosen to make adjustments.
3. Remind all that an important part of the contract between partners is that each takes an equal share of the time.
4. Recapitulate the suggested format for the exercise: person *A* should take 10 to 12 minutes to share, while *B* uses active listening skills. *A* then gives three to five minutes' feedback to *B* on the skills which were supportive and on the interventions which were not supportive. The process is then reversed, with *B* sharing and *A* listening.
5. Ask participants to be back in the group room by 4.00 p.m.

# LIVING THROUGH LOSS LESSON PLAN    LP 3.8

**Title**    Looking after ourselves (relaxation); summarizing the day

**Time**    4.00 p.m.

**Timing**    30 minutes

**Aims**

- To raise awareness of the relationship between breathing and stress.
- To raise awareness of individuals' own breathing patterns.
- To provide an opportunity for a quick evaluation of the day.

**What you need**

- Enough carpeted space for those who wish to to lie down without feeling crowded.
- Comfortable chairs for those who wish to sit up.
- If available, foam mats, rugs and pillows.
- **PM 18: Breathing and the stress connection.**

**What you do**

1. Outline the aims of the exercise.

2. Invite everyone to find a position which is comfortable for them. The optimum position is on the back with a pillow under the knees to relieve any strain. The head can be raised slightly on two or three books. Those seated should have their backs firmly supported, shoes off and feet firmly on the floor (or, for short people, on a small pile of books).

3. Read the relaxation script which follows.

   *Relaxation script*

   Numbers in brackets are a guide to the number of seconds' pause.

   *Be aware of your breathing (4) and place your hand on the spot which rises and falls the most. (4) What about the depth of your breathing? (4) Does it feel as if your normal breathing is deep or shallow? (4)*

   *Put both hands gently on your belly and notice what happens. (10) Does your belly rise as you breathe out and fall as you breathe in? (10) Or is it the other way round for you? (10) Is there a considerable rise and fall or just a slight one? (5) Take a breath in through your nose and let it out through lightly pursed lips. (10) Is your chest moving in harmony with your belly or are they unsynchronized? (5) Does either feel rigid? (5)*

*Notice the sensation as the air enters your nose. Trace that sensation down into your lungs. (8) Notice it again in reverse as you breathe out. (8) Take your attention outside yourself; (4) silently say to yourself what you are aware of through any one of your senses, for example, 'I am aware of traffic noises in the distance' or 'I am aware of the smell of a garden fire'. (15)*

*Now come back to your body. (5) Let its parts come into your awareness in any order. (10) What did you notice first? (4) What next? (4) Has any part of your body little sensation? (15) Take your attention outside of yourself again. (5) Say to yourself silently what you notice, using a different sense from last time. (15)*

*Return to your body. (5) Compare the right and left sides: do you notice any difference? (10) Are you aware of any physical discomfort? (5) Concentrate on it as if you were going to have to write a detailed description of it. (10) What happens as you concentrate on it? Notice if it changes, what happens to it? (8) Let your body do whatever it seems to want to do for a short while. (3 minutes)*

*Bring your awareness to this room. (5) Slowly move your fingers and toes (5) then your arms and legs (5) and lastly have a stretch and yawn. (10) Now, very slowly, sit up and form a circle.*

(Adapted from Jacobsen and Mackinnon 1989)

4.  When participants begin to stir, invite them to stay seated on the floor or to return to their seats, as they wish. The muddled informality of a mixture of the two can enhance and exemplify the easier relationships within the group.

5.  Invite people to evaluate the day briefly, using the following two sentence completion rounds. Remind them that they have the right to pass:

    (a)  'The hardest thing for me to do today was…'.

    (b)  'The easiest thing for me to do today was…'.

6.  Distribute **PM 18: Breathing and the stress connection**, together with any others for the day (**PMs 12 to 17**). Close the day.

---

# DAY 4

Day 4: the group's process will now have developed to a high level of performance and co-operation. You can risk quite a challenging video if you are prepared to support the depth at which participants might experience this. This will not be a passive experience for a group which is at its peak.

The 90 minutes after the coffee break are arranged as parallel sessions with optional topics. Alternative topics, suggested by participants, may be accomodated here (see items 9 and 10 on p.40).

The exercise on giving and receiving support is also likely to contain some potent learning.

The warm-up after lunch is to stimulate the group's flagging energy and to lift the mood of participants. It may also relax tension, so that the second skills' practice is experienced as an improvement on that of the previous day. People will also be ready for a deeper relaxation at the end of the day.

## Programme for day 4

| | |
|---|---|
| 9.30 a.m. | Introduction to the day; review of learning; centring |
| 9.50 a.m. | Mini-lecture: stages of grief; video[*] |
| 10.45 a.m. | COFFEE |
| 11.15 a.m. | Parallel sessions<br>a) Giving and recieving support[*]<br>b) Working with feelings[*] |
| 12.45 p.m. | LUNCH |
| 1.45 p.m. | Warm-up: 'Fruit salad' |
| 2.00 p.m. | Practising skills learnt |
| 3.00 p.m. | TEA |
| 3.15 p.m. | Practising skills – continued |
| 3.45 p.m. | Feedback from skills' practice |
| 4.00 p.m. | Looking after ourselves (relaxation)[*]<br>Summarizing the day |
| 4.30 p.m. | FINISH |

Note: Sessions marked [*] are alternatives, to be negotiated with participants.

## Lesson plans for day 4

<table>
<tr><td></td><td style="background:black; color:white">

# LIVING THROUGH LOSS LESSON PLAN     LP 4.1

</td></tr>
</table>

| **Title** | Introduction to the day; review of learning; centring |
|---|---|
| **Time** | 9.30 a.m. |
| **Timing** | 20 minutes |

**Aims**

- To provide a way of closing the previous day's business and focusing on the present day's work.
- To encourage acknowledgement of the range of feelings possible in the group.
- To help individuals realize that they are neither alone nor unusual in having these feelings.
- To help participants to accept that the trainers are aware that some may feel in turmoil, even fragile, and that you are taking care.

**What you need**

- Flip-chart, pens, paper, glue.

**What you do**

1. For the introduction and learning review, use either of the two methods outlined previously for days 2 and 3.

2. For centring begin as usual, getting people grounded and belly breathing. When their rhythm is established, continue, following the script.

   *Centring script*

   Numbers in brackets, for example (4), are a guide to number of seconds' pause.

   *Think of something about yourself which you are accustomed to seeing as a weakness. (15)*

   *Think of a time in your life when, if you hadn't learned to be that way, you might not have survived that situation or period. (15)*

   *Honour your creativity for helping you to survive at that time. (15)*

   *Then you were relatively helpless, now you are stronger. Perhaps you don't need that behaviour any more. If now is the right time, maybe you can let go of it. This will free your creativity to respond to new situations with a wider variety of choices. Consider that. (60)*

   *Deepen your breathing and bring your mind back into the room. When you are ready, open your eyes and have a good stretch.*

Note for trainers: Some people may have made an instant connection with the suggestion during the centring. The effect can be powerful.

For those who have not, suggest that they remember the questions, and that the next time they notice that they are 'putting themselves down' for something, they might try to centre themselves and ask those questions.

# LIVING THROUGH LOSS LESSON PLAN    LP 4.2

| | |
|---|---|
| **Title** | Mini-lecture – stages of grief; video (optional) |
| **Time** | 9.50 a.m. |
| **Timing** | 55 minutes |

**Aims**

- To provide participants with a framework, or a choice of frameworks, for them to recognize the stages of grieving.
- For participants to experience being alongside a person in pain.

**What you need**

- **FM 10: The grief process, prepared on a flip-chart.**
- **PM 19: Responses to bereavement.**
- A video of your choice. (Some suggestions are in Section 5 under 'Resources'.)

**What you do**

1. Outline the aim of the session, making it clear that there will be a handout and suggested reading to reinforce the brief talk. What you are about to offer is intended to help structure viewing of the video.

2. Present the outlines of two or three different versions of the stages of grieving. Kubler-Ross (1991), Bowlby (1969) and Murray-Parkes (1972) are three possibilities. Timing for stages 1 and 2: ten minutes.

3. Outline the contents of the video. Remind people to look after themselves and to judge if it is appropriate for them to watch the video. Those who stay should be encouraged to remain in the room even if the video evokes tears. If anyone becomes so distressed that they must leave, a trainer will accompany them. Have tissues discreetly available. Re-emphasize the importance of breathing and grounding.

   If participants wish to offer support to a neighbour who is upset, they might place a hand to support the centre of the back, but only after having first checked with the person concerned that touch is acceptable. An arm around the shoulder is not a good idea. This is a gesture of comforting and calming. If feelings are triggered in grieving people, it is important not to give them the message that they should calm themselves and be comforted. The need is to support them to release and experience their pain, and reassure them that it is acceptable that they do so.

4. Show the video. Suggest that each person tries to identify the stages of grief and how they are demonstrated on the video. It is also valid for people to respond to the video in any other way.

   You may need to take 15 minutes after coffee to complete feedback, depending on the length of the video. In this case, adjust the timing for the remainder of the day, for instance, by omitting the 'Fruit Salad' warm-up.

5. During feedback, you should encourage people to accept their feelings, however irrational these seem to be. People should also be encouraged to respect their deeper, non-logical wisdom. For example, if a person was unexpectedly overcome by a need to flee from the room, they might be self-critical and feel a failure. Encourage them to respect the deeper need to look after themselves, and try to reinforce their right to recognize and respect their physical and emotional boundaries and safety limits. This may well be a key to coping with stress in other areas of their lives.

# LIVING THROUGH LOSS LESSON PLAN    LP 4.3

**Title**    Giving and receiving support (optional)

**Time**    11.15 a.m.

**Timing**    1 hour 15 minutes is the *barest minimum*; if possible, allow 1 hour 30 minutes

**Aim**
- To encourage exploration of feelings about giving and receiving support.

**What you need**
- Two carpeted rooms, each large enough to take half the group. Each group should be no bigger than nine participants plus a trainer. If you are forced to use the smaller time slot, reduce the group size by two.

**What you do**    The following exercise can be offered to the whole group split into two sub-groups; or half can pursue this while the other half is offered an alternative.

1. Outline the aim of the exercise.

2. It is important to have even numbers in both sub-groups (for example, a maximum of ten including the trainer), since people will be working in pairs. The trainer will be working with one participant.

3. Ask each person to choose a partner; explain that, in this exercise, both partners will have the opportunity to give and to receive support.

*Giving and receiving support*

*As* sit on the floor, legs straight out in front of them, and a little apart. Emphasize that they should make sure that their backs are well supported against the wall, and that they are comfortable.

*Bs* lie on the floor with their heads between *As* legs. They should make sure that they are comfortable. Some *Bs* may prefer to have their knees bent and feet flat on the floor.

*As* are asked to take their partner's head into their hands, and support it for five minutes. During this time they are asked to concentrate on:

- their own breathing and centring
- making sure they don't strain their back or arms
- what feelings come up for them about this experience of supporting.

*Bs* concentrate on:

- their own breathing and centring
- what feelings come up for them about this experience of being supported.

This exercise is most effective if people can close their eyes.

Avoid answering detailed questions. If necessary, repeat the instructions above and suggest that people interpret them as they choose. There is no 'right' or 'wrong' way to do this exercise.

Tell people that you will let them know when the five minutes are over.

4. At the end of the five minutes, ask *As* to remove their hands from the head of their partners slowly and gently. Pairs then spend three minutes feeding back to each other on their experience of supporting and being supported.

5. Invite feedback to the larger group. It is appropriate for the trainer to begin this process. Demonstrate through your feedback what you did not enjoy, as well as what you did enjoy, and encourage others to do the same.

When listening to the feedback, help people to identify the process of their experience, as well as the content. Here are two examples:

1. *'My arms started to feel tense and shaky, and I was afraid that I would get cramp and drop her head.'*

This person probably did not take in the instruction to make sure that she was supported and to stay with herself. She did not take the support of the floor for her hands, and she focused all her concern on the well-being of her partner, at the expense of her own comfort.

Draw attention to these points very gently and tentatively, so that they do not sound like accusations; they should be presented as interesting discoveries. The person might then be asked whether her observations are consistent with her experience of herself in everyday life.

2. *'I found that I became increasingly resentful at the weight of my partner's head and I really wanted to put it down and go away. I feel quite ashamed saying that.'*

This person has entered fully into the exercise and has made a painful discovery. Validate the wisdom of her discovery, and ask her to consider whether the experience echoes something of her life experience. What sort of feelings are associated with the experience? Do those feelings affect the way that she responds to taking responsibility in everyday life?

Do not expect answers to your questions. They are for the person to reflect on and perhaps to learn from. She may or may not choose to share connections made to lessons learned.

These are only two examples. The general principles for facilitating helpful discussion of feedback from this exercise are:

1.  Ask participants to consider whether their experience of the exercise represents a metaphor of their life experiences. (Do not *assert* that it does; just ask them to consider the possibility.)

2.  Ask participants to consider the earliest period of their lives when they might have learned the behaviour revealed in the experience.

3.  Help them to value their wisdom in making that discovery.

4.  Suggest that they consider how they could make some changes for themselves, if they feel that this is the right time for them to make some change. (You could draw attention to the fact that this was the structure of the morning's centring.) Timing for steps 1 to 5: 35 minutes.

6.  Ask *As* and *Bs* to reverse roles and repeat the exercise.

7.  You may want to take 15 minutes after coffee to feed back on the experience of the exercise with your half-group.

This is a very powerful exercise. Those relatively new to this way of working may wish to use a different structure to look at support issues. Section 4 of this manual includes some alternatives.

## LIVING THROUGH LOSS LESSON PLAN     LP 4.4

| | |
|---|---|
| **Title** | Working with feelings (optional) |
| **Time** | 11.15 a.m. |
| **Timing** | 1 hour 15 minutes |

**Aims**

- To give participants an opportunity to re-experience a past incident where they responded in a way that left them feeling distressed or dissatisfied.
- To help them find an alternative and more satisfying response.
- To enable support of another person who is working through powerful feelings.

**What you need**

- A large room, or several small rooms, for triad privacy.
- **PM 20: Working with feelings.**

**What you do**

1. Ask participants to group themselves into triads, but tell them that, initially, they will be working individually through stages 1a, b, and c of **PM 20**. Time: 10 minutes.

2. If necessary, move people on to stage 2 of the exercise in **PM 20** after ten minutes. Tell them that you will be moving round and working with individual groups. It is unlikely that you will get to all groups, so encourage groups to ask you to join them if they need help. If no one asks, observe for a while. You may then notice a group that seems stuck or confused. Ask their permission to join them. One way in which you might contribute would be to suggest which of various approaches could be appropriate for the issue on which they are working.

   While working with groups, highlight any special aspects of their proceedings that would be useful for discussion in the plenary group. Alternatively, you could ask their permission to use an aspect of their experience anonymously, to make a teaching point to the large group. Time: 50 minutes.

3. Ask groups to ground *As* in the present. Then ask some questions aimed at orienting them to some positive event in the near future. Call the large group together and invite feedback.

Note: Step 3 concentrates on responses from the *As* but this does not imply that the *As* alone are responsible for the painful or destructive effect of the incident that has been recalled (see **PM 20**). One should emphasize, however, that an *A* has power only to change her own behaviour. That change, in turn, may then make it possible to influence responses from others.

# LIVING THROUGH LOSS LESSON PLAN    LP 4.5

| | |
|---|---|
| **Title** | Warm-up: 'Fruit salad' |
| **Time** | 1.45 p.m. |
| **Timing** | 15 minutes |

**Aims**

- To help participants to:
- feel energized
- feel that a heavy day has been lightened
- encourage their 'child' to play.

**What you need**

- A circle of chairs equal to the number of participants who wish to join in, minus one.
- Between one and three 'callers'.

**What you do**

1. Outline the aims of the exercise, and recall that anyone can opt out if they wish.

2. Those who opt out can be offered the opportunity of being a 'caller'. One can call 'fruit salad'. One can call 'vegetable salad'. One can call 'mixed salad'. If there is only one person she can call any of these three at different times.

3. A trainer stands in the middle of the circle and asks each person seated in the circle to tell her the name of a fruit or vegetable which they have chosen for themselves. The trainer also chooses a name.

4. The trainer then calls out the names of any two of the fruits or vegetables chosen. The two people who chose those names then change seats, while the trainer tries to capture one of the two seats. This leaves a new person in the centre of the circle. The process is then repeated.

5. At any time, one of the 'callers' can call 'fruit salad', and all the fruits must change seats. Or she can call 'vegetable salad', and all the vegetables must change seats. Or, if she calls 'mixed salad', everyone must change seats.

# LIVING THROUGH LOSS LESSON PLAN    LP 4.6

**Title**            Practising skills learnt

**Time**             2.00 p.m.

**Timing**           1 hour 45 minutes, including 15 minute teabreak

**Aims**             • As for **LP 3.6**

**What you need**
- Scenarios as for **LP 3.6**. Groups can exchange their role-plays.
- Rooms as for **LP 3.6** on day 3.

**What you do**

1. This second chance to practise skills is important because many participants will now be moving from 'conscious incompetence' to 'conscious competence' (see Figure 3.6 in **FM 9**). However, the day may have been very exhausting for some. Tell them that they should feel free to rest or, circumstances permitting, to take a walk.

2. Tell the whole group that they have the option of working on issues that have come up for them as a result of the course. This should be negotiated with colleagues in their triad. Remind people that the programme for the day does not include any 'paired support'. They may therefore want to take time in their triad to 'dump' unwanted feelings.

3. Remind people that trainers are available for extra support, if required.

4. Remind people about timing. There will be time for two rounds before the tea break, and the last round will be from 3.00 to 3.30 p.m., when all are asked to return for large-group feedback.

Otherwise, the structure is the same as for day 3.

# LIVING THROUGH LOSS LESSON PLAN    LP 4.7

**Title**    Looking after ourselves (relaxation); summarizing the day

**Time**    4.00 p.m.

**Timing**    30 minutes

**Aims**

- To introduce a new nurturing technique.
- To encourage acceptance of the validity of self-care.
- To provide a quick evaluation of the day.

**What you need**

- A carpeted floor large enough for all who wish to to lie down.

**What you do**    An opportunity for deeper relaxation is usually welcomed after an exhausting day, possibly with profound experiences.

1. Positioning: as for day 2 (**LP 2.7**). You could also suggest that, for some people, a 'recovery' position might be an alternative.

2. Explain that this relaxation exercise borrows ideas from the autogenic method. This is a relaxation technique in which 'trigger' words, such as 'warm' and 'heavy' suggest conditions for a relaxed state of individual muscle groups. With practice, it can be used very swiftly to induce deep relaxation. Explain further that the guidelines which you are about to outline should not be taken literally, first because some of them are physiologically impossible, and second because some individuals may not experience what you are suggesting.

   The importance of the words is to give people a focus that will take their brain out of its logical, problem-solving mode (the left brain), and encourage them to use their creative, imaginative mode (the right brain). Ask people to enter into the spirit of the suggestions as far as possible.

3. Encourage people to settle and to start 'belly breathing', as before. Give them 15 to 20 seconds to establish their breathing rhythm. Read out the script.

   *Relaxation script*

   Numbers in brackets, for example (4), are a guide to seconds' pause.

   *Let the words 'release' and 'healing' come into your mind, and allow a colour to emerge for you which is associated with these words. Stay with the first colour that suggests itself to you, if you are willing. (15)*

*Imagine that colour entering your body from your heels, and slowly rising through your ankles, (5) calves, (4) thighs. (4) As it rises, it drives before it the stress and tension in your muscles. You might want to make an image representing your stress and tension. Your healing-releasing colour is now rising past your buttocks, (5) waist, (5) rising up through your back (5) to your neck, (5) up over the top of your head (5) and down over your face, throat (5) and chest. (5) Watch the colour washing out the stress from your body. Now your healing colour is passing through your belly, (5) hips, (5) thighs (5), past your knees, shins and ankles. (8) Try to see your stress streaming out through the end of your toes, and your body suffused with healing colour.*

*Take your attention to your left arm, and imagine that you can breathe warm air down into your arm, with every breath out. (Make an image which feels comfortable for you. (3) It might be of a gentle spray of warm water, bathing your muscle, (4) a stream of warm air, (3) contact with a soft fabric, (4) or the hand of someone trusted and close to you.) Feel the muscles yielding, (5) becoming heavy and warm. (8) Let the floor take the full weight of your arm, the strong muscles spreading soft against the floor. (10) Your arm is becoming heavier and warmer with each breath. (5) Your left arm is heavy and warm.*

Repeat the latter instruction for the right arm, but abbreviate the reference to an 'image'. Then repeat the same instruction for the left leg, followed by the right leg.

*Your arms and your legs are heavy now and warm. (5) Enjoy your warm, heavy legs and your warm, heavy arms. (5)*

*Breathe in and allow your belly to inflate like a balloon. (5) Feel the warmth right up to the top of your chest (5) and right down to the floor of your pelvis. (10) With each successive breath feel your trunk become warm, (4) heavy, (4) tension rinsed away. (10) Your buttocks are spreading against the floor, (5) your hip joints are loosening, (5) your shoulders are letting go of their tension. (10) Feel the floor taking your weight, you don't need to hold on. (20)*

*Now direct your breath towards your neck. (10) Feel the muscles in your neck yielding, loosening, becoming heavy and soft. (10) Feel the ligaments binding your vertebrae together, softening, (5) loosening the tightly bound bones, (10) allowing your neck to be heavy and warm. (4) Your neck is heavy and warm. (20)*

*Let your warm breath flow over your face, washing out the worry and frown lines on your forehead, cheeks and around*

*your mouth. (20) Direct your warmth towards your jaw. (5)
Push your lower jaw forward and then rotate it round to the
right, then to the left. (5) Let your jaw fall loosely, (5) your
mouth a little open. You don't need to compose your face
right now. (10) The muscles of your face are
warm,...smooth,...heavy.*

*Check over your whole body now, starting with your left
arm. Direct one breath to each part, renewing its warmth
and heaviness and connecting all of your body with your
healing colour. (30)*

*Your warm, heavy body is safe. (10) Trust the floor to
support you. (10) Feel the warmth and see the colour flowing
through your body. You are connected, whole, soft and safe.
Stay with that feeling for a while, repeating some of the steps
you have just been through or using words of your own
which give you a peaceful feeling. (Allow four minutes, or
longer if people don't show signs of fidgeting.)*

*Now, taking your time (5) deepen your breathing and slowly
bring yourself back into this room (20) and when you are
ready (10) open your eyes and, if you wish, have a stretch
and a yawn.*

4.  Encourage sharing of feedback on the experience for two
    or three minutes. Then invite feedback to the large
    group. Encourage and acknowledge feedback from those
    for whom the method was not effective. (It feels lonely to
    be the odd one out. Not all methods work for all people.
    This is why one offers a wide repertoire of methods.)

5.  Invite an evaluation of the day with two rounds of
    sentence completion:

    (a) *'What I want to leave behind me from today is...'.*

    (b) *'What I want to take away with me from today is...'.*

    Warn people that their reactions might be slowed down.
    They should therefore allow a little time before starting
    to drive, and should drive very carefully.

# DAY 5

On day 5, participants will be anticipating the end of the group. The programme is designed to support this transition into everyday reality, where the level of honesty and support which people will have shared with each other during the course, is not (unfortunately) the norm.

There are no split sessions on day 5, because people seem to prefer to work as a group on the last day.

The session on 'Managing change' (**LP 5.2**) helps people to affirm and identify their strengths, so as to achieve changes which they might want to make.

The session on 'Exploring spirituality' (**LP 5.3**) may help them to focus on, and clarify their understanding of, an important and often neglected aspect of their experience and creativity.

The last activity, before course evaluation, provides an opportunity for participants to identify where and how their new skills and insights can contribute to enhancing their work and life experience.

Evaluation, and the closing exercise, allows participants to recognize and honour what they have done, and to give and receive appreciation as a celebration of the culmination of the course.

## Programme for day 5

| | |
|---|---|
| 9.30 a.m. | Introduction to the day; review of learning; centring |
| 9.50 a.m. | Managing change |
| 10.30 a.m. | COFFEE |
| 11.00 a.m. | Exploring spirituality |
| 12.30 p.m. | LUNCH |
| 1.30 p.m. | Taking course learning back to the work place |
| 2.45 p.m. | TEA |
| 3.00 p.m. | Course evaluation |
| 3.50 p.m. | Closing exercise |
| 4.15 p.m. | FINISH |

**Lesson plans for day 5**

## LIVING THROUGH LOSS LESSON PLAN    LP 5.1

| | |
|---|---|
| **Title** | Introduction to the day; review of learning; centring |
| **Time** | 9.30 a.m. |
| **Timing** | 20 minutes |
| **Aims** | • As for first sessions on previous days. (Centring aims to promote integration.) |
| **What you need** | • As for first sessions on previous days.<br>• Spare copies of **PM 21: Spirituality (poem)**, for distribution to participants. |
| **What you do** | 1. Try to keep the learning review fairly short and snappy, to leave the maximum time for the first exercise. |
| | 2. People will now be familiar with grounding and breathing when you signal that it is centring time. When they are settled, read the poem **PM 21: Spirituality**. Leave the group in silence for one minute before gently bringing them back to their normal level of functioning awareness. Leave space for comments before moving on. Distribute copies of the poem to those who want it. |

Note: It is possible that the religious views of some participants may not allow them to accept assumptions implicit in this poem. The views of such participants are listened to and respected.

# LIVING THROUGH LOSS LESSON PLAN    LP 5.2

| | |
|---|---|
| **Title** | Managing change |
| **Time** | 9.50 a.m. |
| **Timing** | 40 minutes |

**Aims**

- To help participants to identify their behaviour patterns when faced with change.
- To help participants to recognize their strengths in managing change.

**What you need**

- **PM 22: Change.**

**What you do**

1. Outline the aims of the exercise. Ask each participant to choose a partner, although initially, individuals will be working on their own.

2. Distribute **PM 22** and ask everyone to work through it (allow 15 minutes).

3. Ask participants to share with their partner as much as they wish of what they have noted about their change, and what this meant for them (allow 15 minutes).

4. Re-assemble the group and invite comments.

# LIVING THROUGH LOSS LESSON PLAN          LP 5.3

| | |
|---|---|
| **Title** | Exploring spirituality |
| **Time** | 11.00 a.m. |
| **Timing** | 1 hour 30 minutes |

**Aims**

- To encourage individuals to examine their concepts of spirituality.
- To encourage individuals to consider how to recognize and promote their spiritual needs, and those of others.

**What you need**

- **PM 23: Spirituality (statements).**
- **PM 24: Spirituality (some definitions).**
- **PM 25: One definition of spirituality, with examples. (PM 25** is for possible use, if there is sufficient time. The handout includes reference to a compact disc: *Black and White. (Ewan McColl – The Definitive Collection.* Cooking Vinyl CD (Cook CD 038).
- Flip-chart and pens, loose flip-chart paper.

**What you do**

1. Outline the aims of the session and explain that the format will be for some plenary and some small-group work.

2. Introduce the first activity and distribute **PM 23**. Allow the group a few minutes to reflect individually on the statements. Then invite people to share their thoughts and feelings on each statement in turn, in groups of five or six.

Note: A number of differing viewpoints may emerge in discussion. The purpose of the activity is to encourage consideration of the concepts more broadly. Make it clear that you are not looking for 'right' answers; the discussion is more important than the conclusions. (Timing for steps 1 and 2: 20 minutes.)

3. Give each group of five or six people a piece of flip-chart paper and a pen. Working from insights gained so far, invite groups to spend 20 minutes creating their definition of spirituality and writing this on the paper.

4. Display posters and invite further discussion.

5. Distribute **PM 24** for comparison and comment. (Timing for steps 3 to 5: 35 minutes.)

6. If there is time, distribute **PM 25**: offer the definition given as just one possible viewpoint.

You might want to pre-record a reading of the poem *On a Sunny Evening* (**PM 25**). Alternatively, you could read it, or ask a volunteer to read it. Play the song *The Joy of Living*. Invite responses. (Timing for step 6: 20 minutes.)

## LIVING THROUGH LOSS LESSON PLAN      LP 5.4

**Title**          Taking course learning back to the work place

**Time**           1.30 p.m.

**Timing**         1 hour 15 minutes

**Aims**
- To provide an opportunity for individuals to identify a goal: something learnt from the course which they intend to use as a support in their lives.
- To encourage each participant to make a contract with another that will provide support towards achieving their goal.
- To arrange a date for the follow-up day.

**What you need**
- **PM 26: Setting goals.**
- Sample goal, in two stages, see **FM 11: Setting goals**, with description of the example on a flip-chart.
- Paper and pens for participants.
- Three or four suggestions for dates for follow-up day.

**What you do**
1. Give a mini-lecture on how to set a goal, using the information in **FM 11**. A mini-brainstorming session can generate a list of advantages to be derived from goal-setting.

2. Work through your example. Participants should help you to check that the example fulfils all of Egan's criteria. (Timing for steps 1 and 2: 25 minutes.)

3. Ask people to work with a partner. This could be, but need not be, their paired support. If they want to take some sort of action that involves working with a work colleague on the course, they should feel free to do this.

   *A* takes 15 minutes to identify what changes she wants to make in her life as a result of something she has learned during the last week. This learning does not have to be connected with course content. It could be something learned about herself and her own needs.

   *B* uses her active listening skills to help *A* identify something suitable and to formulate a goal which will help her to incorporate learning into her life.

4. After 15 minutes, suggest that *A* and *B* reverse this process.

5. After a further 15 minutes, invite everyone to write two copies of a contract that states what they will expect to

have achieved by follow-up day. One copy is kept; the other is given to the partner.

Re-convene the plenary group and invite brief feedback from the preceding goal-setting exercise (10 minutes).

Note: Emphasize that the exercise is meant to support people to make changes or achieve aims that will be helpful and enriching. If one finds that the goal becomes a pressure or a burden, then there is an important lesson to be learned from recognizing this and abandoning, or modifying, the goal.

6.  Suggest possible dates, about six months hence, for the follow-up day. When a date has been agreed, ask everyone to record this in their diaries. Announce that you will be sending a reminder letter two weeks before the agreed date. A retrospective evaluation form will be enclosed with the letter. This will ask participants to review the course and to evaluate its effects on their working practice. These retrospective evaluations will form the basis for the first part of the follow-up day.

    If you do not plan to have a follow-up day, then suggest that people fix a date in their diaries for six months hence, to meet or to telephone each other, to discuss their progress towards achieving their goal.

## LIVING THROUGH LOSS LESSON PLAN    LP 5.5

**Title**      Course evaluation

**Time**      3.00 p.m.

**Timing**      50 minutes

**Aims**
- To enable participants to review their original requirements for the week, and their daily responses to their experiences.
- To allow time for participants to feedback their assessments to each other and to the trainers.

**What you need**
- All the sheets with feedback from daily learning reviews, displayed around the room.
- Each group's 'Sharing expectations' poster from day 1.
- **PM 27: Evaluation form**.

**What you do**

1. Invite everyone to wander around the room and look at the displayed daily learning reviews.

2. Ask participants to re-assemble into the groups they were in on day 1, when sharing their expectations from the course. (The names should be on the bottom of the poster.) Groups should work through the poster, checking whether, and to what extent, their expectations have been met. (Timing for steps 1 and 2: 10 minutes.)

3. Ask someone from each sub-group to report to the plenary group on their sub-group's assessment (five minutes).

4. Distribute the course evaluation handout (**PM 27**) and ask individuals to complete one. Ask them to place the completed forms on a chair, designated for that purpose, when they are ready. Tell them they have 20 minutes for this.

5. If you have been asked to supply an evaluation of the course to managers, discuss this with the group now, explaining the way in which this might be done.

   Participants' evaluations may be collated in two ways. The first would include all comments, but with participants' names replaced by a letter of the alphabet. The second would give examples of a spectrum of typical comments in each section of the form. The second is more anonymous, and participants are usually happy for the evaluation to be passed to managers in this format. The first, more detailed collation, they may like for themselves. An appreciated practice is to send a collated evaluation to each participant within one month of the end of the course.

## LIVING THROUGH LOSS LESSON PLAN     LP 5.6

| | |
|---|---|
| **Title** | Closing exercise |
| **Time** | 3.50 p.m. |
| **Timing** | 20 minutes |

**Aims**
- To give participants an opportunity to show their appreciation of each other.
- To acknowledge the process of parting.

**What you need**
- A piece of flip-chart paper for each participant and for the trainers.
- Plenty of poster pens – one for each person.

**What you do**

1. Ask each participant to draw a very large shape, perhaps a vase, on their piece of paper and to write their name inside the shape.

2. Participants then circulate around the room, filling the shapes with a comment for each person they wish to appreciate.

3. Closing circle

   1  Ask the group to form a large circle, standing close to each other.

   2  Ask everyone to rub the palms of their hands together briskly for one minute.

   3. At the end of the minute, ask that they put out the left hand with the palm facing upwards, and the right hand with the palm facing downwards, over and close to, but not touching, their neighbour's left hand.

   4. Ask them to close their eyes, breathe into their bellies and concentrate attention on the palms of their hands. (Invariably, there are reports of tingling, and of a feeling of energy passing from person to person around the group.)

   5. Group leaders share the following comments between them, by prior arrangement:

      (a) *'We share our energy now as we have shared it with each other over the last five days.'* (Pause ten seconds)

      (b) *'Open your eyes, and let your palms make contact with your neighbours' on either side.'*

(c)  *'Feel how with your left hand you are supporting,
     and with your right hand you are supported.'*
     (Pause ten seconds)

(d)  *'This is the way we have related to each other
     during our time together. If you have found this a
     useful way of relating to others, find a way of
     incorporating it into your life'.*

(e)  *'Thank you and goodbye.'*

Note: Remind people to take away any blankets and pillows that they might have
brought with them.

# FOLLOW-UP DAY

Write a letter to participants to arrive two weeks before the date set for follow-up day. Include a **Retrospective Evaluation Form** (**PM 28**), and ask them to complete this *before arrival on the follow-up day*.

No formal structure is provided for the follow-up day. A suitable structure will suggest itself during the first two sessions on the day itself.

## Lesson plans for follow-up day

# LIVING THROUGH LOSS LESSON PLAN     LP F.I

| | |
|---|---|
| **Title** | Welcome and centring |
| **Time** | 9.30 to 9.45 a.m. |
| **Timing** | 15 minutes |

**Aim**

- To allow the group to formulate a programme for the remainder of the day.

**What you need**

- An outline, on a flip-chart, of a possible structure for the day. This can be completed on the basis of feedback from the morning's work.
- A centring script.

**What you do**

1. Greet people, and ask if a quick name-round would be helpful.

2. Introduce the day by suggesting that one purpose is for all group members, participants and trainers, to say farewell to each other within the context of the group. An important part of grieving is the willingness to accept the finality of separation. It is useful to set this boundary for the day's proceedings from the start, to avoid unrealistic expectations of what can be achieved. Within this boundary, time can be taken to separate appreciatively, and to recognize with whom one wishes to maintain contact.

3. Outline the structure of the day, making it clear that the afternoon has been left clear so that participants can decide for themselves how best to use the time, based on what occurs during the morning.

4. Introduce centring as previously. Once people are grounded, and 'belly breathing', read the following centring script or another of your choice.

CENTRING SCRIPT

Numbers in brackets, for example (4), are a guide to number of seconds' pause.

*Ask yourself four questions. See what answers come up for you. (5)*

*First, ask yourself: 'What do I want to get out of today?'. (20)*

*Next, 'How am I going to get it?'. (20)*

*Third, 'How could I stop myself getting what I want?'. (20)*

*Lastly, 'How will I know when I have got it?'. (20)*

*Get in touch with a pulse or your heart beat and be aware of this and of your breathing. Stay with yourself for a short time. (3 minutes)*

*Deepen your breathing, (5) allow yourself to be aware of the room and the noises around you, (5) and when you are ready (5) open your eyes and have a stretch and a yawn.*

*You might want to write down your answers to the four questions, and to check with your paired support partner at the end of the day, whether each of you has achieved your aims, or how you stopped yourselves from achieving them.*

*Allow a little time after centring for people to make comments, before moving on.*

# LIVING THROUGH LOSS LESSON PLAN     LP F.2

**Title**

Feedback in groups and large-group feedback

**Time**

9.45 a.m. to 12.30 p.m.

**Timing**

1 hour 45 minutes (excluding 15 minute coffee break) in small groups. Forty-five minutes in the large group.

**Aims**

- To share information with colleagues about the difficulties and joys encountered in using our skills, in any or all aspects of our lives.
- To discuss the usefulness or otherwise of setting a goal on the last day of the course. What lessons were learnt from that exercise?
- To suggest topics that might be discussed in the afternoon session.

**What you need**

- Flip-chart paper and poster pens.
- A large enough room for work in four groups, without overhearing each other; or several small rooms.
- A few blank **Retrospective evaluation forms (PM 28)**. (Someone may have forgotten to bring theirs.)

**What you do**

1. Outline the aims of the session and ask the group to construct a poster summarizing their discussion. Headings might be:
   - how and where skills have been effective
   - the difficulties in using skills
   - setting goals: useful or not useful?
   - subjects for discussion later in the day.

2. Ask people to divide into four groups. They might want to include in their group the person with whom they worked on contracts on the last day of the course (see the exercise on Setting goals: item 5 in **LP 5.4**, p.96).

3. Remind participants to take a coffee break between 10.30 and 10.45 a.m., and to return to the plenary group room at 11.45 a.m.

4. When the groups have re-assembled and displayed their posters, invite spokes-persons from each group to report. Discussion of issues may occur spontaneously, with other groups voicing their own views. Make sure that all groups have the chance to raise aspects of their experience that are not covered by other groups. This might mean setting time limits for discussions, while

acknowledging that the topic can be returned to in the afternoon.

5. Negotiate what can be dealt with realistically from the list of subjects for the afternoon. Ask participants to be prepared to share sources of information about topics which will not be covered, so that needs can be fulfilled.

6. Offer evaluation forms to anyone who has forgotten theirs.

# LIVING THROUGH LOSS LESSON PLAN    LP F.3

| | |
|---|---|
| **Title** | Discussion of issues raised |
| **Time** | 1.30 p.m. |
| **Timing** | 2 hours, excluding 30 minutes' coffee break |

**Aims**

- To discuss agreed issues.
- To share information about resources to explore issues that cannot be discussed in the time available.

**What you need**

- Flip-chart and pens.

**What you do**

Divide the time according to the number of discussion topics that can be covered reasonably, leaving 20 minutes for the 'resource' session at the end. Include a 30 minute coffee break.

Vary the methods used to discuss topics, for example, brainstorming, large group, small groups with feedback, and pairs or triads. Select the method to suit the topic.

# LIVING THROUGH LOSS LESSON PLAN    LP F.4

| | |
|---|---|
| **Title** | Ending |
| **Time** | 4.00 to 4.30 p.m. |
| **Timing** | 30 minutes |

**Aims**
- Group relaxation
- Saying goodbye

**What you need**
- Relaxation script – those from day 3 or 4 of the course would be appropriate.
- **PM 29: Excerpt from Williamson 1996**.

**What you do**

1. Ask everyone to assume their relaxation position, lying down or seated. Use the introductory breathing and releasing instructions from your script. Tell the group that you will leave them to relax in silence for three minutes.

2. Talk them up into an everyday awareness level, but invite them to stay relaxed with their eyes closed while you read the excerpt from William's 1996 speech. Ask them to stretch and to sit up slowly.

3. Ask for the completed 'Retrospective evaluation' forms. If you are prepared to collate these and send copies to everyone, say so.

4. Invite participants to join you in a closing circle (see **LP 5.6**).

Note: It usually takes some time for the group to disperse, since addresses and telephone numbers may be exchanged at this stage. There is also a reluctance to separate – a part of grieving. You may therefore want to use your discretion about getting caught up in lengthy discussions.

# ADDITIONAL LESSON PLANS

No time of day is specified for the following nine additional lesson plans. They can be used as alternatives to lesson plans used in the five day course.

## LIVING THROUGH LOSS LESSON PLAN     ALP I

**Title**          Getting to know each other (alternative)

**Timing**         35 minutes

**Aims**
- For people to share something of themselves and their interests with one other, and then with increasingly larger groups of people.
- To create an ice breaker.

**What you need**
- Large sheets (A3) of plain paper.
- Coloured pencils or pastels.
- Plenty of floor space.

**What you do**

1. Using a demonstration example, invite people to divide their paper into quarters and write their name in the centre. In each section, ask them to draw an illustration of the following:

   (a) a happy day from my childhood

   (b) a happy day from my adult life

   (c) something I am good at

   (d) something I want to learn.

   Emphasize that this is not a test of drawing ability; stick figures are acceptable. Time: 15 minutes.

2. When the pictures are finished, each person looks around for another and they share their pictures with each other.

3. When a pair have finished sharing, they can join another pair, and each person introduces her partner's picture.

4. When the quartets are ready to move on, they join another group. This time each person in the octet talks about their picture (a). This is followed by a round on picture (b), and so on. Time for steps 2 to 4: 20 minutes.

5. Ask the large group to re-assemble and invite feedback on the experience of the activity. What similarities? What differences? What surprises?

Adapted from Williams and Lockley (1989)

# LIVING THROUGH LOSS LESSON PLAN ALP 2

**Title**    Exploring loss through creative writing

**Timing**    45 minutes to 1 hour

**Aim**
- To facilitate participants' use of another creative medium (prose, poetry, song) to explore feeling associated with loss and bereavement.

**What you need**
- Flip-chart, paper and pens.
- A selection of poetry and prose dealing with experiences and emotions related to loss. Alternatively, a cassette of a relevant song might be used; see **FMs 13, 14** and **15**.

**What you do**
1. Read or pre-record a piece of poetry or prose, or ask a volunteer to read this to the group. Alternatively, play a cassette of a song.

2. Invite people to note down, without discussion, the first two or three words that come into their minds on listening to the trigger piece chosen.

3. Ask people to share their words, and to list them on a piece of flip-chart paper.

4. Read or play the piece again.

5. Ask people to form small groups for the following activity. (Timing for stages 1 to 4: 15 minutes.)

6. *Activity*

   (a) What were the feelings of the people in the group?

   (b) How did these feelings affect them?

   (c) What did they do with the feelings? For example, did they try to suppress them, acknowledge them, deny them? Did they feel embarrassed, ashamed or confused about having those feelings?

   (d) What did they say, or want to say; do, or want to do?

   (e) Who would they have liked to be there with them as they were experiencing those feelings?

   This activity could then continue in various directions. For example:

   (a) Invite people to draw a picture of a scene or memory which the prose, poetry or song helped them to recall. They might then choose to talk about their picture with the small group.

(b) Role-play the trigger piece, or a memory evoked by it for someone in the group.

(c) Individuals can write a poem or short story based on the list of words shared by the group.

(d) Write a group poem, based on the words shared by the group.

(Adapted from Ward and Associates 1993)

## LIVING THROUGH LOSS LESSON PLAN    ALP 3

| | |
|---|---|
| **Title** | Reflecting on death |
| **Timing** | 1 hour (to be used only on day 3 or 4) |

**Aims**

- To provide an opportunity for group members to explore the fears they have when thinking about their own death. (Unacknowledged, such fears can impair one's effectiveness in helping others who are facing their own death or that of a loved one.)

- To allow participants to discover whether the extent of their fear about their own death suggests that this is not a good time for them to be working with such clients.

**What you need**

- Each person needs a notebook or paper and pen.
- **PM 30: Reflection on death.**
- Enough space for each person to feel private while remaining together in the same room.
- **PM 36: Seven stages of transition.**

**What you do**

1. Ask everyone to find another group member with whom they will work once the individual activity is complete.

2. Outline the aims of the activity.

Note: It is particularly important to emphasize that the second aim is for a positive discovery. It is not a failure to be fearful; indeed, some people may be well aware of the origin of their fears. Those who are not thus aware, may be contemptuous of their feelings. The most enabling way to view such a discovery, is that it provides information that allows for choices that will safeguard the well-being of both counsellors and clients.

3. Distribute activity sheets (**PM 30**) and allow group members time to find space and settle. Be available for support and guidance while the groups are working.

4. Ask individuals in pairs to share:

    (a) how easy or otherwise it was to get in touch with the thought of their own death

    (b) their thoughts, feelings and physical sensations.

5. Debrief; bring participants' attention back to the group and invite feedback.

6. Distribute **PM 36**.

# LIVING THROUGH LOSS LESSON PLAN ALP 4

| | |
|---|---|
| **Title** | Impact of loss |
| **Timing** | 1 hour (to be used only on day 3 or 4) |

**Aim**

- To allow participants to examine their responses to loss.

**What you need**

- A room large enough for work in pairs without being overheard.
- **PM 31: Impact of loss.**

**What you do**

1. Introduce the session and its aims, and distribute **PM 31**.

2. Explain that, initially, participants will work alone through steps 1 to 8 of **PM 31**. This should take about 25 minutes.

3. After 25 minutes invite everyone to share, with a partner, their experience of doing the exercise alone. Allow 20 minutes for this step.

4. After 20 minutes ask the large group to re-assemble and to share what they wish with the whole group.

# LIVING THROUGH LOSS LESSON PLAN ALP 5

**Title**        Setting up a staff support group (optional)

**Timing**        45 minutes

**Aim**
- To share and collect experiences about establishing and running a staff support group.

**What you need**
- Flip-chart and pens.
- **PM 32: Staff support groups.**
- Enough space for participants to work in groups without disturbing each other.

**What you do**
1. Introduce the aim of the exercise.

2. Ask for suggestions about the advantages and disadvantages of such a group, and record these under separate headings on the flip-chart.

3. Ask people to form groups of three or four. If there are those who share a place of work, it could be to their advantage to work together.

   Using the questions raised on the handout, and any others identified, the groups should formulate the outline of a proposal for a support group. If this is not relevant to their work context, they should formulate an outline proposal for a group of people with occupations similar to those of their own. (Allow 30 minutes for this activity.)

4. Re-convene the plenary group and invite feedback.

5. Distribute **PM 32**.

# LIVING THROUGH LOSS LESSON PLAN     ALP 6

**Title**   Setting up a bereavement support group for clients

**Timing**   45 minutes

**Aim**
- To provide participants with an opportunity to explore how to set up a support group for clients.

**What you need**
- Enough space for people to work in groups without disturbing each other.
- **PM 33 and 34: A bereavement support group for clients.**

**What you do**
1. Introduce the exercise and state its aim.
2. Invite division into groups of three or four. Distribute **PM 33** and ask everyone to take 30 minutes to work through it together.
3. Re-convene the plenary group.
4. Collect responses to the various worksheet questions on a flip-chart.
5. Invite those who already have experience of working in a client support group to share that experience with the group.

   Encourage discussion of the points raised.
6. Distribute **PM 34**.

# LIVING THROUGH LOSS LESSON PLAN    ALP 7

**Title**          Allegations of abuse; confidentiality

**Timing**         1 hour

**Aims**
- To enable participants to explore the issue of confidentiality.
- To provide an opportunity for participants to experience the dilemma of dealing with an expectation of confidentiality.

**What you need**
- Flip-chart and pens.
- Prepared summary (flip-chart or acetate) of material covered by **PM 35: Allegations of abuse: confidentiality**.
- Enough space for people to work in pairs without feeling as if they can be overheard.
- **PM 35: Allegations of abuse: confidentiality.**

**What you do**
1. Introduce the session and outline its aims.
2. Ask participants to help you list, on the flip-chart, the difficulties they have experienced, or expect to experience, if they:

   (a) agree to absolute confidentiality

   (b) don't agree to absolute confidentiality

   in connection with child abuse.
3. Review with the group the summary of **PM 35** that you have prepared on flip-chart or acetate. (Time for steps 1 to 3: 20 minutes.)
4. Distribute **PM 35**. Ask the participants to work through the exercise in pairs, each of them taking a turn at role-playing and responding to the situation. Suggest that they monitor what feelings, thoughts and physical sensations they experience, and that they share these with their partners. They might also give each other feedback on how their responses could be made more effective, taking into consideration tone of voice, non-verbal communication and use of language. (Time: 30 minutes.)
5. Re-convene the plenary group for feedback.

## LIVING THROUGH LOSS LESSON PLAN ALP 8

| | |
|---|---|
| **Title** | Working with parents of grieving children |
| **Timing** | 1 hour 30 minutes or 1 hour 15 minutes |

**Aim**

- For participants to discover the skills required to support parents in communicating with their sick or grieving children.

**What you need**

- **FM 16: Sample leaflet: helping children.**
- Paper and pens.
- Two pieces of flip-chart paper for each group.

**What you do**

1. Outline the aims of the session.

2. Ask individuals to work alone, noting any memories they have from childhood when they knew something really serious had happened and were:

   (a) not told about it even when they asked

   (b) knew that what they were told was only part of the truth or was false.

   What thoughts, feelings and sensations do those memories evoke?

   Next, recall any occasions when, as adults, participants had to give sad or disturbing news to children. What aspects of this were difficult? What assumptions about children might have caused the difficulties? (Allow ten minutes.)

3. In groups of six, share experiences and list them on flip-chart paper (30 minutes).

4. As a group, list:

   (a) the sort of behaviour that helps one to recognize that a child is reacting to loss

   (b) practical ways of dealing with that behaviour (15 minutes).

5. Display the sub-groups' lists for large-group discussion (15 minutes).

## LIVING THROUGH LOSS LESSON PLAN　　ALP 9

**Title**　　Looking at love

**Timing**　　1 hour 45 minutes

**Aims**
- To help people to:
- clarify what love means for them
- identify how love or the absence of love affects them and their clients.

**What you need**
- Flip-chart paper and pens.
- The book *Love You Forever* by Munsch and McGraw (1992).
- Art materials.

**What you do**

1. Ask participants to form groups of five or six. Distribute flip-chart paper and two pens to each group and ask them to do a silent brainstorm. This means that, in silence, people take a pen and write a word or phrase associated with 'love'. Others in the group do the same, responding to what is already written or adding their own thoughts (15 minutes). The group then discusses their list, focusing on the relevance of the presence or absence of 'love', as they have defined it, to their lives and to the lives of their clients (30 minutes).

2. The large group re-convenes, and sub-groups report on their discussions.

3. Read the short book *Love You Forever* to the group, sharing the illustrations as the story proceeds.

4. Invite people to respond to the story without discussion, using paints, pastels or clay, or writing prose or poetry.

5. Invite a brief large-group discussion.

# PART 3

# Facilitators' Materials

The following materials for facilitators (FMs) are arranged in three groups. The first three (**FM 1** to **3**) relate to preparations for the course. **FM 4** to **11** deal with the conduct of the course itself, and are therefore linked with the lesson plans in Section 2. Finally, there are five additional materials (**FM 12** to **16**) on other relevant aspects of grieving. Note also that the workshop structures incorporated into the course programme (Section 2) allow facilitators to adapt some of the materials distributed to participants (see Section 4).

## PREPARING FOR THE COURSE

## GROUP SKILLS CHECKLIST                    FM 1

Spend a little time reading and responding to this checklist of 14 questions. Circle the place on the scale which best describes your behaviour in the group.

1.  Ability to listen to others understandingly
    *Inattentive and insensitive*                    *Observant and sensitive*
    1    2    3    4    5    6    7    8    9    10

2.  Ability to influence others
    *No influence*                    *All my suggestions accepted*
    1    2    3    4    5    6    7    8    9    10

3.  Willingness to be influenced by others
    *Resistant*                    *Flexible*
    1    2    3    4    5    6    7    8    9    10

4.  Inclination to build on the ideas of others
    *Go my own way*                    *Use others' ideas*
    1    2    3    4    5    6    7    8    9    10

5.  Inclination to discuss personal feelings
    *Reticent*                    *Free*
    1    2    3    4    5    6    7    8    9    10

6.  Inclination to trust others
    *Distrust*                    *Trust*
    1    2    3    4    5    6    7    8    9    10

7.  Inclination to seek close relationships with others in the group
    *No interest*                    *Seek close relationships*
    1    2    3    4    5    6    7    8    9    10

8.  Awareness of the feelings of others
    *Unaware*                    *Sensitive*
    1    2    3    4    5    6    7    8    9    10

9.  Reactions to critical comments or disagreements with one's opinions
    *Defensive*                    *Receptive*
    1    2    3    4    5    6    7    8    9    10

10. Reaction to expressions of affection and warmth

    *Embarrassed*                                              *Pleased*

    1    2    3    4    5    6    7    8    9    10

11. Reaction to conflict and antagonism in the group

    *Avoidance*                                                *Creative*

    1    2    3    4    5    6    7    8    9    10

12. Awareness of self and the effect of one's behaviour on others

    *Unaware*                                                  *Aware*

    1    2    3    4    5    6    7    8    9    10

13. Clarity in communicating one's thoughts to others

    *Unclear*                                                  *Clear*

    1    2    3    4    5    6    7    8    9    10

14. Contributing original ideas

    *Seldom*                                                   *Often*

    1    2    3    4    5    6    7    8    9    10

Choose one or two statements where you feel you could improve to be more effective in groups. Next time you facilitate a course, concentrate on improving these skills, and re-evaluate yourself at the end of the course.

(Adapted from the Teacher Training Programme in Health Education (1983, out of print) Health Education Bureau, Republic of Ireland)

## DAILY RECORD FORMS                                        FM 2

- Spend a little time reviewing the day's plan and events in your mind.
- Make notes under the appropriate headings.
- Using these, compare your response to the day with your co-trainer(s).

1. Learning climate – was it:
    (a) extremely productive?
    (b) productive?
    (c) satisfactory?
    (d) not very productive?
    (e) unsatisfactory?

2. What went well?

3. What changes would you make for next time? How and what would you handle differently?

4. Did anything go badly? Say what and, if you can, why.

5. What did you do which really pleased you?

6. Specify what you did to promote a safe climate.

7. What was the range of feeling you experienced today?

8. What challenges did you offer and how were they responded to?

9. Which individuals raise what questions in your mind?

10. What have you learned about yourself today?

11. What did you especially appreciate about your co-trainer(s) today?

12. To what extent were the aims of the day achieved?

(Adapted from Jacobsen and Mackinnon 1989)

## EXERCISE: CO-TRAINER DIALOGUE     FM 3

**Aim**     To help trainers explore and compare their teaching and learning philosophies and styles.

**What you need**     A copy of this exercise for each trainer.

**What you do**     Make brief notes in answer to the following questions:

1.  What do I think are the broad educational aims of this course?

2.  Ideally, what should participants gain from the course?

3.  What relationship do I aim to establish between myself and the participants?

4.  What do I see as my job on a course dealing with grief support?

*© 1997 Fay W. Jacobsen, Margaret Kindlen and Allison Shoemark*

5.  What are my strengths and limitations in teaching counselling skills?

6.  What are my strengths and limitations in working with groups?

7.  How do I feel about myself as a trainer?

8.  How do I want to change?

9.  Do I want to make changes in my training style?

10. What skills will I need to fulfil those changes?

❦ ❦ ❦ ❦ ❦ ❦

Now talk through your answers while your co-trainer uses active listening skills.

Now your co-trainer should talk through her answers while you listen.

11. Note points of difference between you.

12. Are these likely to enhance or disrupt your co-training partnership?

13. What can you do to minimize the latter effect?

14. Note points of similarity between you and agree how you can best exploit these.

(Adapted from Ewles and Simnett 1985)

## RUNNING THE COURSE

---

**Living through loss facilitators' materials**

---

# JOHARI WINDOW: TRAINERS' GUIDE      FM 4

---

Prepare a flip-chart or an acetate of the diagram shown in Figure 3.1, before the session. Build up the diagram as indicated in the following text and illustrations. This diagram represents the different levels of self-awareness and aspects of ourselves which we feel more or less comfortable to share with others. It symbolizes a notional starting point in a process of change, where every individual is now; it is not intended to imply neat and equal divisions of the four elements shown.

|  | *Known to self* | *Unknown to self* |
|---|---|---|
| *Known to others* | Free and open | Blind self |
| *Unknown to others* | Hidden self | Unknown self |

*Figure 3.1 Johari window: outline*

Part of each person's self is known both to themselves and to others. It is 'free and open'.

Another part of each person's self is known to themselves, but is not shared with others. This is the 'hidden self'.

A third part of each person's self is unknown to themselves, but known to others. This is the 'blind self'.

The fourth part of each person's self is unknown to them and to others. This is the 'unknown self'.

Counsellors use their skills to encourage clients to become more aware of aspects of their 'blind self' and to share some aspects of their 'hidden self'. Consequently, clients often recall events, and experience feelings, that were buried in their 'unknown self'.

This is a two-way process. When working with a client, a counsellor's own prejudices may be challenged, memories stirred and emotions triggered, as the client's disclosures chime with the counsellor's own unresolved issues. If the counsellor was previously unaware, or in denial, of these problems, then she can become de-skilled and ineffective. For example, one might limit the depth of a client's disclosures to protect one's personal vulnerability. Some personal prejudices and misapprehensions could thus be projected on to the client, resulting in a loss of the objectivity that is so crucial in the counselling process.

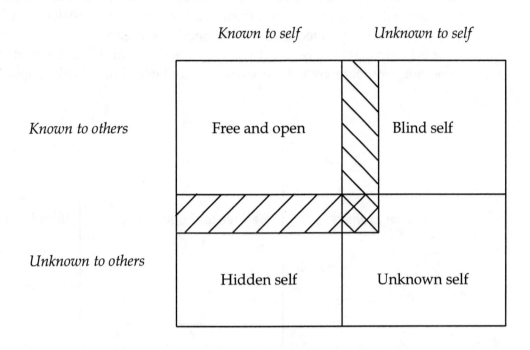

Figure 3.2 *Johari window: blind and hidden self reduced*

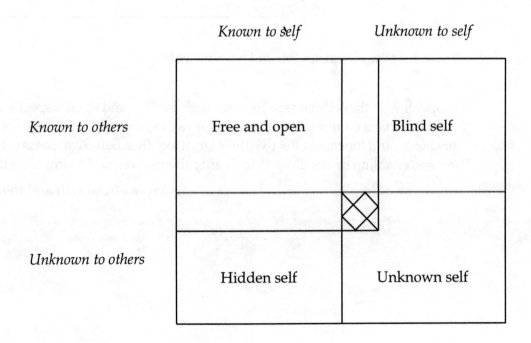

Figure 3.3 *Johari window: unknown self reduced*

Training courses that teach counselling skills need to provide opportunities for participants to explore their own vulnerability in a supportive environment. This is better than some hidden or unknown trauma emerging while attempting to support someone else.

The self-awareness exercises offered on this course aim to reduce those areas of your awareness referred to as the 'blind self' and the 'hidden self'.

People have a right to keep part of themselves private. It is important also to be conscious and respectful of one's personal boundaries. These will vary depending on the individual and the situations involved. Yet the self-awareness exercises that are provided may reveal some of the more destructive and restrictive messages that may have been implanted during childhood (see Figure 3.3).

It is likely that, as a result of reducing the 'blind and hidden' parts of the self, something entirely new will be learned from the 'unknown self' (Figure 3.4).

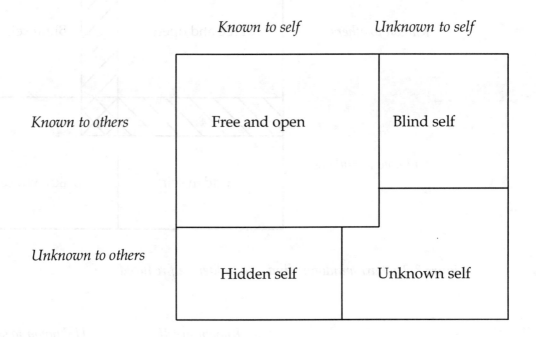

*Figure 3.4 Johari window: free and open self enlarged*

By opening up these three aspects of the self, the 'free and open' aspect is expanded. The more that a counsellor is able to achieve this, the more available she will be to her clients, and the more effective their work together. Self-awareness is an ongoing process, enabling counsellors to look after themselves and to improve their skills.

(Adapted from Luft and Ingham 1955)

# FEELINGS: THEIR PURPOSE AND DISTORTIONS
## FM 5

| Natural feeling | Purpose | Distortion |
| --- | --- | --- |
| Grief | To deal (not cope) with tears; to express remorse ('*I could have done better*') | Self-pity; shame; guilt |
| Anger | Assertiveness; self-esteem; power to say 'no' and to change things | Rage; hatred; powerlessness; low self-esteem; need to hurt self and/or others |
| Fear | Self-preservation | Anxiety; phobias |
| Love | To express who I am; feel free to love and be loved; to give and receive freely with no conditions; to nurture myself and others; to experience the joy of life | 1. Conditional: '*I'll love you if...*'<br>2. Clinging vine: '*I need you to be with me, never leave me*'<br>3. Possessive: '*You belong to me, you're mine*' (reflected in the lyrics of many 'love' songs) |
| Envy | Stimulant to:<br>1. Emulate a mentor or model ('*I'm glad you're the way you are. I want to be that way too*')<br>2. Growth ('*I can grow out of this situation, seeing how you handle it more effectively*'; to be curious; to be inspired by | Critical: self-critical; low self-esteem; powerlessness; undermine self with the successes of others; jealousy |

The ideas suggested by these notes are presented as a basis for reflection and discussion, to challenge the common categorization of feelings into 'good' and 'bad'. Viewed in this way, it is possible to begin to examine the validity of some of the deeply rooted messages from our past, which might be counter-productive and distorting to relationships.

(Adapted from material presented at an E. Kubler-Ross 'Life, Death and Transition' workshop, Edinburgh, 1992)

# EXAMPLE OF A ROLE-PLAY IN THREE PARTS

FM 6

SUMMARY

Sharing bad news – breast cancer.

PART A: COUNSELLOR

You have been asked to see Mary Marris, a 35-year-old woman who has been diagnosed with breast cancer. Mary saw the consultant earlier today, and he gave her the result of her biopsy. He suggested that she come to talk over her feelings with you.

PART B: CLIENT

You are Mary Marris, a 35-year-old woman just diagnosed with breast cancer. You have been feeling absolutely stunned since the consultant told you the result of your biopsy earlier today. Before the biopsy was taken, you saw a different doctor who reassured you that there was '...nothing to worry about'. You have two children, a four-year-old boy and a girl aged seven. Your husband is usually very supportive, but he is squeamish about illness and operations. You don't know how he will react to this bombshell. The consultant saw how shaken you were and suggested that you speak to the counsellor.

Note: If you are working with a lay group, small changes can make this example appropriate. For example, at the end of Part B, after '...*speak to the counsellor*', add, '*But you declined, since you have a dear and trusted friend (or sister) to whom you instinctively want to turn in this crisis*'. The counsellor then becomes the friend (or sister), with appropriate changes in the Part A summary.

## THE KARPMAN (OR DRAMA) TRIANGLE (I): DIAGRAM    FM 7

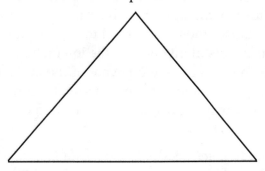

VICTIM
helplessness, martyrdom, 'I'm weak',
refuses to act on possible alternatives

PERSECUTOR
blaming, knows it all,
dominance, aggressiveness.
Persecution through passivity,
stubborn silence, withdrawal

RESCUER
pacifying, protecting
and defending others,
covering up, trying to
solve other people's problems

*Figure 3.5 The Karpman (or drama) triangle (see Berne (1971) and Harris (1975))*

# THE KARPMAN (OR DRAMA) TRIANGLE (2): TRAINERS' GUIDE      FM 8

The Karpman (or drama) triangle (Figure 3.5) is a concept originating from transactional analysis (Berne 1971). It symbolizes a 'game' into which people sometimes become locked, and which leads to a perpetuation of mutually destructive relationships. 'Game' means here that people are relating to each other with hidden motives. It is a form of manipulation that can perpetuate and reinforce old patterns of behaviour. It causes those concerned to feel misunderstood and confused, and to blame the other person involved in the interaction.

Participants in the game are unaware of the cycle of behaviour – until one of them breaks the pattern and behaves assertively. Initially this may trigger anxiety, but ultimately new ways of responding can emerge.

Figure 3.5 depicts three roles in the game:

1.  The victim (*I'm not OK. You're OK, and I'll do anything you say*).
2.  The persecutor (*I'm OK. You're not OK, and I'll punish you*).
3.  The rescuer (*I'm OK. You're not OK, but I'll help you*).

These different roles might be played by any one person at different times; or by two or three people, with one or other person perhaps switching roles as the game proceeds.

One way of recognizing when one becomes locked into the triangle is when one is working very hard to help somebody, but there is no response to any of the suggestions offered. The would-be 'rescuer' feels that no effort is being made. Anger and impatience begin to emerge, so that the 'rescuer' has switched to the role of 'persecutor'. The other party in this particular game might then also begin to feel and to show anger, because the presenting problems are not being solved. Thus the initial 'rescuer' turned 'persecutor' may now feel that *she* is the 'victim'.

The concept of the drama triangle is closely linked with that of co-dependency, familiar to those working in the field of alcohol abuse (Cermak 1986). Co-dependency refers to situations in which someone relates to an addict in a way that supports the addiction. For example, an alcohol-addicted partner in such a game might alternate between playing 'victim' when sober and the 'persecutor' when drunk. The non-alcohol-addicted partner might have a compensating addiction to the 'rescuer' role when the alcoholic is sober, and to the 'victim' role when he is drunk. A similar dynamic has been identified in sexually and physically abusive relationships (Norwood 1985).

The way out of the triangle is to insist on relating to the other person in the 'transaction' as an equal (*I'm OK, you're OK*). This requires use of assertive responses (Harris 1975).

# EXPERIENTIAL LEARNING PROGRESSION: A TRAINERS' GUIDE          FM 9

Experiental learning can be thought of as preparing through four stages.

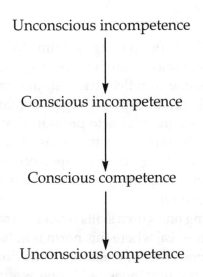

Unconscious incompetence

Conscious incompetence

Conscious competence

Unconscious competence

*Figure 3.6 Experiential learning progression*

UNCONSCIOUS INCOMPETENCE

People come to courses with some degree of confidence in their professional and other skills. They want to learn new skills, and to validate and improve those they already have. Few would claim to be infallible; but one cannot know what is not known.

CONSCIOUS INCOMPETENCE

As participants discover what they do not know, they begin to realize that they may have handled some past situations less effectively than they previously imagined. For those whose self-esteem is fragile, or for those who work in a very competitive or judgemental professional environment, this realization can be both painful and de-skilling. This occurs frequently among people involved in 'skills' learning, particularly those who have just used role-play for the first time. There may be expressions of guilt, of hopelessness and of distress for '...*doing it wrong all these years*'.

It would be unethical and irresponsible to undermine people's sense of professional expertise and then send them back to the work place. It is important, therefore, that the planning of any course should include a second chance to role-play, thus providing a chance for people to progress to the next stage of learning.

## CONSCIOUS COMPETENCE

Following a second chance to practise their skills, people often make remarks such as, '*I feel so wooden and artificial*' or '*I am struggling to think of which skill is appropriate, and my mind just goes blank*'.

In these situations, it can be helpful if participants are reminded of what it was like during their first driving or typing lesson. Many will remember experiencing similar feelings in the early stages of learning these, or other, skills. They will recognize then that they subsequently progressed to competence.

## UNCONSCIOUS COMPETENCE

This stage is reached after having had time to practise and consolidate skills. The acquisition of unconscious competence is a gradual process. Something may then occur that causes one to reflect back, so that one then recognizes that using the newly acquired skills is now increasingly spontaneous. One function of a follow-up day, after three to six months, is to promote that recognition.

It is particularly important that those with a poor sense of self-worth are supported to acknowledge their competence. Sometimes one hears dismissal of achievements with denigrating remarks, such as, '*It is not really such a big deal. I mean, anyone can learn it*'.

Acknowledging one's own skills is not generally encouraged in Western society. Even in North America, where this norm is adhered to less rigidly than in the UK, overt self-assertions of what one knows one does well are not encouraged. There is a fear of being thought 'boastful' if one asserts one's competence. But a trainer who fails to establish her competence because of inappropriate modesty, will thus reduce her effectiveness in passing on her skills.

Note that an apparently 'modest', self-effacing remark by a trainer in a teaching situation may be interpreted as implying, '*If a fool like me can do it, anyone who finds it difficult must be really dumb*'.

This would not be a helpful position from which to approach someone struggling to learn skills that are new to them. An awareness of this danger can help one to take the first steps in self-affirmation.

## THE GRIEF PROCESS                                    FM 10

The grief process has been described by various authors in terms of patterns, rather than a sequence, of responses. Bowlby (1969) refers to the grief process as ebbing, flowing and meandering. The journey from loss to adjustment is gradual and cannot be rushed. People oscillate between stages; some will 'get stuck' and require assistance. Others will take varying amounts of time to complete the process.

### PROTEST

What Bowlby terms 'protest' is similar to acute grief as described by Lindeman (1944), Engel (1961) and Kubler-Ross (1991). Inwardly there are feelings of disbelief, denial, shock, anger and self-recrimination. Outwardly the person might weep, cry, search and sigh. They may experience symptoms of somatic distress and some disturbance of sleep, of memory and of concentration.

Somatic distress is characterized by waves of symptoms, persisting for 20 to 30 minutes, and re-emerging each time the loss is remembered. Physical symptoms experienced might include shortness of breath, tightness in the throat, overwhelming tears, sighing, exhaustion, a feeling of detachment, sweating, numbness, nausea and a fluttering in the stomach.

Hopson (1982) considers that denial is a positive reaction. It is a creative response to a crisis that is too overwhelming to confront. Exhaustion, numbness and feeling detached can similarly be seen as strategies for temporary withdrawal, allowing people to internalize the event, to gather thoughts, and to begin to understand the extent of the changes that the crisis has injected into their lives.

### DESPAIR

Despair incorporates developing awareness, as described by Engel (1961); anger, bargaining and depression, identified by Kubler-Ross (1991); and facing reality and depression, as incorporated in Hopson's (1982) model. Inwardly, the person is sad, depressed, despairing, feels powerless and is subject to mood swings ranging between anger and periods of hopelessness. Outwardly, the person continues to experience somatic distress, may become less spontaneous in responding to events, and may be reluctant to socialize and resume their previous living pattern.

Hopson (1982) refers to this depression as a signal that the person has begun to face the reality that a change has occurred; a growing awareness of a need to re-orient oneself to the world and to other people.

### DETACHMENT

Bowlby (1969) describes the absence of attachment as a kind of behaviour immobilization. Inwardly, there is a feeling of meaninglessness, of isolation and of apathy. Outwardly the person withdraws from social contacts and takes refuge in routine, rather than pursuing a planned or purposeful lifestyle.

Hopson (1982) considers detachment to be an 'unhooking' from the past – the process of letting go and moving on towards the future.

## PERSONALITY REORGANIZATION

Personality reorganization begins when a grieving person is able to accommodate the loss: the absence of a loved one, a lost object (for example, a home destroyed or repossessed), a lost body part or body function, or a loss of self-image (for example, the loss of social status on becoming unemployed). There might be a period of experimenting with new modes of behaviour, new lifestyles and new ways of coping. Mistakes may be made if there are efforts to model oneself on others. Restlessness, exhaustion, irritability and anger may all be experienced as the search for a new meaning in life proceeds.

Progress can involve sliding back and forth between protest, despair and detachment. Full adjustment to the loss, or personality reorganization, may be said to be complete when the person feels able to live without the lost person, object or status. Hopson (1982) describes this stage as 'internalization': the person has come to understand the changes that have occurred, accepts the new circumstances, and is prepared to deal with them.

In his later work, Bowlby (1988) refers to the strength and nature of attachments as significant factors influencing the intensity of individuals' experiences of grief and mourning, and of the way they progress through the process.

## SETTING GOALS                                    FM 11

### BACKGROUND

Setting goals occurs at every level of human activity: personal, domestic, professional and corporate. It also has a role to play in counselling. When people have explored and understood the issues that were confusing and distressing them previously, they then begin to realize that they can take action to change some aspects of their lives. Counsellors need to support them to do this in a way that will strengthen, rather than undermine, their confidence in themselves.

Locke and Latham (1984) describe some of the advantages of goal-setting:

1. Goal-setting focuses attention, and it gives direction to action.
2. Goal-setting mobilizes energy and effort. Planning and thinking about the goal is the first step towards its achievement.
3. Having a goal increases resolve to work harder and longer to achieve it. The clearer, more relevant and realistic the goal, the less likely that it will be abandoned.
4. By setting goals one is motivated to search for ways and means by which they can be achieved.

Egan (1986) refers to eight criteria for setting goals:

### CRITERION 1

Goals should be formulated in terms of *accomplishments*, rather than forms of behaviour. For example, a woman who states that she intends to leave an abusive partner has thereby stated her goal. Her possible further statement, that she intends to join a 'Battered Wives Support Group', is not a *goal*, although it may be one way in which the goal might be achieved.

### CRITERION 2

Goals need to be *specifically stated*, if they are to motivate behaviour. For example, it is neither specific nor focused for a person to say that he needs to get more exercise. It would be more helpful to say something like, *'By my birthday I will have been swimming twice a week, every week'*.

### CRITERION 3

Progress towards achievement of a goal should be *measurable*. For example, if a man who has had his leg amputated says, *'I'll be up and about soon'*, he cannot measure his progress. However, he can if he says, *'In five days' time I will have walked to the end of the ward and back with my artificial leg'*.

### CRITERION 4

Goals need to be *realizable*. The resources required to achieve the goal must be available in practice. An unemployed woman with children may declare that she intends to have found work by the end of the month. If no child care facilities are available in her area, then this might be an unrealistic, unrealizable goal.

### CRITERION 5

Goals need to be *adequate*. They should contribute directly to resolving or managing the problem that motivated the goal-setting. For example, a man may decide to marry a woman friend because he believes that this will help him feel better about himself. If the underlying problem is his 'shame' about his homosexual orientation, then he is not likely to achieve his goal.

### CRITERION 6

Goals need to be the person's *own* goals. The manager who sets arbitrary time limits on tasks to be accomplished by his staff is likely to be less successful than one who encourages his staff to set their own goals for streamlining their time management.

### CRITERION 7

Goals need to be *in harmony with one's values*. A personnel manager who is feeling stressed by overwork may set herself a goal to introduce an appointments system for seeing staff on only one specific day of the week. However, if her view of her role is to be freely available to staff, to discuss personal issues affecting their work, then she might experience increased stress arising from the dissonance between her convictions and the goal she has set herself.

### CRITERION 8

Goals need to be on a *clear time scale*. For example, '*I would like to work freelance*' does not generate a drive as effectively as, '*By this time next year I will have built up sufficient clients and training consultancies to be working freelance*'.

Note: some people have commented that criteria 2, 3 and 8 seem to replicate each other. In many cases this is true, but not in all.

### PROCEDURE

Put a semi-formulated goal, similar to example 1 below, on to the flip-chart.

> *Example 1* (a semi-formulated goal)
>
> I want to move into a bigger house soon

Invite the group to identify which of the eight criteria for goal-setting are met. Note these on the flip-chart.

Participants are sometimes slow in getting started on this exercise. It helps to work through the list with them: '*Is the goal stated in terms of an accomplishment?*'; '*Is it* specifically *stated?*' and so on.

You will need to contribute to the exercise by indicating (preferably in response to participants' questions) whether or not sufficient resources are available to make the goal *realizable* (criterion 4), and whether it is *adequate*, in the sense that it will contribute to the solution of a problem that, you confirm, needs to be tackled (criterion 5). Criterion 6 will be met if you state explicitly that it is really 'your' goal. You may also want to indicate whether or not the goal poses any conflict with your 'values' (criterion 7).

Now prepare a second example which will fulfil more, but not all, of the remaining criteria.

*Example 2* (an almost fully formulated goal)

In six months' time I want to move into a house with one more living room, two double and one single bedrooms, a garage and a small garden front and back

This still does not fulfil criterion 1. (A participant may suggest changing '*I want to move…*' to '*I will have moved…*'.)

Criterion 2 is fulfilled because the goal states *specifically* how much bigger the house has to be. (Some participants may want to quibble about the lack of precision regarding the size of the garden, or how many cars the garage has to accommodate.)

Ask if criterion 3 is met. In fact, the goal is not *measurable* unless the date is included in the statement. In this example, criteria 2 and 3 are closely linked. Criteria 4, 5, 6 and 7 have already been dealt with, above.

Fulfilment of criterion 3 defines a clear time scale for achievement of the goal, six months from the date written on the acetate. In some examples it may be necessary to specify the achievement date.

When editing of the goal is complete, so that all criteria appear to be satisfied, invite comments and criticisms. Someone might note, for instance, that *external factors* could prevent achievement of the goal (see criterion 4 – the kind of house required may not be available at an affordable price within the nominated time period). Such a comment would allow you to draw attention to the danger of accepting a bogus achievement of the goal (a house that falls short of the defined requirements). It would be better to modify the goal from the outset, for instance allowing more time for its achievement.

## ADDITIONAL MATERIALS

> **Living through loss facilitators' materials**

# OFFERING PHYSICAL SUPPORT          FM 12

Very occasionally, during a course, a participant may become painfully aware of the absence of support throughout her life. Such individuals may have become expert at supporting others, but may never have given themselves permission to *accept* support. This would not be surprising if they have never had an opportunity to learn to trust the support of others.

If recognition of a lack of support is articulated during the course, then some other participants may want to offer physical support. If this is accepted, proceed as follows:

1. Ask for able-bodied volunteers to assist you to physically lift and hold the 'supportee'.
2. Tell the 'supportee' that she can stop the exercise at any time.
3. If you have enough volunteers (in most cases, six or eight will be enough), position them on each side of her. Those positioned near her head and shoulders will take her weight as she leans back. Those supporting her legs and hips then lift her to a horizontal position. Warn people to lift with bended knees, taking the strain on their thighs, not their backs.
4. Once she has been lifted, ask people to center themselves and silently to focus their attention on the 'supportee'. Ask her to belly breathe and to try to allow her weight to be carried by the group. It may take a little while for her to be able to relax and accept the support (she may not achieve it at all).
5. Often the group starts to sway gently, rocking her to and fro; sometimes they will also start to hum a tune. This can be a profound emotional experience for her and, indeed, for the whole group.
6. When she is ready to be put down, or when the group tires, lower her gently and support her to a chair. Alternatively, she may prefer to lie on the floor.
7. The group may share anything they wish about the exercise. No pressure should be put on the 'supportee' to share what she has learned. It can take time to process the experience and make sense of what it means for her.

### ALTERNATIVE SUPPORT

If a 'supportee' is too heavy to be lifted, she can stand facing a wall, so that her feet will not slide forward. A group of people can then support her body weight from behind, to an angle which feels appropriate for all concerned.

# POEMS AND SONGS: AN INTRODUCTION

Poems and songs have been valuable in past courses as aids for centring and as discussion triggers. Some of them are reproduced in the following two sections (**FM 14** and **15**). We are also privileged in being able to offer some original poems which deal with issues around grief, loss and abuse. For these we are indebted to Kate Robinson, a young sculptor who contributes to the Arts in Glasgow; and J.M.D., whose poems witness stages on her journey to reclaim herself after suffering sexual abuse as a child.

You will identify and collect similar materials of your own, once you are convinced of their power and value.

The first two poems may need a little introduction.

In the pre-history of the Aegean, the part of Greece known as Attica based its social relationships and culture on a matriarchal system. The myths that originate in that period reflect the struggle of the system to retain its dominance against the encroaching threat of patriarchy.

Persephone was the daughter of Demeter, Earth goddess and goddess of fruitfulness. One day, when Persephone was lured into a grove by the lovely flowers that grew there, her mother's brother, Aidoneus, or Thanatos, raped her and carried her back to his kingdom, Hades, or Death. Grief-stricken, Demeter searched for, and finally found, her. Such was her power, that she was able to return with her daughter to the Earth. However, because Persephone had eaten pomegranates given to her by Thanatos, she had to return to live with him for one-third of every year.

At one level, this myth symbolizes the storage of the seed corn underground during the winter months, and its growth and fruitfulness during the remaining two-thirds of the year. Thus the rape and abduction of Persephone is regularly transformed into an affirmation of the triumph and fruitfulness of the Earth. At another level the rape reflects the struggle of a matriarchal society against encroaching patriarchal forces. It is also one of many precursors to the Christian theme of 'death and resurrection'.

It is interesting that, in the following poems, the poet speaks not of rape, but of seduction. This raises some interesting issues for discussion, for example:

- What is the difference between seduction and rape?
- Is it reasonable to call seduction psychological rape?
- Does the age of the person being seduced have a bearing on our view of seduction?
- If seduction is seen as acceptable after the age of consent, what does this imply about a woman's 'no'?
- What are the therapeutic issues which are likely to be accentuated in a 'loving' seduction?

In a personal communication (Kate Robinson 1996), the poet has provided further insight into her thoughts:

When I talk about seduction…it is when Persephone is presented with the possibility of escaping from Hades – the ground has opened and she has seen the sky. But because she has eaten the fruit of the pomegranate, she has to return to the underworld.

The poet continues with a further connection between classical and Christian iconography, with regard to the rich imagery of the pomegranate. Using Botticelli's painting of the Madonna and the Pomegranate as an example, she writes:

…the Christ child holds the pomegranate to his body where his heart is. The pomegranate *is* his heart, sliced open to reveal its jewel-like contents. Close up, you can see the membrane, the pith of the pomegranate dividing the seeds in the shape of the cross; above this, the top part of the pomegranate forms a small gold crown. Encircling the fruit are the left hands of both the child and the Madonna; the Madonna's thumb, ever so gently, touches the jewels of the fruit. In this tiny element of the painting, Botticelli refers to love (the heart), death (the cross), power (the crown), and sex (in the active/passive relationship of the central figures to the fruit).

*Persephone (1)*

Mother,
He took me
Downstairs,

your brother,

and plaited
my hair
while I

Stared straight
ahead and did not
speak.

I laughed
When he dallied
in a glade of white poplar
and mint.
Then I was alone.

When I was found
the ground opened
and a blue brook
ran down
over the waters of the Styx.

I looked up
and saw the sky.

But your brother
My lover
and downfall
returned to seduce me
with the seeds of a pomegranate
and my life
is reduced.

I must abide here
until I can see your fields
of ripening corn, again.

Kate Robinson (1990)


*Persephone (2)*

Persephone
Reborn
Is surprised
That the love
She bore
For Thanatos
Returned
Reborn

As Eros,
Cradles her hands
(her thin boned hands)
So the palms show
Outwards
(that her hands
now will mould the clay)
And the fingertips
Point downwards
To earth showing
No wound;
That
Now
She laughs.
(Persephone begins
to think
She is laughing
at Thanatos)

Kate Robinson (1995)

*This*

This is the last
Song I will sing for you:

You are all the love
I could have loved
You are all the life
I could have lived
You are all the hope
I have hopcd for and
You are all
I have desired.

Kate  Robinson (undated)

❦ ❦ ❦ ❦ ❦ ❦

As a child you could not afford to feel the full extent of your terror, pain or rage. The agony would have been devastating (Bass and Davis 1992).

*Why?*

The garage doors opened wide
Crouched inside
Sits a bundle
Body taut
And closed inside
Wanting love,
Needing hands
To crouch down low
And offer themselves,
To be lean't on
Held in

Loved by.
Never coming
Close down systems.

J.M.D. (1990)

Deep healing happens only when you choose it and are willing to change yourself (Bass and Davis 1992).

*Hope*

Hands outstretched
A simple gesture
Given to one
Whose hands are clenched.
Hands so open
Reaching out
To grasp the pain

And comfort the hurt.
Can't accept
Won't accept
Need to accept
Want to accept
Will not accept
THIS TIME!

J.M.D. (1990)

While it is always worth it, healing is rarely easy (Bass and Davis 1992).

*Life*

Before I was dead
And closed up tight
Now I'm alive
And seeping strong
Grasping for emotions
To fill the hole,
Begging for someone to fill its gap.

Increasingly wider
It lets out the hurt,
Overflowing the brain
With too much pain.
Thinking dissolves
Feelings emerge,
Out come the tears
And everything  dread.
Anger, Sadness, Hurt, Loneliness
And most of all Fear.
My only gain in all this
Is that now I feel
Before I was dead!

J.M.D. (1990)

*Survival*

Lost within a minefield of thought
Feelings, embedded within
Shells erupting
Shrapnel flying
Scaring, piercing the edges of my mind.
Nightmares begin
Relentlessly pushing
Forcing me into choiceless moves,
Defending myself from death
An instinct to survive evolves
and I BEGIN AGAIN

J.M.D. (1990)

*The inner child — big me and little me*

Little me says 'hello
Hold me gentle but hold me tight'
Feel my quivers and hear my frights
Let me Cry, Scream and Shout'

Big me then pops out
Full of logic, programmed to the full
A frozen facade plays the game
Rules set, dice rolled, cards at hand
I played my lot.

Little me packed up tight
Squeezes out and shouts aloud,
'Play my lot, play my lot!
I need time and space and thought
To sort me out!'

Big me squiggles and squirms
'Rest your case little one
I cannot deal with all your pain
My mind does not compute.'

Down I go, little me
With my pain complete
I quiver silently
'Goodbye big me
I'll see you soon
Cos me and you
Are part of Jean'

J.M.D. (1990)

*Jean*

Jean exists
Between the two
Inseparable from either
Yet belonging to neither.

No man's land
is where I sit
Struggles resist
my very being.
Bars my feelings
Creating conflicts.

'SHUT-UP you two' I shout
'I need to referee the fight
Little one spill your fears,
Feel your tears, quivers and frights.

Big me hold tight
Your mind will not ignite
You'll have your logic
and compute your fate.'

In the end
I'll control the way
and play the game
Fair and square.

J.M.D. (1990)


If you were abused within your family, or if your family is generally unsupportive, critical or withholding, continued relations can be very difficult (Bass
and Davis 1992).


*Untitled*

Mum, where are you?
Mum, you're not here,
Mum, I need you
My very being's in despair.

Mum, where were you?
Mum, why did you not hear?
Mum, I crave to have you near.

Mum, I hate you
I despise your fear
I loathe your attitude to my life.

I heard your tears
and dried your eyes,
I sorted your troubles
Just to feel you cared I was alive.

Mum, I lost my life
My innocence and my child,
and you did not wish to see or hear.

I played a part
To please your need
but where were you to see my fear?

I needed you to look at me
and see my desperation
I needed you to hold me tight
and stop the world encroaching on my rights

J.M.D. (1990)

A big part of moving on is integration. You see yourself as a whole, not compartmentalized... (Bass and Davis 1992).

*Me*

I'm here
I'm there
I'm everywhere
So there!

J.M.D. (1990)

*Standing tall*

Don't explain
Don't justify
Leave it
We'll understand why

You are yourself
No one else
You're in command

Unique
Important

Alone to decide
In this crazy
Mixed up world.

J.M.D. (1990)

*This is what it feels like to be me*

It's the dead of the night
But my mind is alight,
Is this what it feels to be me?
Can this truly be real?

I feel TREMENDOUS!!
ABSOLUTELY STUPENDOUS
My life is alight
My light shines bright.

I float with the stars
Yet my feet are enrooted in the ground
Is this what it feels like to be me?
Is this truly real?

I feel all my fingers and toes and remember
Yep! this is me
before they crippled my core
and left me for timber.

I stand like a tree
Majestic and free
Branches outstretched
Grasping at life
Reaching high into the sky.

I'm awesome and strong
With a heart like fire
that warms all my limbs
and disperses the sins
of all those others
who decided I was just their bin.

This is what it feels to be me
There is a way for this to be real,
I'll pick a seed
from this battered old tree
I'll replant it and reclaim me!

J.M.D. (1990)

## SONGS                                                    FM 15

The following two groups of songs (available on audio cassettes or CD, as indicated) can stimulate and promote discussion on topics relevant to the course. Inform participants about the content of the songs, so that they can choose to listen or not.

GROUP I FROM *BLACK AND WHITE. EWAN MACCOLL -- THE DEFINITIVE COLLECTION.* COOKING VINYL CD (COOK CD 038)

Track 3. *My Old Man* An appreciation of the struggles and philosophy of life of a dead father. Also an attempt to establish continuity, as the 'old man's' experiences are passed on to his children.

Track 5. *Black and White* Written as a protest against Apartheid. Does it have any relevance to our experience of life? How would an unemployed person, or one in menial, poorly paid employment, relate to this?

Track 6. *Brother Did You Weep*? Written at the time of the war in Vietnam. Some memorable images of war:

> Hymn of rubble and powdered stone,
> Anguished flesh and splintered bone...

and

> Showing a ditch where a dead girl lies
> Courted by death and hungry flies...

Feelings and ideas stimulated by this song could be helpful for those working with people who have been in combat zones (for example, the Gulf war) and who are suffering from the after-effects of that experience.

Track 10 *The Sheath and the Knife* This is a song about brother/sister incest. Its usefulness is hampered by being in a dialect which, though beautiful, is inaccessible to many.

Track 14 *Moving On* This song deals with homelessness – among travelling people. It is likely to be relevant to other homeless groups. Its link to the homeless family in Bethlehem 2000 years ago, challenges Christian ethical values.

Track 15 *Nobody Knew She Was There* The writer realizes that his mother became invisible beneath her 'shroud of self-denial'. Again, there are memorable images:

> The bucket's steam like incense coils,
> Around the endless floors she toils...

and

> How could it be that no one saw her drowning,
> How did we come to be so unaware?
> At what point did she cease to be her,

> When did we cease to look and see her?
> How was it no one knew that she was there?

The issue of self-denial and self-sacrifice, ever present in the caring professions, should be addressed by those intending to practice counselling.

Track 16. *Looking for a Job* A harsh, agonizing look at the emotional turmoil caused by unemployment:

> Sick of being outside in the street,
> Sick of being last in the queue,
> Sick of being looked through as if I'm not there...

and

> Tired of the bickering rows,
> Ashamed of the things I say,
> And tired of feeling ashamed...

Track 18. *The First Time I Ever Saw Your Face* A simple love song, with an emphasis on expression of emotion, rather than ownership. A useful introduction to exploring what sort of love we have experienced and what sort of love we are looking for in our lives.

Track 20. *The Joy of Living* The writer says goodbye to the people and places he loves, as he accepts his approaching death. He celebrates life, and transforms his farewell into a love song:

> Scatter my dust and ashes,
> Feed me to the wind,
> So that I may be
> Part of all you see
> The air you're breathing.
> I'll be part of the curlew's cry and the soaring hawk,
> The blue milk wort and the sundew hung with diamonds.
> I'll be riding the gentle wind that blows through your hair,
> Reminding you how we shared in the joy of living.

This is likely to promote exploration of acceptance of death and the obstacles to such acceptance. The song is also an example of spirituality (see the participants' handout **PM 23**).

GROUP 2 FROM *I WILL STAND FAST*. FRED SMALL (1988). FLYING FISH RECORDS INC. (FF90491) C/O ROUNDER RECORDS, I CAMP ST, CAMBRIDGE MA 02140, USA (CASSETTE)

The tape sleeve is headed with the words, 'The stories in these songs are true'. All the songs have important things to say.

Track 3. *I Will Stand Fast* Popular at Elizabeth Kubler-Ross' 'Life, Death and Transition' workshops, this song is about supporting those working through early childhood trauma:

> I will stand fast,
> I will stand fast
> You are safe in the daylight at last

Nightmare and fear, they have no power here.
I will stand fast...

and

You will walk with no fetters to bind you
Cold wind beating out of the past
All the love that you have wanted will find you
Hold on, I will stand fast.

Track 5. *If I Were a Moose (and You Were a Cow)*. An amusing exploration of the serious issue of marriages which challenge social norms:

Would your parents watch us graze
Shake their heads
'It's just a phase',
Or would they thank the stars above
Their precious heifer's found her love.

Track 6. *Every Man* The socialization of boys into 'macho' attitudes, suppressed feelings and violence. The recurring chorus is:

Every man gonna be a soldier
Every man be cut to kill
Every man looking over his shoulder
Every man be shaking still.

The final chorus changes to:

Every man got love abiding
Every man got a hurt unhealed
Every man got a heart in hiding
Every man gonna be revealed.

Track 7. *Scott and Jamie* Two abused children are successfully fostered by a gay couple, until a homophobic media campaign forces the social work department to take them back into care:

The kitchen's clean and quiet, we change the furniture around
Still keep Scott's rabbit – in the middle of the night sometimes wake up to the sound
Of a little one crying when there's nothing there at all
David holds me says 'Go back to sleep'.

Track 8. *Denmark 1943* An account of the national response of the Danes to the German intention to deport and exterminate Danish Jews:

Christian policemen, shopkeepers and teachers
Tell their friends of the quickening storm
While students on bicycles race through the streets
Searching for Jews to be warned...

and

'We're not heroes or martyrs,' so say the Danes
'We were just looking after our own.'

The events recalled are a part of history for many, but the song could touch a chord among those working with survivors of the holocaust, or later generations from those families, who may still be deeply affected by the trauma. This is valid whether the connection is with the victims or the perpetrators. The song might also be relevant to those traumatized by current struggles in Ireland, Bosnia and other places. In any case, in a course of this kind, it is useful to be reminded that human behaviour can be noble and uplifting.

Track 9. *This Love* An affirmation of the power of love. By the end of this type of course, people are very aware of a closeness which may be quite new to them. The song affirms that feeling and could be appropriate as an ending:

> When you get this close to someone
> There's no blaming, no mistaking
> You know what they've been through
> And the courage it's constantly taking.

Below is the text of a leaflet designed to support bereaved parents with children. It might be worth enquiring at local hospitals and social work departments to see what is available in your area. Samples of these could be made available for participants to look at.

### Helping children…when someone dies
### A guide for parents

The death of someone close to us is perhaps one of the hardest events in life we have to face up to, and the same is true for our children. As parents we have not only our sadness to deal with, but we also have to help our children with their own grief.

We cannot protect children from sadness and pain following the loss of someone close. It is very important to allow children to grieve, just as adults must. Sometimes children can surprise us by coping better than we think.

**Your child's grief**

Children react to grief in different ways. These are some of the ways they might react:

- Children may first feel numb and shocked when someone has died. They may become withdrawn or perhaps have an outburst of screaming. They may act as though nothing has happened.

- Despair and sadness may follow, or the child may become very angry. Younger children may break their toys in anger. Older children may be aggressive to brothers, sisters and friends. Children may say angry and hurtful things to members of their family, like 'I hate you', but this is part of learning how to cope with their feelings and the change that has happened in their life.

- Some children might feel blame for the death of a loved one.

- Most children will feel insecure. Children may change or regress and act in an immature and babyish way. Some children refuse to go to school, fearing you might not be there when they get back. They might find it hard to concentrate once at school and might fall behind with their work. Others might have problems going to sleep and become afraid of the dark. Eating habits may change, becoming fussy, not eating or hoarding food. Young children may wet and soil again, or want a long-forgotten bottle or dummy. Children of any age may wet the bed.

- They may become more prone to illness.

- The way they behave can vary a lot from day to day. Young children have problems knowing what death means. They may seem to have taken in what has happened one day and then ask after the dead person the next day.

- Children are likely to be disturbed in the first few weeks after someone's death, but a lot of children still have problems for up to one or two years later.

## How to help your child

### The need for honest, open talking

Remember you cannot stop the pain of losing someone. It is right that children are sad when someone dies. Trying to protect them from unhappiness may make problems for them in later life.

Most adults feel awkward talking about death, especially to children. They are afraid they might scare their child or say the wrong thing. You need to talk about death and provide honest and truthful answers to your child's questions. Often the meaning of a child's question is unclear. It may be wise to ask, 'why do you ask me that?' before trying to answer. It is best to avoid answers like 'Daddy has gone to sleep', as the child may fear going to sleep, or 'Grandma has gone away', as your child may believe she will come back.

Children are better able than we think to take on board an honest attempt to explain death. They may ask the same question again and again. This is normal. It is your child's way of coming to understand what has happened.

Make sure your child does not feel to blame for the death.

### The importance of the funeral

The funeral plays an important part in grieving. The family can say goodbyes with the support of family and friends. It is important for children to be involved in getting ready for the funeral. You should explain what will happen and let them attend the service, but don't force your child. Explain that when they are ready they can visit the grave or garden of rest.

### The need for reassurance

Your child needs plenty of reassurance. Let them know you love them and will be there for them. Give them lots of cuddles. Let your child know that feelings are important. Take time to listen to them. If you have not got the time when they ask a question, make sure you make time later and tell them that you will do so. Teenagers may want to spend more time on their own; let them.

### Practical ways to help your children through their grief

- Grief is tiring, so change between active and quiet activities. Think about an early bedtime for young children.

- Extra clothing during the day can reduce the coldness of shock. It can make your child feel loved and protected. Soft sheets and blankets on your child's bed will be comforting.

- Give special foods. Soft foods remind your child of being young and protected.

- Try to keep to your usual routine. Maintaining a routine reassures your child. Try not to worry or get cross if their behaviour seems strange and babyish.

- Don't tell your child not to worry or be sad. They can't control their feelings, just as you can't control your own.

- Don't try to hide your pain. It is alright to cry in front of your child. You will need to talk to people yourself through the difficult times.
- Do let your child know that you understand how they are feeling and that you are there for them whenever they want to talk.

*Tasks to help your child's grieving*
Remembering how things used to be is an important part of grieving. It can be comforting to realize that the person who has died can still be an important part of our lives. As time goes on, your child should find it easier to talk about their own loss. It is important to allow and encourage your child to look back on their memories, when they seem ready. Reading a book, [see 'Resources' in Section 5 of this manual], looking through old photographs or perhaps making a scrap book, can help your child to talk about their thoughts and feelings.

- Young children may not understand what is said to them and are unable to tell you how they feel. They may be able to use toys or drawings to help them let you know.
- Visiting the grave or garden of rest (from time to time) is also very important. Encourage your child to take an active part, for example, arranging flowers on the grave.
- Often your child can gain great pleasure from being allowed to keep an object which reminds them of the person who has died.
- Do let your child's school know about your child's loss. Your child's teacher can be there to provide an extra hug and reassurance. Keep the school informed. Some teachers may not realize how long the effects of bereavement can last. School friends can help children a lot, but sometimes children will be cruel and it might help to prepare your child for this. You could discuss ways of answering unkind remarks.

There is no right or wrong way of grieving, and each child is unique and special. Take things one day at a time, and remember your family's sadness and pain will heal in time.

[The leaflet continues here with references to books for young children, older children and adults. These are included in Section 5 of this manual.]

*Local contacts*
If you have further worries about your child, you might contact the health visitor or school nurse, family doctor, MacMillan nurses or self-help groups.

*Leaflet produced by Alison Gray and Fiona Parry for West Cumberland Hospital, Whitehaven.*

# PART 4

# Participants' Materials

All documents in this section may be photocopied for distribution to participants in a course, *provided that* facilitators ensure that in all such cases, participants also receive the first in this series (**PM 1: Professional and ethical guidelines**) – see the 'Note on ethical issues' at the front of this manual.

The materials are numbered consecutively, **PM 1** to **PM 52**, for ease of reference. Those numbered **1** to **29** are grouped to correspond to the five days of the course and the follow-up day. **PMs 30** to **36** are linked with the additional lessons plans that are included in Section 2. **PMs 37** to **43** are a mixture of support information, exercises and centrings. Facilitators can use these as a basis for other lesson plans that they may want to construct, using appropriate learning structures. **PMs 44** to **50** are structured role-plays, and the last two (**PMs 51** and **52**) are alternative evaluation forms.

## MATERIALS FOR THE STRUCTURED COURSE

# DAY 1

# PROFESSIONAL AND ETHICAL GUIDELINES

**PM 1**

*Please keep this handout with you for reference throughout the course*

Regardless of the level of counselling skills a person possesses, a warm and empathic personality can induce a needy client to disclose problems that are pressing for attention. A relatively inexperienced listener can thus find herself confronted by issues which she may feel are beyond her in terms of her training, and perhaps because of her own emotional state at the time.

Participants in this course should note also that although the activities in the programme, and the associated handouts, will be seen as a challenge by many, others may view them as threatening in part, perhaps because of some recent personal experience or temporary emotional vulnerability.

The following suggestions should help everyone on the course, trainees and trainers alike, to extract the maximum benefit from working together in a professional and ethical manner.

### DURING THE COURSE

- Play an active part in choosing the optional activities in which you want to be involved.

- Opt out of sessions that are not appropriate to your needs; choose an alternative activity.

- When you are involved in an exercise, state clearly if you wish to stop.

- Use the support structures provided by the course to deal with any problems that arise, as they emerge. You may want also to seek additional or alternative support elsewhere.

### AFTER THE COURSE

- Counselling may be an accepted part of your responsibility in your work place. In that case, when considering what sort of commitment you can offer to clients, first make a realistic assessment of how much support you are likely to be able to negotiate among colleagues at work.

- If you plan to use counselling skills outside your work environment, then you will need to create your own support network. Alternatively, you may take advantage of the support that would be available if you were to work with, say, a voluntary agency. However, you should always match your commitments to the current state of your support structures.

- In any case, if you undertake a continuing commitment to counselling, it will be necessary for you to monitor your skills constantly, and to develop them further with additional training.

- Before committing yourself, consider carefully your own emotional state. For example, if you have had a recent bereavement, this may not be the best time to take on demanding new counselling commitments.

*© 1997 Fay W. Jacobsen, Margaret Kindlen and Allison Shoemark*

- Discover whether the client chose to come for counselling or whether she was sent. If the latter, then, after explaining what counselling might provide, support her in choosing to stay or to withdraw.

- Be clear about your level of training and experience when starting to work with a client.

- Be clear about the length of each session that you offer, and whether there are any limits to the number of sessions.

- Be clear about confidentiality, and about situations (for example, in supervision) where, with the client's agreement, you may wish to discuss the work with your supervisor.

If the issues emerging during a session with a client seem to be developing in a direction where you feel inexperienced or unprepared, discuss this with your supervisor. She will help you to decide whether to refer the client to a more appropriately qualified counsellor, and, if so, how to help the client over the transition.

If you decide to continue working with the client, then the supervisor will help you plan to deal effectively with the issues raised, and advise you on what extra support you might need. (This could be in the form of reading or of networking with others who are working with similar issues.)

## SHARING EXPECTATIONS WORKSHEET    PM 2

1.  Take five minutes to make notes under the following headings. These can be private thoughts, and there is no obligation to share them with anyone. However, please also include some thoughts which you are prepared to share with the larger group at the next stage of the exercise.

    What I want from this course is

    What I don't want from this course is

    What I bring to this course is

2.  Now spend 15 minutes with your group sharing what you choose of your responses above.

3.  At the end of this time you will be asked to construct a poster which conveys your group's response (allow ten minutes). *Write your names on the poster.* (We will review this at the end of the course.)

4.  Posters will be discussed in the large group. They will be the basis for contracts between participants and trainers.

|                        | *Known to self* | *Unknown to self* |
|------------------------|-----------------|-------------------|
| *Known to others*      | Free and open   | Blind self        |
| *Unknown to others*    | Hidden self     | Unknown self      |

*Figure 4.1 The Johari window*

Figure 4.1 illustrates two ideas. First, everyone has different levels of self-awareness. Second, everyone has aspects of themselves that they are more or less able or willing to share with others. The diagram is not meant to imply that these different aspects of personality are divided neatly and equally, as depicted; it represents only a notional starting point in a process in which individuals may progress.

Part of each person's self is known to them and to others. It is 'free and open'.

Another part is known to themselves but is not shared with others. This is the 'hidden self'.

A third part of an individual's personality is unrecognized by the person concerned, but is known by others. This is the 'blind self'.

Finally, there is a part of one's personality that is not recognized by oneself or by others. This is the 'unknown self'.

Counsellors try to relate to clients in a way that will encourage them to become more aware of aspects of their 'blind self' and to share some aspects of their 'hidden self'. During this process, clients often become aware of memories of events and feelings that were previously buried in their 'unknown self'. By reducing the areas of the 'blind self', the 'hidden self' and the 'unknown self', the client becomes more 'free and open' (Figure 4.2).

*Known to self*        *Unknown to self*

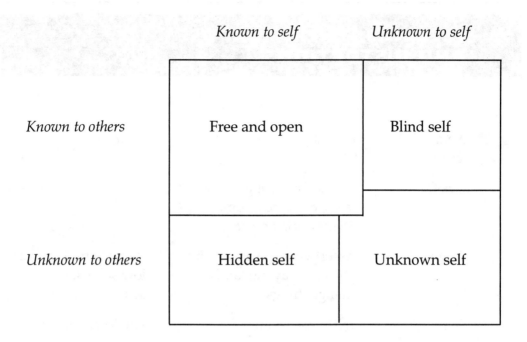

*Known to others*        Free and open        Blind self

*Unknown to others*        Hidden self        Unknown self

*Figure 4.2 Johari window: more 'free and open'*

However, this increasing insight is a two-way process. When working with clients, counsellors' prejudices are challenged, their memories stirred and their emotions are triggered, as the client's disclosures ring a bell with the counsellor's own unresolved issues. If these have been out of awareness previously, or denied, then the effect can be to de-skill the counsellor and reduce the effectiveness of her work. In a subconscious effort to protect her own vulnerability, the counsellor may then restrict the depth of the client's disclosures. She might also project some of her own prejudices and misapprehensions on to the client, thus losing the objectivity which is crucial for successful counselling.

This is why this training course in counselling skills includes opportunities for participants to explore the kinds of issue that clients may raise in a way that will help participants to discover their own vulnerabilities. It is better that such discoveries are made here, in a supportive environment, rather than that some hidden or unknown trauma emerges while attempting to support someone else.

But of course, everyone has a right to keep part of themselves private. Recognition of, and respect for, personal boundaries is part of looking after oneself. Personal boundaries vary, depending upon the people involved and the situations that they are experiencing. One aim of this course is to help people to free themselves from some of the more restrictive and destructive messages that are often implanted in awareness during childhood.

Self-awareness is an ongoing process for counsellors. It helps them to look after themselves and to improve their skills.

(Adapted from Luft, J. and Ingham, H. (1995) *The Johari Window: A Graphic Model of Interpersonal Relations*. Los Angeles: University of California Western Training Laboratory in Group Development.)

## FEELINGS: THEIR PURPOSE AND DISTORTIONS                                   PM 4

| Natural feeling | Purpose | Distortion |
|---|---|---|
| Grief | To deal (not cope) with tears; to express remorse (*'I could have done better'*) | Self-pity; shame; guilt |
| Anger | Assertiveness; self-esteem; power to say 'no' and to change things | Rage; hatred; powerlessness; low self-esteem; need to hurt self and/or others |
| Fear | Self-preservation | Anxiety; phobias |
| Love | To express who I am; feel free to love and be loved; to give and receive freely with no conditions; to nurture myself and others; to experience the joy of life | 1. Conditional: *'I'll love you if...'*<br>2. Clinging vine: *'I need you to be with me, never leave me'*<br>3. Possessive: *'You belong to me, you're mine'* (reflected in the lyrics of many 'love' songs) |
| Envy | Stimulant to:<br>1. Emulate a mentor or model (*'I'm glad you're the way you are. I want to be that way too'*)<br>2. Growth (*'I can grow out of this situation, seeing how you handle it more effectively'*); to be curious; to be inspired by | Critical: self-critical; low self-esteem; powerlessness; undermine self with the successes of others; jealousy |

These ideas are presented as a basis for reflection and discussion. They challenge the common categorization of feelings into 'good' and 'bad'. They help one to begin to examine the validity of some deeply rooted messages from the past. Those messages may now be counter-productive, and distorting one's relationships.

(Adapted from ideas presented at an Elizabeth Kubler-Ross 'Life, Death and Transition Workshop', Edinburgh, 1992.)

# CONSTRUCTIVE USE OF FEEDBACK　　PM 5

Sensitively offered and constructive feedback is invaluable for improving counselling skills and deepening self-awareness. It also helps to improve communication between people in many other situations. Unfortunately, however, in Western culture, there are common messages that discourage effective communication:

1. *It's not nice to criticize; if you can't say something nice, don't say anything; don't draw attention to people's faults.*

2. *If you can't do a job well, don't do it at all; spare the rod and spoil the child; single-minded commitment is essential for...*

Both sets of these familiar messages are destructive in different ways. The first suggests that it is socially unacceptable to comment on counter-productive or potentially damaging behaviour. This denies others knowledge of how such behaviour is perceived, and thus the opportunity to make changes. Those who give such uncritically positive feedback are also denied the right to be genuine or congruent in the way they express their feelings. This type of response rapidly loses credibility and compromises the giver's integrity.

The second set of messages reflects the attitudes of those who feel they have a monopoly of the truth, and that their 'truth' is applicable to all. Such a person is likely to give highly critical and perfectionist feedback and little, if any, praise.

Constructive feedback implies taking a middle course: the offering of both positive and constructively critical information during an interaction between two people. This is done in a way that will promote self-awareness and growth. Here are some simple guidelines to help you to achieve this:

1. Concentrate on what you observe, rather than on your interpretation of what you observe, for example, '*I saw you shift in your chair when I said...*', not, '*You looked uneasy when I said...*'.

2. Use neutral rather than judgemental language, for example, '*You say your wife sometimes raises her voice at the kids*', not, '*You say your wife screams at the kids continuously*'.

3. Be specific and avoid generalizing, for example, '*You told him the date of his next appointment four times*', not, '*You went on and on at him*'.

4. Focus on behaviour that the person can change, for example, '*I find it difficult to concentrate when you are clicking your pen*', not, '*I find it difficult to concentrate because of that wart on your nose*'.

5. Give amounts of information appropriate to the needs of the recipient. (This may be much less than you have available.) Offer ideas and information as your perceptions; they are not necessarily accurate. For example, '*I imagine...*', '*It seemed to me...*', '*It was my impression...*', not, '*You were...*'.

6. Whenever possible, sandwich critical feedback between two layers of positive feedback, and check that the person has taken in both. A useful check is to invite the recipient to summarize your remarks. Feedback shared in this spirit is usually experienced as supportive.

(Adapted from Jacobsen, F.W. and Mackinnon, H. (1989) *Sharing Counselling Skills: A Guide to Running Courses for Nurses, Midwifes and Health Visitors.* Edinburgh: Scottish Health Education Group.)

Working in the area of loss, whether it be abuse, death or bereavement, is not easy. It can be exhausting to bear witness to the depth of pain and hurt being experienced. 'Looking after ourselves' implies that while the client *and* the counsellor find ways of being open and vulnerable with each other, both are able also to experience nourishing change and growth.

When working in helping relationships, counsellors often protect themselves so well that they become unreachable. (Sometimes they become saturated and over-burdened with the client's problems.) If they are to allow themselves the freedom to feel vulnerable, counsellors need first to acknowledge and express their own store of pain. But this is the spectre which they fear will overwhelm them when working in this area. So, wisely, they find ways of distancing themselves from pain; or if their generosity disallows this, then they collapse.

The core of the work described in this package is about the therapeutic relationship. The twin strands that hold that core together are *self-awareness* and *self-nurturing*. The therapeutic relationship is seen as a partnership between counsellor and client. Both are open to change and influence by the other, using sensitive listening and communication skills. This two-way process is painful and enriching. It is essential that it takes place within clearly defined boundaries which establish a safe environment. Both counsellor and client may then allow themselves to be open and vulnerable. For example, boundaries of time, suitable context, space, and permission to touch and to express feelings without censoring are negotiated.

Counselling involves use of intuition and curiosity while maintaining respect for the client. To do the first without the second negates the idea of a partnership in the therapeutic relationship, and degenerates into pseudo-therapeutic manipulation.

'Looking after ourselves' in this course includes all the above aspects of self-awareness. Self-nurturing is also built into the programme for each day. Space is reserved for some of the many aspects of *self-care* with which caring professionals are becoming increasingly familiar; things such as relaxation, centring, meditation, massage, aromatherapy and reflexology. Yet another aspect of self-nurturing promoted in this course is this idea of seeking *support structures*. Paired support and group support are two examples.

All these skills are more convincingly conveyed to clients if they are integrated within the counsellors' own lives. Sound therapeutic relationships develop a high degree of sensitivity to nuances of language and non-verbal communication. Attempting to convey these self-caring concepts to clients without practising them oneself implies a lack of conviction that is likely to be detected by the client. In consequence, the work is likely to be less effective and the counsellor–client relationship could be jeopardized. However, if counsellors use these methods for themselves, then they have available powerful additional tools for work with clients. Moreover, even if these methods are not being used overtly when working with clients, a counsellor's own self-awareness and self-nurturing represents a valuable model of positive self-regard and good practice.

# DAY 2

# THE HIDDEN CHILD                                    PM 7

Read the following article by John Southgate (1989). Your reading can only be cursory in the time allotted but no matter; just record your first impressions. A detailed analysis is not being sought.

As you read, make notes about ideas or statements:

- that are new to you
- with which you disagree
- that strike an unexpected chord of sympathy in you
- that you don't understand.

When you have finished, discuss your notes with a partner.

---

## The Hidden Child Within Us

### Introduction – the experience

When people grow up they tend to think that childhood is in the past, leaving only memories, some of which can be recalled – a bit like a family album stored on videotape within the mind. To some degree this is what happens. But when an adult behaves frivolously, or is enchanted by a view, or feels inside like a scolded child, or stifles a scream at a horror movie, or makes a daisy chain, or plays with a toy train, then she[1] is in touch with her *inner child*. The inner child is alive there and then, within the adult body. A person who is out of touch with her inner child has no fun or flair, she is always serious and ponderous. That is because the playful, energetic inner child has been stifled, hidden away, or 'made unconscious'.

It can be that another side to the inner child is also hidden from view. This is the child who is sad, miserable, lonely or terrorized. For some adults it is so unbearable to be in touch with these bad feelings that they do not allow them into their consciousness. The price that they have to pay for this is to lack all feelings and emotions, to live in a flat and colourless world. This may have been absolutely necessary in order to survive. In this process of surviving, *both* the bad experiences and the good experiences may have been suppressed.

No matter what happens, a baby strives towards gaining love. At this stage to gain love and approval is life itself – it is all the baby has. She has to believe that her caretakers are good. If she is mistreated and there is no one to help her, she has to 'die' – that is, to stifle all the feelings that result from being mistreated, such as anger and rage. She then shuts these feelings out of her consciousness to avoid further hurt. This enables her to pretend and imagine that her caretakers are good – she idealizes those who have mistreated her. This process leads the child to build a 'false self' which, apparently, says and does the expected or normal things in life. She may try to build relationships and to some degree

---

1 Wherever she/her are used in this chapter, he/his should be read as possible alternatives.

succeed. However, underneath she may feel empty, and find it difficult to make real emotional contact with other people.

Sometimes close relationships are avoided altogether, in case the lonely, frightened or terrorized child bursts forth and overwhelms the person. If the early experience was that love is followed by vulnerability and then terror, closeness to an adult in the present can bring fear of repetition. Usually the early experiences are not consciously recalled and the person does not know or understand why relationships seem to go wrong.

Traumatic experiences often take place before spoken language has developed. Our earliest language is in the form of body sensations and visual images, as in dreams. The terror can be symbolized as fleeing from monsters, as in a nightmare. In therapy, when a person starts to recover these memories into consciousness, it can feel to her like opening a 'Pandora's box'. Dreams are important as they can describe symbolically a baby's preverbal experience. Dreams and body sensations, in this case, are the 'voice' of the inner child, expressed in the language of the unconscious. Attempts to stifle the unhappy inner child are in vain because she can never simply disappear. Her voice, if it is not heard by the grown-up self, 'speaks' via the languages of the unconscious, through physical sensations or symptoms, dreams and behaviour in relationships. The body may develop migraine, rashes, asthma, ulcers and, some think, even cancer. Another common 'indicator' is refusing food (anorexia) or gorging and then vomiting food (bulimia). At an unconscious level, starving oneself is like the inner child saying, 'I won't have bad things inside myself, I don't deserve to live, it's all my fault'. Compulsive eating is like the inner child trying to fill the space up inside herself to stifle the feelings of pain and terror.

Of course, neither 'solution', starving or gorging, is dealing with the real problem and *in extremis* can be life threatening. Orbach (1979) and Chermin (1985) have written about this subject.

Most disrupting for our intimate sexual and social life is the fact that the unhappy inner child influences relationships. This may cause the grown-up self to repeat an early trauma within a current relationship.

If the early scenario was of abandonment and neglect, the adult may repeatedly choose partners who run away or leave. If there was early physical or sexual violence, the adult may choose partners who are violent and sadistic, or who are passive and masochistic. If the inner child is not 'heard' the message will be repeated over and over again in terms of disruptive feelings, symptoms or behaviour. This can make the adult feel inexplicably compelled by an inner force. This force often seems to say that the inner child is guilty and bad and is to blame for others' unhappiness. The same voice implies that parents (and later parental figures in society) are always right and good. The overall effect is that the inner child takes upon herself all the blame and guilt and shame that really belongs to those who have abused or abandoned the child. For many people the whole process remains within the unconscious for a lifetime.

### The child is innocent: the viewpoint of Alice Miller

Alice Miller was a world-famous psychoanalyst and had herself been analysed twice. While painting some pictures she began to get in touch with the hurt little girl inside her who had not been reached before. After much research and investigation she came to the conclusion that all children are born innocent and this fact is hidden by our culture. She has written books (Miller 1986, 1987a and 1987b) that are read worldwide and have influenced many people regarding child abuse, therapy, politics and social life. The descriptions at the introduction to this chapter derive largely from her work and therapists influenced by her. A number of important points lead from the premise that a child is born innocent, that is, 'not guilty'. Among these Miller includes the following:

- Each child needs among other things: care, protection, security, warmth, skin contact, caressing and tenderness.

- These needs are seldom sufficiently fulfilled: in fact, they are often exploited by adults for their own needs (trauma of child abuse).

- Society takes the side of the adult and blames the child for what has been done to her.

- The victimization of the child has historically been denied, even today.

- This denial has made it possible for society to ignore the devastating effects of the victimization of the child for such a long time.

- The child, when betrayed by society, has no choice but to repress the trauma and to idealize the abuser.

- Repression leads to neuroses, psychoses, psychosomatic disorders and delinquency.

- The therapeutic process can be successful only if it is based on uncovering the truth about the patient's childhood instead of destroying that reality.

- A past crime cannot be undone by our understanding the perpetrator's blindness and unfulfilled needs.

- New crimes, however, can be prevented, if the victims begin to see and be aware of what has been done to them.

- Therefore, the reports of victims will be able to bring about more awareness, consciousness and a sense of responsibility in society at large.

As you can see, Miller believes that neurosis, psychosis, delinquency and addictions are rooted in the mistreatment of children. This implies that forms of child abuse are quite widespread. This is now being accepted more generally as true. If we define 'abuse' widely to include psychological invasion, abandonment and neglect, then almost *everyone* in our culture has suffered abuse. The implications of this view are radical and for many people hard to accept. It means that our families, culture and social system are partly based upon the mistreatment, manipulation, deprivation and exploitation of children. It follows that the unconscious aspects of abuse permeate our thoughts, ideas and education. The term that has been coined for this process is 'adultism'. This means that the needs, desires, wishes and demands of adults are, or may be, satisfied *at the expense* of those of the child. An extension of this argument is that adultism is at the root of all situations where the strong exploit the weak – for example, sexism, racism and imperialism. Throughout recorded history, wars and violence have been endemic in these processes. The thesis here is that the unconscious repetition pattern, where the adult repeats a childhood experience, is the mechanism that passes potential violence down the generations.

The reader may think this is all very well at an abstract historical level, but how does it affect one personally? What about you and me? As a parent have I mistreated my children? Have you mistreated yours? And what about all those who come under our care and control – lovers, friends, students, colleagues, clients, patients or even pets? An understandable reaction is to feel guilty, to blame ourselves or others or to dismiss the whole theory entirely. Alice Miller's argument is that it is not helpful or relevant to lay blame. She suggests that we unconsciously, unwittingly and *innocently* repeat compulsively what has been done to us in our childhood. We do this partly as an attempt to exorcize or deal with early experience and partly because our ethical, political, religious and educational beliefs unknowingly collude in this process and make it feel 'natural'.

The obviously abused child who comes to the attention of social workers, doctors and the police is but the extreme example – the 'tip of the iceberg'.

When early abuse is unconscious, people choose different ways of coping with anxiety and body symptoms. For some it can be drink or drugs, for others smoking, gambling, overwork or even neurosis and psychosis. These are the slightly more visible victims of adultism. There is, therefore, no one reading these words who has not, in a very general sense, suffered abuse as a child – to a greater or lesser degree. So what can be done? Is the process reversible? Miller and those influenced by her work have an optimistic answer. Yes. It *is* reversible, though not easily or without pain. To develop this answer we need to consider in more detail the processes for countering the effects of abuse.

### The advocate for the child

In the best of circumstances a baby feels that she is held safely by a warm person who conveys without words that she is beautiful, good and worthwhile. This gives a self-confidence which lasts a lifetime. In time the growing child, and later the teenager, develops an internalized version of this person who nurtures. This internalized figure can be thought of as the inner advocate who supports the child. Consequently, later in life the adult also feels supported and thereby develops a personality that can cope with adversity and basically feel real and true. This person will easily be able to be an outer advocate for a child or grown-up. Each person needs to develop an 'inner advocate' who supports the child inside themselves, and also an 'outer advocate' who can support others. Quite often people who are good as outer advocates may be attracted to one of the helping professions – for example, nursing, therapy – or they may be people to whom friends and neighbours frequently turn for help and advice. When someone has never had the chance to develop an inner advocate, they can be helped to do so by an outer advocate/therapist. No matter how bad the experience in early life, for most people some spark of the creative self survives from babyhood. An advocate for the inner child can help this part of the person grow. As a therapist I sometimes find it hard to believe that a person could survive the experiences that are shared with me. But it can be, and it sometimes is, possible to regain health and well-being.

The reason that this is possible is not due to something special about the therapist, but the fact that nature has provided creative and repair cycles that enable us to cure ourselves (with a little help from our friends!).

**Nature's two cycles**

There is a *creative cycle* in nature (see Figure 4.3) which we may know even though we may not conceptualize it. Even a mundane task has elements of nurturing – energizing – peak – relaxing. Take gardening as an example. You may nurture yourself with a cup of tea and reflect upon the task. You prepare tools and materials. You put more energy into working as you dig and prune. Then, *voila*! You reach a peak. It's done! You step back and admire your creation. You may now relax and tidy up and ask others to share your pleasure and achievement. An outer advocate or mother helps the inner or actual child through a similar process. First, to nurture, hold and encourage the child, physically and emotionally. It is important that the child's needs take priority – it is possible to over-love or smother. Then, in the energizing part of the cycle, the advocate/mother facilitates play and activity. Again it is important that it is the play the child desires and not the play the adult decides is for the child's own good. At the peak of pleasure and laughter the advocate is a witness and one who recognizes the child's achievements: for example, where the child builds her first sandcastle and says with joy, 'Look what I've made!'. In the relaxing phase the advocate/mother encourages rest, day-dreaming and sleep. An adult's own inner advocate can encourage the inner child to enjoy this process, or a therapist/advocate can encourage the child within the adult to do the same. (An excellent example of such advocacy is given in Pinney and Schlachter 1983.) Although one needs to pay attention to the hurt or abused child within a person, it is important to develop the creative child at the same time. Sometimes the experiences to be worked through are so appalling that they cannot be faced without the help of the creative child within the person. The creative cycle was formulated by Randal and Southgate (1980), by a synthesis of the work of Reich (1961) and Bion (1968).

The *repair (mourning) cycle* (Figure 4.3) provides nature's healing and 'repair' for trauma. A lot of work has been done to try to understand the curative process of mourning the death of a loved one; the key researcher in this area is Bowlby (1985). Most of us think of the mourning process as weeping or crying. In fact there is more to it than this. Miller describes how mourning is a natural curative process not only for the trauma of bereavement, but for any trauma – sexual abuse, violent attack, abandonment or whatever. (Bowlby suggested this many years ago but few people seem to have taken it up until recently.) Below are described the basic elements of mourning (in actual fact there would not be a neat movement from one phase to another).

1. *Traumatic event*. Emotional and physical shock galvanize the body and psyche. In bereavement this would be witnessing the moment of death or hearing about it. In abuse it would be the actual moment of the abuse happening or reliving and remembering the event. An immediate reaction may be to scream, shout or wail. It is not usual to remain 'stuck' in this phase, as the sheer physical exhaustion will lead to the following phases.

2. *Numbness*. This is experienced as the loss of sensations and feelings, and sometimes a feeling of deep depression. It has been described as

**The hidden child within us**

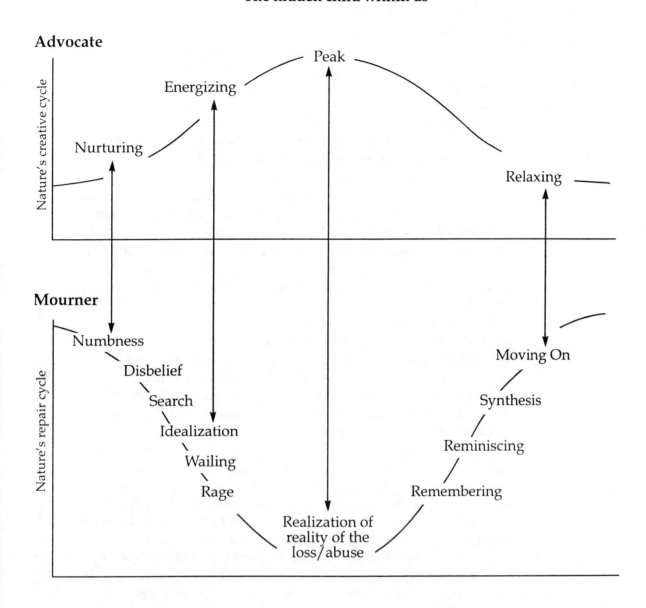

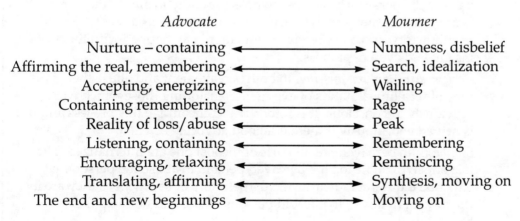

*Figure 4.3 Relationship and process between advocate and mourner*

falling down a black hole'. As in all phases it is possible to get stuck here and be unable to move on.

3. *Disbelief.* An initial reaction in bereavement is often to deny that the loved one is really dead. Social influences on the person are likely to support reality rather than fantasy. However, in the case of the abused person, she is first of all likely to deny an experience that blames someone loved. And even when other family members are told, they too may disbelieve that it happened. Unfortunately, until recently, social influences and pressures tended to deny the reality of abuse.

4. *Search.* In bereavement this is the belief that the lost one is alive and may be found in the street or some familiar setting. In abuse it may be the search for the good, idealized person who, it is imagined, will protect and look after the child.

5. *Idealization.* In bereavement this is where the loved one's good side is remembered and idealized. In abuse the perpetrator is idealized, as described earlier. It is not uncommon to become stuck in this phase. There is enormous social and cultural pressure to 'honour thy father and thy mother'. But the effect is to halt the mourning process and leave the person in a very unhealthy state.

6. *Weeping and wailing.* This is the most commonly accepted part of mourning in the case of bereavement. Unfortunately many well-meaning people try to ignore or stop this process. In abuse it happens when the person can really let themselves feel the gravity and awfulness of what has happened to them.

7. *Raging anger.* Often people are angry that someone has left them by dying. It is helpful to express this with someone they can trust. Again many well-intentioned people try to stifle this phase. In the case of abuse it can be a time when the inner child finally rages back at the perpetrator – encouraged by the inner or outer advocate. It is possible to get stuck in this phase too – often in combination with the previous one, so that active anger is followed by quieter weeping and so on.

8. *Realization of reality – depressive creative contradictions.* In bereavement the person begins to accept the reality of the loss. Both the good and bad parts of the person are seen as a whole. Similarly in abuse, the person feels both the cruelty and the kindness of the other as a whole. But it is contradictory, and a depressive rumination may happen with times of insight and even happiness.

9. *Remembering and reminiscing.* In both bereavement and abuse there is a time of recalling all kinds of experience, including those which were previously unconscious. It is important to encourage this process and it is helped enormously if there is a good advocate listener.

10. *Synthesis.* In bereavement all parts of the lost one are internalized. The lost one lives on inside the bereaved person. In abuse the person may either be indifferent towards the perpetrators or see them as they are in the present (if alive), that is, old persons who could not help their behaviour.

11. *Moving on.* Mourning is over and life is to be lived. Therapy changes to encouraging creativity and finally finishes altogether.

## Therapists as advocates

The Institute for Self-Analysis was set up in 1986 to train therapists as advocates for the inner child. Our first inspiration was Alice Miller; our second Karen Horney (1942), who was a pioneer in encouraging people to write a self-analysis with occasional help from a therapist. Many people spontaneously write letters and diaries when trying to deal with anxieties arising from childhood. We have found the combination of face-to-face work with an advocate, plus the exchange of letters, poems and paintings, to be an effective way to do therapy (see, for example, the letter from one of our members – what we call a 'LISA', a Live Interactive Self-Analysis – in the *Journal of the Institute for Self-Analysis*, April 1988).

The most important thing an advocate does is to *listen* and *be* with a person, giving undivided attention. This sounds simple and easy, but although this is true in one sense, people in our culture rarely give or receive such attention. It is important to create a safe place where the inner child can tell her story. This can only happen when considerable trust, confidence and even love has grown between the outer advocate and the inner child. The inner child may 'speak' of preverbal experience, so that listening includes messages from the body and the unconscious (as in dreams). Such messages need 'translating' into ordinary language and this is a skill an outer advocate needs to learn. Another skill is facilitating the person so that the creative and repair cycles described earlier can be encouraged. None of the above will work unless the inner child or infant feels safely held – in the sense of a baby feeling safe in her mother's arms (see Bowlby 1988; Winnicott 1971). This is not a skill, but a way of *being* and of each person relating to the other. It takes time to build such a relationship. It is very important that the advocate is *never* parental or adultist – even benevolent paternalism is bad for the inner child. Finally, it is crucial for a therapist to be in touch with her own inner child and to have worked through her own abuse and mourning. The function of the advocate for the inner child can be summarized in five roles:

- nurturer
- witness (accompanying the person as they relive traumas)
- protector against what has been done to the person
- translator
- supporter of the person's inner advocate and creativity.

However, it is important that the reader does not conclude that only a specialist can be an advocate. In daily life, at work and at play anyone can, and most of us do, some kind of advocacy. Nurses can be advocates for patients, teachers for pupils, play workers for toddlers and so on, using the principles already discussed. It is only when a person has been severely abused in early life that it is advisable to consult an inner child advocate/therapist.

## References

Bion, W.R. (1968) *Experiences in Groups*. London: Tavistock.

Bowlby, J. (1985) *Attachment and Loss*. Volume 3. Harmondsworth: Penguin.

Bowlby, J. (1988) *A Secure Base: Clinical Applications of Attachment Theory*. London: Routledge.

Chermin, K. (1985) *The Hungry Self: Women, Eating and Identity*. London: Virago.

Horney, K. (1942) *Self Analysis*. New York: W.W. Norton [Paperback (1962): London: Routledge and Kegan Paul.]

Miller, A. (1986) *Thou Shalt Not be Aware*. London: Virago.

Miller, A. (1987a) *For Your Own Good*. London: Virago.

Miller, A. (1987b) *The Drama of Being a Child*. London: Virago.

Orbach, S. (1979) *Fat is a Feminist Issue*. London: Hamlyn.

Pinney, R. and Schlacter, M. (1983) *Bobby, the Story of an Autistic Child*. London: Harville.

Randal, R. and Southgate, J. (1980) *Co-operative and Community Group Dynamics: Or Your Meetings Needn't Be So Appalling*. London: Barefoot Books.

Reich, W. (1961) *The Function of the Orgasm*. New York: Farrar, Straus and Giroux.

Southgate, J. (1989) 'The hidden child within us.' In W.S. Rogers, D. Hervey and E. Ask. *Child Abuse and Neglect: Facing the Challenge*. Milton Keynes: Open University.

Winnicott, D.W. (1971) *Playing and Reality*. Harmondsworth: Penguin.

# WHAT IS CHILD ABUSE? PM 8

**PM 9** is an activity sheet with descriptions of ten different kinds of situation. Read through them, and then cut them out from the page. Make two markers for 'most abusive' and 'least abusive', so that you have 12 small pieces of paper: ten descriptions and two markers.

Place the 'most abusive' marker on your left and the 'least abusive' on your right. Put the ten descriptions in front of you in a line. Place the one you think is the most abusive on your left, under the 'most abusive' marker. Place the one you think is the least abusive on the right, under the 'least abusive' marker. Arrange the other eight in between, in a sequence that reflects decreasing abusiveness from left to right. When you have finished, write the description numbers in the line of boxes below.

MOST ABUSIVE                                    LEAST ABUSIVE

☐   ☐   ☐   ☐   ☐   ☐   ☐   ☐   ☐   ☐

You may find this very difficult. Don't worry; the point is to stimulate you to think about the problem, and to confront you with the different issues and dilemmas raised by having to make the choices. You will probably find that you are asking yourself all sorts of questions. You may feel that you cannot decide between some of the descriptions. Again, don't worry. *There are no right or wrong answers.* The main point of this activity is to demonstrate, through experience, just how impossible it is to decide what is, and what is not, 'abusive'.

Write brief answers to the following questions:

1. What were the most important factors you took into account when making your decisions?

2. What decisions did you find most difficult? Can you think what it was that was making your choice so hard?

3. You may have found yourself saying, '*Well it all depends*'. If so, what sort of things would influence your judgement?

4. In each case who or what did you think was responsible?

Discuss and note the similarities and differences of your answers with those of a partner.

(From Open University – Child Abuse and Neglect, p.554, *What is Child Abuse?*, Course Book 1 pp.9–10)

# WHAT IS CHILD ABUSE?
# ACTIVITY DESCRIPTIONS                                    PM 9

DESCRIPTION 1

Miss Winter is Lee's teacher. Lee is eight, is disruptive and difficult, and has behaviour problems, such as wetting his pants. In a moment of frustration when he had been particularly naughty, Miss Winter called him a, '…dirty stinking boy' in front of the whole class, and made him wear a pair of girl's pink shorts as a punishment.

DESCRIPTION 2

Rita is 15 and from a strict Muslim family who have been very protective of her all through her childhood. Today Rita's father found out she had gone to a pub with her friends when she said she was going to her friend's house. He has forbidden her to go out after school again, and says she must leave school as soon as she is 16, and he will arrange a marriage for her.

DESCRIPTION 3

Tracy is six, and for the last couple of years her father has been persuading her to fondle his penis. Last night he got Tracy to masturbate him. When it was over he kissed Tracy lovingly, told her she was a good girl and he loved her and that this was her special way of showing him that she loved him.

DESCRIPTION 4

Petra is almost two years old. Her mother frequently leaves her alone at night while she goes down to the pub. Petra has frequent nightmares and wakes up screaming and frightened with nobody to comfort her.

DESCRIPTION 5

Ken is ten months old. This morning his father was looking after him while his mum was at work, and he got so frustrated with Ken's constant crying that he snatched him from his cot and shook him until he stopped.

DESCRIPTION 6

Mary is a single parent bringing up two teenage sons, Paul and Mark. Both are feeling terribly depressed because they are unemployed and there is no prospect of a job. Mary finds it hard enough to keep going, and has reached the point of ignoring them, leaving them to watch TV and play tapes in their room most of the day and night. This morning Paul took an overdose, and is unlikely to survive.

DESCRIPTION 7

Megan is three. Her mum, Alice, and her dad, Tom, are both unemployed teenagers, and they live in a very damp, cold, high-rise flat. Alice gets very depressed and takes tranquillizers. She and Tom row a lot, and last night, after a particularly bad row, Tom walked out saying he was never coming back. As Alice lay sobbing on the bed, Megan managed to knock an electric fire on top of herself, and she has been badly burned.

DESCRIPTION 8

Polly is the only daughter in a family of five children. She has become the family drudge, always called 'dumbo' and made to eat her meals (when she gets them) in another room; she is never allowed to watch TV with the family, or go out with them. She wears her brother's cast-off clothes, and is always very dirty, smelly and unkempt.

DESCRIPTION 9

Holly is 15. She has had a steady boyfriend for two years. Yesterday Holly's father returned home unexpectedly during the day, and found Holly in bed with her boyfriend. The boyfriend was thrown out, and Holly given what her father called, '...a sound hiding' with his belt. She has several large, fresh bruises and some cuts, even though she was fully clothed when the beating occurred.

DESCRIPTION 10

Rodney is 13, and attends a minor public school. Although he says he is a pacifist, he is forced to join the school Combined Cadet Force (CCF) and forbidden to wear his CND badge. His parents, despite his pleadings, refuse to take him away from school or intervene – even though he is now 'grounded' and exposed to public ridicule, because he will not put on his uniform or join in with CCF activities.

# HOW TO WRITE A ROLE-PLAY SCENARIO

**PM 10**

PART 1: THE SUMMARY

This will provide the trainers with a brief outline to be written on a flip-chart, for the skills' practice session, together with other summaries. It gives people the opportunity to choose or not to choose a topic which might be close to their own experience.

PART 2: THE COUNSELLOR

This should contain a brief outline of the personal and domestic details of the client, and of the issue or issues about which they need to see you.

PART 3: THE CLIENT

All the information in *part 2*, together with more information about the client's personal and domestic situation, should be included here. Some clues about hidden fears that are troubling the client will give the person playing her role some idea of how to approach this task.

ROLE-PLAY EXERCISE IN TRIADS

1.  Working alone, think of a situation which you have experienced, and construct a scenario in three parts as shown above.

2.  Working with your colleagues, compare your role-plays and relate how you dealt with the situation, identifying what felt effective and what felt ineffective at the time. Ask each other questions, to clarify any aspects of the written scenario that are unclear.

3.  When all three scenarios have been discussed, rewrite them making any changes which may have been suggested. They should be clearly written or printed in ink on one side of a piece of A4 paper.

4.  A selection of these role-plays will be made available as material for the skills' practice session. Individuals can use experiences from their own group, or may choose a scenario based on the experience of someone from another group.

# HEAD AND NECK MASSAGE                                     PM 11

This massage is based on one taught and practised by Ian Holland, an experienced masseur who has practised for more than 15 years in Glasgow. He claims that, using the massage, he can remove eight out of ten simple tension headaches.

The massage is a combination of Eastern and Western styles. The Eastern method is Shiatsu, in which fingers press on pressure points that are related to those used in acupuncture. The Western method is a version of Swedish massage, as adapted and taught by the Essalin Institute in California.

### POSITIONING

Ideally *A*, the person giving the massage, should sit on the floor with her back well supported against the wall. Her legs should be open so that *B*, the person to be massaged, can lie on the floor with her head a comfortable distance within reach of *A's* arms. If this position is used, *B* might want to flex her knees or have a small pillow under them.

This is a vulnerable position for *A*, however, and unless the group has reached an appropriate level of trust, it might not be acceptable. In any case, this position may be physically impossible for some participants.

### *ALTERNATIVE POSITION*

Although this alternative does not provide either partner with the same level of support as the position described above, many participants have enjoyed using it for massage.

*B* sits in a chair with a good back support. It should not be too low, since this would strain *A's* back. But *B* should be able to place her feet firmly on the ground, or, if she is a short person, on a pile of books. *Bs* should remove ear-rings, necklaces and contact lenses, and loosen any tight clothing.

Both *A* and *B* should preferably remove their shoes.

*A* stands behind the chair with knees unlocked.

Whatever positions are adopted, pairs should be arranged in such a way that *As* can see the trainers, who will demonstrate the massage step by step.

### *B*, THE RECEIVER

Close your eyes, feel the ground under your feet or body, and let it take your full weight. Breathe down into your belly, letting it expand with your 'in' breath and fall back with your 'out' breath. Keep your breathing easy and rhythmic, not unusually deep, and with a slight emphasis when you breathe out through lightly pursed lips.

If any thoughts come to you, try to let them float away while you enjoy the massage.

### *A*, THE GIVER

In the first position, make sure that your back is well supported and your knees do not feel strained. A small pillow or rolled up cardigan under the knees can improve your comfort. In the second position, keep your knees softly unlocked. If you need to change position during the massage, do so. Discomfort or tension building up in you might be transmitted to your partner.

Breathe in the same way suggested above to *B* and, during pauses, try to synchronize your breathing with your partner's and relax your body. You don't have to be busy all the time; a pattern of activity followed by rest enhances the relaxation process.

Transfer the weight of your body to achieve the pressure strokes. This saves unnecessary expenditure of energy by the arms and shoulders.

COMMUNICATION

*As*:    from time to time invite your partner to guide you on whether you would like lighter or firmer pressure or strokes.

*Bs*:    give your partner clear guidance. She has no other way of knowing how this feels to you. Your accurate feedback is her best way of learning. Don't hold back spontaneous sighs or other gentle sounds. These are the most expressive of all feedback. Apart from this, keep talking to a minimum.

OILS AND LOTIONS

The skin produces enough of its own oil, so massage oil is unnecessary. A choice of two or three light toilet waters should be available for *A* to put on her hands, to freshen them, and to give the pleasure of their smell to *B*. (Elderflower water and honey water have been popular.)

THE STROKES

*As* place your hands gently on either side of your partner's face and synchronize your breathing with hers (30 seconds).

1.   Place the pads of your thumbs side by side in the centre of her forehead, just above the brow line. Using firm pressure, slide the thumbs apart, smoothing out the brow until you reach the temples (Figure 4.4).

*Figure 4.4 Massage (1)*

© 1997 Fay W. Jacobsen, Margaret Kindlen and Allison Shoemark

Return your thumbs to the centre point, but an inch higher than before. Again, smooth out the brow to the temple. Check with your partner about the degree of pressure she would prefer.

Repeat this stroke, raising your thumbs an inch further up the forehead each time, until you have reached the hairline. Rest your hands gently on either side of your partner's face, relax and breathe (15 seconds).

2. The next strokes concentrate on the Shiatsu pressure points around the eyes. Place the pads of your thumbs on the inner extreme of the eyebrows, about an inch apart on the brow ridge (Figure 4.5). Ask your partner to take a breath, and as she exhales, press firmly and hold for five seconds. Ask your partner to inhale again, and repeat the pressure on this point as she exhales. Check with your partner if she wants more or less pressure. Move your thumbs to half way along the brow ridge, and repeat the procedure. These two points are worked twice as they are significant sites for tension, causing headaches. The procedure is the same for all other points shown in Figure 4.5, but you need only work these once.

*Figure 4.5 Massage (2)*

The third pressure point is at the end of the brow. The fourth point is alongside and about an inch from the outer point of the eye. The bone here is very fragile, so here use only half the pressure that you have used on other points. Point five is on the cheek bone under the centre of the eye, and point six is right up against the nose, under the inner point of the eye.

3. Press the eyeballs gently with your thumbs (check with your partner first that she wants this stroke), cup your hands over her eyes, relax, breathe and give her 30 seconds' soothing darkness (Figure 4.6).

*Figure 4.6 Massage (3)*

*Figure 4.7 Massage (4)*

4.  Using the thumbs and the tips of your fingers, pick up and knead the cheek muscles. Move around the cheek, loosening the muscles and those of the upper lip. These latter can become very tight and dehydrated in people who smoke. Moving your thumbs to the point of the chin and with your finger tips under the jaw, pick up and knead the muscles along the jaw line until your fingers reach the angle of the jaw (Figure 4.7). With a firm, circular movement of your fingers, massage the area around the angle and hinge of the jaw. This is the powerful muscle which tenses when we are

angry.[1] People who hold on to their anger and rarely express it, can be very tight here and the slightest pressure can be painful for them. Check with your partner that the pressure is appropriate for her.

5. This part of the massage is most effective if your partner is lying down. Slide your fingers around so that your hands are side by side, palms level with the nape of your partner's neck. Now push your hands as far down under her back as you can.

   (*Bs*: let the full weight of your back lie on your masseur's hands. If you are sitting in a chair you might even want to press back a little.)

   Now, raise the tips of your fingers so that they push into your partner's back. Hold for a count of three and then release. Repeat this procedure twice more. Pull your hands towards yourself about one inch; and repeat the entire sequence above (that is, three times in all). Continue moving your hands about one inch and repeating the sequence, until your thumbs are free of your partner's back. Now place your thumbs over the front of her shoulders and, using them as a counter-pressure, move your fingers in a circular, squeezing, kneading fashion, to massage the powerful, but often painfully tense, pads of muscle on either side of the spine at the top of the back. As you massage you might find knots in the muscles, which will become softer as you work on them. (If no other stroke has elicited 'oohs' and 'ahs' of pleasure, this one is likely to do so.)

   Withdraw your hands and rest them over your partner's ears to give her quiet. Check that your knees and body are relaxed, and synchronize your breathing with your partner's (30 seconds).

6. Pinch the lobes of your partner's ears. Continue pinching around the entire ear, then, taking the whole ear, one in each hand, move them in a small circular movement.

7. Move the hands to the base of the neck. Using a small, circular movement with the pads of your fingers, massage the strip of muscle on either side of the spine, slowly moving up towards the head. Follow the muscles up to where they attach the neck to the head, continuing to massage, until you find a hollow, just below the bulge at the back of the head (or occiput). This is another prime site for tension associated with tension headaches, and can be tense and sore. Check with your partner what pressure to use, as you work on this area.

   (If your partner is seated, move a little to her right side and, using your right hand on her forehead to steady her head, use your thumb and fingers on either side of the spine, for this entire sequence.)

   Rest your hands on either side of your partner's face; relax and breathe.

8. Turn your partner's head to one side and, while steadying it with one hand, spread your fingers over the uppermost part of the scalp, and work into the entire sheet of muscle, moving it over the underlying skull (Figure 4.8). Gently turn the head to the other side and repeat.

---

© *1997 Fay W. Jacobsen, Margaret Kindlen and Allison Shoemark*

---

1    A participant gave us a dramatic confirmation of this. She worked with a surgeon who specialized in reconstructive surgery on the bones of the face. He had operated on several clients to reconstruct their jaws, destroyed by this type of tension. He insisted on counselling before and after surgery to help the person to express rather than suppress their feelings.

*Figure 4.8 Massage (5)*

(Ian Holland asserts that this manoeuvre is particularly effective for relieving hangovers; a claim supported by independent accounts from some participants in courses.[2])

9. Re-centre your partner's head, ready to work on some of the many powerful pressure points on the scalp (Figure 4.9).

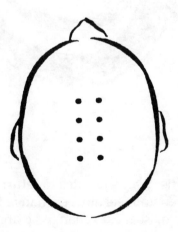

*Figure 4.9 Massage (6)*

2    Imbibing a lot of alcohol dehydrates this sheet of muscle, effectively 'shrink wrapping' the skull. Massage stimulates the blood flow, rehydrates and relaxes it.

Place your thumbs on either side of where a centre parting in the hair would be, about an inch apart. Ask your partner to take a breath and, as she breathes out, press down very firmly, holding for a count of five.

Now, move your fingers back about an inch, and repeat this process.

Move your fingers back a further inch, and repeat again.

Move your fingers back a further inch, and repeat for the third time. There are eight points in all. Rest your hands on your partner's face; relax and breathe.

10. Place the pads of your thumbs in the centre of the forehead, between and slightly above the eyebrows. Smooth them up the forehead to the hair line.

Return to the starting point, but separate your thumbs an inch (Figure 4.10). Repeat the stroke. Continue in this way, separating the thumbs by a further inch at the beginning of each stroke, until you reach the outer point of the eyebrow. Massage the temples with gentle, circular motions. Rest your hands for the last time on your partner's face; relax and breathe (30 seconds). Gently peel your hands away from her face, so that your fingertips are the last to leave.

*Figure 4.10 Massage (7)*

Give your partner a few minutes to return gently from the depths of her relaxation. When you feel able, exchange feedback on how it felt to give and receive the massage. Exchange positions so that the whole procedure can be repeated.

Adapted from: Holland, I. (1986) Head and Neck Massage.
In *Connections: Health and Arts in Scotland*, No.7, pp.22–24.

# DAY 3

# LISTEN (POEM)                                         PM 12

When I ask you to listen to me
And you start to give me advice,
You have not done as I asked.

When I ask you to listen to me
And you begin to tell me why I shouldn't feel that way,
You are trampling on my feelings.

When I ask you to listen to me
And you feel you have to do something to solve my problems,
You have failed me, strange as that may seem.

Listen! All I asked was that you listen.
Not talk or do – just hear me.
Advice is cheap:
25 cents will get you Dear Abby and Billy Graham in the same newspaper.
And I can do for myself. I am not helpless;
Maybe discouraged and faltering, but not helpless.

When you do something for me that I can and need to do for myself,
You contribute to my fear and weakness.

But when you accept as a simple fact that I do feel what I feel
No matter how irrational, then I can quit trying to convince you
And get on with the business of understanding
What is behind this irrational feeling.
And when that's clear, the answers are obvious and I don't need advice.
Irrational feelings make sense when we understand what's behind them.

Perhaps that's why prayer works, sometimes, for some people,
Because God is mute, and he doesn't give advice
Or try to fix things. 'They' just listen and let you
Work it out for yourself.
So please listen and just hear me. And, if you want to talk,
Wait a minute for your turn, and I'll listen to you.

Author unknown

# AN ADULT REMEMBERS A CHILDHOOD EXPERIENCE OF HOSPITAL                 PM 13

I spent two years in hospital between three and five years of age. The details in this account are taken from an amalgam of descriptions from my parents, two staff who worked in the hospital in the early 1950s, my own memories of other stays in the same hospital and insights which emerged from individual therapy and psycho-dramas.

What was it about? Fear – a churning in my stomach as I think of what two years of mind-numbing boredom must have been like – but I don't remember – at least my mind doesn't – my body sometimes recalls glimpses – lying on my back, legs in the air, my head turns back to the right and shouts in angry cries – 'I want my mummy! I want my mummy!' – another visiting hour is over – once a week on Sundays, so my mother says. The anguish for her and dad as they said each painful, guilty goodbye – I feel sick – at their pain – at my suffering – at my endless months of cheeriness – of being a good girl so mummy and daddy would come back.

And the clowns, they were the highlight – the circus came on the lawn but I guess I couldn't see much – except the clowns – they'd dance round the cot bars in their funny faces and bright colours. Was I just a little afraid? – but thrilled as well. And their sad faces told my story back to me. They knew – you had to put a mask on – it was the only way to survive.

What did they do to my legs? I didn't want to know. They weren't part of me. I could get by if I cut myself off from them. The nurses talking over me as they made the beds and tucked us in so tight – controlled – trapped, like flies in aspic – all tidy and sterile – 'Don't wrinkle the clothes, matron will be round soon' – bosom like a continental shelf, daring even a whisper of dissent. Puffed up with her own importance. Could she see us over that non-maternal cliff?

And what did she see? Rows of silent faces – they didn't dare tell their tale. It would have been too painful for her and them – so the routines and rules took over.

'Are the wheels straight nurse?'

'Don't let me see a speck of dust in *my* hospital nurse!'

'Nurse, get that hair tidy – *my* nurses must always be smart.'

'You were cuddling a child – *that's no excuse* – I've told you before you'll spoil them.'

'Look at Sister B____. She's a perfect example, discipline, tidiness and dedication – that's what I expect.'

What did we do between meals, bed baths, changing bandages, the weekly visiting and ward rounds? There was no radio, no record player, no 'school' for the under-fives. TV – what was that? Did the nurses read to us? I don't know. I think my mum did, on her visits when dad went outside to look after my brother Ian. Mum was shy and found it hard to talk, so we both escaped to the land of fairy tales together. Was Squirrel Nutkin there or did he come later? It's all a blank.

And where was teddy? Teddy who was taken away from me at night. The ultimate cruelty – he couldn't keep me safe in the dark. He had to go with all the other toys into the toy box – he didn't like it there. He missed me. My stomach tightens writing this and I remember the psychodrama where 'Sister B' took teddy away. The 'night nurse' with golden curls and a pretty face tucked him back in beside me, and then she told me I was her brave girl. I howled – nearly took the roof off – the pain was so intense...it's a release to write this down. It feels like my declaration to the world of just how bad it all was.

I'm wondering if I can face Jimmy's painting again – it's like a pelvis that grips my guts when I look at it. I remember as a teenager meeting my surgeon at some social event and he said, 'Hello, you're the hip aren't you?'. He was kind, but that wasn't how I wanted to be remembered.

I wanted to be seen as *me* – not just as my problem hips – to be bandaged and pulled and X-rayed. Legs scraped and oiled every other day to stop the skin flaking – in the dressing room – there, the most hated smell of all – *ether*. Victory V lozenges still make me heave. All the shining brass and chrome, the clunk of noisy brakes as the beds were let down on to the hard, clean marble floor and then rolled back into the softer ward.

But the nurses were too busy rushing back and forth to spend much time with us. It took all morning and sometimes into the afternoon to get through all the routines. And then there were the bedpans. 'Have you done a mark today?' If not, it was Syrup of Figs for you. Then temperatures, pulses and respirations...*why*? We were healthy children apart from our orthopaedic problems. But it was a hospital rule, so it was followed – never mind if the time would have been better spent cuddling and playing with us. The nurses did their best, but nobody really understood.

And that says it all... the dedicated but unthinking regiment, trained never to question authority.

Those who did soon left because they couldn't stand the rigidity. Is this why I'm such a rebel now – refusing to conform to mindless rules? I rarely make my bed. Is that another remnant?

And I'm just beginning to listen to my body – to notice when it's tired or painful, to attend to its needs rather than pushing on regardless. It's difficult – I've been dead to it for so long – but I have to hear those feelings if I want to be a whole person – if I want to be gentle with myself and in so doing, learn to be gentle with others.

POST SCRIPT

Today health care staff are far more aware of children's needs. Mothers can stay overnight, and visiting is almost unrestricted.

Last year I went back to the same hospital. Outside and in the corridors it felt much the same, but I didn't recognize the ward – it had been moved. Much more significant, however, was the warm and human atmosphere.

The ward was smaller with bright cartoons on the walls. Sister was sitting on a wooden child's chair with a book on her lap, one child by her shoulder and another playing by her feet. The ward was full of happy noise and chatter. The priority was clearly children, not routines, and the fear of authority had gone.

Contributed by Carol, a colleague

## TALKING TO BEREAVED CHILDREN      PM 14

In wanting to protect children we sometimes exclude and isolate them from experiences associated with death and dying. Children can sense when something serious is happening and their fantasies are often worse than the reality. We may be disturbed by what appears to be children's casual or callous behaviour or attitudes, but this is often a type of bravado, a 'whistling in the dark'. Beneath this facade, children are sometimes very sad. Their vulnerability may make them suppress feelings which may then emerge as sleep disturbance, clinging or bed wetting.

Ideally we need to prepare children before the death occurs, and provide opportunities for them to ask questions. It is not helpful to try and protect them from their sadness. It is helpful to support them in fully experiencing their sadness. Because young children do not understand what death is all about, they need to talk about it. Caring adults should help them to talk about the dead person, and to recognize, name and express their feelings.

When talking to parents about 'telling children', acknowledge that this will not be easy. Warn them to be prepared for resistance from other adults to the idea of talking with children about death. Alert parents to the facts. Children will:

- sense the emotions around them

- respond to body language

- overhear conversations

- ask questions directly or indirectly.

Children need:

1. *Information:*

    - Clear, simple, truthful, repeated. Offer parents help to express themselves in appropriate words.

    - Avoid confusing explanations of death, and avoid use of euphemisms. For example, if death is described as 'going to sleep for ever', a child may accept this very literally, and may subsequently fear going to sleep.

    - Link explanations to things children have noticed already, for example, the death of a pet, finding a dead bird, relevant incidents in television wild life programmes.

2. *Reassurance to help them deal with:*

    - Practical anxieties such as, 'Is this going to happen to other people I love?', 'Will I be left all alone?'.

    - Fear that illness for themselves or others is likely to result in death.

    - Guilt, that they, in some way which they don't understand, might have been responsible for the death, perhaps by 'being naughty'.

3. *Encouragement to express their feelings. (But take care not to tell them how to feel:)*

- Acknowledge the child's loss.
- Allow involvement.
- Warn parents that grief may be acted out in behaviour rather than words.
- Discuss discipline. Gentle, firm maintenance of non-punitive boundaries, as guidelines to acceptable behaviour, can be a support when a child is experiencing the chaos of the emotions of a grieving family.

4. *Help on how to release their feelings in safety:*
   - Let them know that anger is normal and that sadness is not for ever.
   - Give them room to act out emotions. Kicking and punching large cushions can help.
   - Encourage them to scream and shout their rage in an appropriate place.
   - Join them in talking to their toys about their sadness.
   - Join them in crying.
   - Drawing, painting and using clay can help a child to express feelings.
   - An older child may like to write a letter to the dead person.
   - Look at photographs; provide books, leaflets, scrapbooks.
   - Let them choose a memento of the dead person.
   - For an older child, a walk is often helpful. The release of energy and feeling of companionship during walking, tends to encourage expression of thoughts and feelings that were previously blocked. The side-by-side position during a walk provides a helpful degree of privacy – of not being directly observed.
   - Remember the child's right to fun and hope.

Parents need *support* and *advice*. (Often you will not work directly with the child:)

- Increase parents' feelings of competence by giving them tools to use for themselves, for example, books and leaflets.
- Offer parents suggestions for conversations with the children.
- Professionals should model for parents. This might include allowing tears. When what is being conveyed to parents is relevant and supportive, they will learn quickly that what is being offered to them is also relevant to their children's needs.
- Encourage parents to involve others. Involving others, for example, teachers, friends and relatives, not only helps to provide a support network for the parents and children, but also helps to ensure some consistency in the way issues are handled.
- Be aware of the family belief system. Do not conflict with it.
- Encourage parents not to be too hard on themselves.
- Be realistic.
- Emotional pain is contagious. Remember your own supports.

# THE KARPMAN (OR DRAMA) TRIANGLE　PM 15

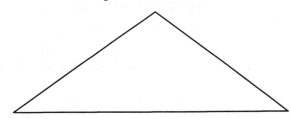

VICTIM
helplessness, martyrdom,
'I'm weak', refuses to act
on possible alternatives

PERSECUTOR
blaming, knows it all,
dominance, aggressiveness.
Persecution through passivity,
stubborn silence, withdrawal

RESCUER
pacifying, protecting and
defending others, covering up,
trying to solve other people's
problems

*Figure 4.11 The Karpman (or drama) triangle (see Berne (1971) and Harris (1975))*

REFERENCES

Harris, T.A. (1993) *I'm OK – You're OK*. New York: Avon Books.

Berne, E. (1971) *What Do You Say After You Say 'Hello'?* New York: Bantam Books.

## GUIDELINES FOR COUNSELLING PRACTICE
## PM 16

In the time available it is unlikely that you will be able to resolve the issues presented by the role-play you have chosen. Pace yourselves and concentrate on offering good quality listening.

Each of you should have the opportunity to adopt the roles of counsellor, client and observer. There will be 20 to 25 minutes for each cycle. Decide quickly who is to do what. Then divide your time. Allow 15 minutes for the preparation and role-play, then ten minutes for feedback and discussion before moving on to the next cycle.

### COUNSELLOR

It is difficult to stay alongside your client if performance anxiety takes over. It sometimes defuses tension if you can identify and acknowledge to your colleagues how you feel. At any stage, feel free to say '*I'm stuck*' and ask the observer or trainer for suggestions. Keep yourself centred and breathing, with your feet on the floor.

### CLIENT

Your role descriptions will be sparse. Use aspects of your own experience and your imagination to flesh them out. A name might be provided in the role-play scenario, if not choose a name different from your own. Spend a little time centring yourself, and imagining what it would feel like to be the person whom you are representing. Try to work from this, and you will learn more about the person and her situation. Role-play is not acting (except perhaps the kind of acting where the actors try to find an empathic understanding of their character).

Respond to helpful interventions from your counsellor and, while not being obstructive, do not offer information unless the counsellor provides the appropriate openings to 'trigger' the response.

Look after yourself by limiting the depth of your emotional involvement to what feels right for you.

### OBSERVER

During the role-play you have three very important tasks:

1. Note down examples of skills used well and not so well by the counsellor; note opportunities that are missed and those that are taken. Record enough information, and in sufficient detail, to allow you to offer specific and constructive feedback later.

2. Be ready at any time to offer supportive suggestions to the counsellor, if she asks for them. Consider yourself as her 'consultant'. Be clear that this is not because you know 'better' what should be done; but because you can offer a different perspective, and this may, or may not, be helpful.

3. You are the time keeper. Let your colleagues know when they have only three minutes left to role-play. This gives them the opportunity to practise bringing the session to an organized close.

© 1997 Fay W. Jacobsen, Margaret Kindlen and Allison Shoemark

After the role-play you have two further tasks:

1. 'Chair' the discussion, inviting feedback in the following order:
   - The counsellor feeds back first. (It is irritating to be told what you have already learned from your own experience.)
   - The client then feeds back, staying in role to do so.
   - Lastly the observer asks if the counsellor wants further feedback. Only if she says 'yes' do you then add your comments. Remember to start and end with positive remarks, sandwiching any negative feedback in between. Be constructive and specific and offer comments only about matters which the counsellor can control or influence.

2. De-role the client at the end of each cycle, using the following format:
   - *'Who are you not?'*
   - *'Who are you?'*
   - *'What will you be doing in the next few days which you are really going to enjoy?'*.

N.B. Remember to observe small-group confidentiality during the large-group feedback.

(Adapted from Jacobsen, F.W. and Mackinnon, H. (1989) *Sharing Counselling Skills: A Guide to Running Courses for Nurses, Midwifes and Health Visitors*. Edinburgh: Scottish Health Education Group)

# EXPERIENTIAL LEARNING PROGRESSION PM 17

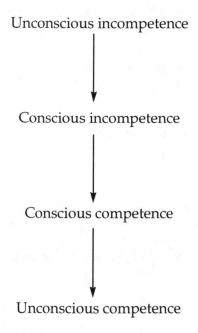

Unconscious incompetence

Conscious incompetence

Conscious competence

Unconscious competence

*Figure 4.12 Experiential Learning Progression*

### UNCONSCIOUS INCOMPETENCE

People come to courses with some degree of confidence in their professional and other skills. They want to learn new skills, and to validate and improve those they already have. Few would claim to be infallible; but one does not know what is not known.

### CONSCIOUS INCOMPETENCE

As one discovers what one does not know, one begins to realize that one may have handled some past situations less effectively than had been imagined. For those whose self-esteem is fragile, or for those who work in a very competitive or judgemental professional environment, this realization can be both painful and de-skilling. This occurs frequently among people involved in 'skills' learning, particularly those who have just used role-play for the first time.

### CONSCIOUS COMPETENCE

Following a second chance to practise their skills, people often make remarks such as: '*I feel so wooden and artificial*' or '*I am struggling to think of which skill is appropriate, and my mind just goes blank.*'

In these situations, it can be helpful to remind them of what it was like during their first driving or typing lesson. Most people will remember experiencing similar feelings in the early stages of learning these, or other, skills. They will recognize then that they progressed to competence.

*© 1997 Fay W. Jacobsen, Margaret Kindlen and Allison Shoemark*

UNCONSCIOUS COMPETENCE

This stage is reached after having had time to practise and consolidate skills. The acquisition of unconscious competence is a gradual process. Something may then occur that causes one to reflect back, so that one then recognizes that using the newly acquired skills is now increasingly spontaneous. One function of a follow-up day, after three to six months, is to promote that recognition.

It is particularly important that those with a poor sense of self-worth are supported to acknowledge their competence. Sometimes one hears dismissal of achievements with denigrating remarks, such as: *'It is not really such a big deal. I mean, anyone can learn it'*.

Acknowledging one's own skills is not encouraged in Western society. We are afraid to be thought 'boastful' if we assert our competence. As a result we deny ourselves the self-affirmation that could nourish our self-esteem.

## BREATHING AND THE STRESS CONNECTION

PM 18

Because breathing is autonomically controlled, people pay little attention to it in normal circumstances. But breathing and anxiety are inextricably linked, and breathing exercises have been shown to be highly effective in relieving anxiety and stress.

One way of viewing anxiety is that it is a condition resulting from breathing difficulty during blocked excitement (Perls, Hefferline and Goodman 1984, p.128). During excitement of any sort, heightened concern or close contact, either aggressive or erotic, there is an energy surge and an associated increase in metabolic processes. The normal response is to increase breathing, so as to cope with the larger volume of oxidized nutrients. But in our culture, and particularly in the caring professions, a high value is placed on self-control; remaining cool, calm and collected; not showing fear, anger, disgust or grief. Thus, goes the theory, to control the energy surge, or rather to control the feelings associated with it, people often restrict their natural responses and so constrict their breathing.

It is common to hold one's breath when one is afraid, or to stop an outburst of rage, or even in the excitement of pleasant anticipation. But when one is culturally or professionally conditioned to conceal one's feelings, constricted breathing becomes a routine pattern for coping with all excitements. As a result, one may stop oneself from consciously feeling or expressing feelings appropriate to one's experience. A muscular rigidity, particularly, but not exclusively, of the chest, back, shoulders and neck, may be associated with this. This was described as 'character armour' by physician and psychotherapist, Wilhelm Reich (1980). The purpose of character armour is to protect the 'self' from the invasion of an environment that is perceived as hostile. When muscles have reached this state of rigidity, they no longer facilitate free and unfettered movement, but work against themselves in order to perform their normal function.

In this way, many people cope successfully for years, but at a cost. The physical cost includes, first, the energy used to maintain rigid musculature to keep feelings under control. This results in a feeling of exhaustion, even when there has been no physical activity. People are sometimes perplexed by this, and ask, *'Why am I so tired when I haven't been doing anything?'*.

A further physical cost is the inevitable extra wear and tear on joints that are held too tightly clamped together, and on organs that are constricted by over-tightened bands of muscles.

But there are other costs. When one suppresses feelings habitually, one is unable to be selective about which feelings to suppress. Thus, while one is apparently relieved of the awareness of 'unacceptable' emotions, one is also denied the value of experiencing emotions that are prized and enjoyed. One does not usually notice this until one becomes aware that life seems to have lost some of the sparkle remembered from the past. It is easy then to dismiss the loss as being part of 'getting older and wiser'. Having rationalized and accepted one's loss, one is not motivated to do anything to reverse the process.

As for the suppressed 'unacceptable' emotions, these are retained within; an emotional time-bomb of which one is aware at some level of consciousness. The half hidden time-bomb may become a source of considerable anxiety when working with people who are confronted by their own death, the death of a loved one or some other great loss, and where the presence of extreme emotion is unavoidable.

A variety of responses to this situation are possible for a counsellor. One may choose to avoid the release of feelings, by reassuring and comforting the client. This might be appropriate to the counsellor's needs, but would be inappropriate to the needs of the client. Another may choose to 'steel' herself to the pain, and to encourage clients to express their feelings. This may be appropriate for the clients, but the counsellor is then at risk of being overwhelmed by her own accumulated and unexpressed emotions. Or the 'steel' of self-control might hold emotions in check yet again, but some physical symptoms could manifest themselves later.

An alternative approach is to seek to come to terms with one's feelings. Several of the exercises in this course will help participants to develop more effective breathing patterns. This, in turn, may encourage some to allow themselves to acknowledge the validity of their strong, perhaps even painful, emotions more freely, and to express them in a safe and supportive environment. You are invited to use these opportunities to benefit yourself as an individual and as a counsellor.

*REFERENCE*

Perls, F., Hefferline, R. and Goodman, P. (1984) *Gestalt Therapy: Excitement and Growth in the Human Personality*. London: Souvenir Press Ltd.

Reich, W. (1980) *Character Analysis*. New York: Farrar and Giroux Incorporated.

# DAY 4

# RESPONSES TO BEREAVEMENT    PM 19

| | |
|---|---|
| Shock: | *'I felt cold and numb.'* |
| Disbelief, denial: | *'This can't be happening to me.'* |
| Yearning: | *'Don't leave me…'* |
| Emptiness: | *'Inside me is an aching void.'* |
| Searching: | *'Is that her across the road, there?'* |
| Anxiety: | *'How will I manage? Must I sell the house?'* |
| Anger: | *'She had no right to desert me like this.'* |
| Guilt: | *'If only…'* |
| Depression: | *'I feel as if I am plunging into a bottomless black pit.'* |
| Loss of identity and status: | *'When I filled in my tax return it hurt to tick the "single" box.'* |
| Stigma: | *'Friends never know what to say to me.'* |
| Sexual deprivation: | *'Oh, to have someone to hold close!'* |
| Loss of faith: | *'Why did it happen to him?'* |
| Loneliness: | *'I dread weekends and holidays.'* |
| Acceptance: | *'She would have laughed about that.'* |
| Healing: | |

STAGES OF GRIEF

1. A state of shock.
2. Expression of emotion.
3. Feelings of depression and loneliness.
4. Experience of physical symptoms of distress.
5. Feelings of panic.
6. Feelings of guilt about the loss.
7. Seething, hostile and resentful feelings.
8. Inability to pick up usual life activities.
9. Occasional, then increasingly frequent, periods of hope.
10. Struggling to adjust to our new reality.

## WORKING WITH FEELINGS                                    PM 20

1. At first, work individually. Think of a time when either:

   (a) you felt really powerful feelings and expressed them in a way that you felt bad about afterwards; *or*

   (b) you felt powerful feelings and did not allow yourself, or were not in a position, to express them; and you felt bad about that afterwards; *or*

   (c) you received powerful feelings from another, felt paralysed and unable to respond, and felt bad about that.

   When each person has thought of an example, and perhaps noted briefly an outline of the situation, the three of you assemble in a quiet place. Each one recounts their recalled memory to the other two. When recounting the memory, tell it in the present tense, as if it is happening now. For example: *'I am 10 years old and I am standing next to the piano in my grandmother's house…'* (15 minutes).

2. The triad agrees on one example to work through. (In what follows, the person whose scenario is being used will be called *A*, and the others in the group *B* and *C*.)

   The facilitator will make herself available to groups, suggesting which of the following methods might be most appropriate for the example chosen. Invite her to join your triad if you need suggestions or support.

   METHODS OF WORKING WITH SCENARIOS

   *METHOD I*

   *A'* takes the role of 'the other person' in the exchange that has been recalled. *B* plays *A's* part, responding first in the way that *A* recounted the incident, and then as *B* herself would have handled the situation.

   The scenario is then replayed with *C* responding both ways, as described for *B* above.

   *B* and *C* both tell *A* how they felt responding in the two different ways: *A's* and their own.

   *B* and *C* should not feel that they have to 'get it right'. *A* may well feel supported if *B* and *C* learn through the experience how difficult and painful it is, for example, to be trapped in a position of powerlessness.

   Thus *A* has seen two alternative ways of dealing with the recalled situation, suggested by *B* and *C*. If *A* feels able to, she replays the scene using one or both alternative strategies, and she notes how it feels using them. *When replaying your scenario, remember to do this in the present tense. Bring all the power and skill of your present self to the situation.*

   The alternate strategies are not to be regarded as 'right' or 'better'– unless they help *A* to feel more powerful in the situation when she uses them.

   If *A* does not feel able to use either of the alternatives, then the triad concentrates on helping her to work out some other strategy.

*© 1997 Fay W. Jacobsen, Margaret Kindlen and Allison Shoemark*

208

*METHOD 2*

*B* and *C* take both parts in the exchange, directed by *A*. First, *A* tells them how to re-enact the scene as it originally happened. As in Method (1), replay the scene as if it is happening in the present. *B* and *C* feed back to *A* how they felt. For example:

> *When she insulted me and I didn't let myself respond, I felt powerless, my body tensed and I really despised myself...'*

or

> *When she insulted me and I just insulted her back, there was a temporary satisfaction and I felt a surge of triumph, but then I felt that I had just let myself down.*

*B* and *C* can then replay the scenario responding as they choose. *B* and *C* exchange roles and repeat the replay.

*METHOD 3*

*A* sits opposite an empty chair. *B* and *C* encourage her to ground herself and to belly breathe. *A* then imagines that the other person in the recalled interaction is sitting on the chair opposite her. She reconstructs, in her imagination, the room in which the original events occurred; what both are wearing, and any other relevant details.

*A* then says what she would have liked to have said on that occasion, *or* she repeats what she said originally, but in the way she wishes she had said it. *B* and *C* help her to be fully effective by giving feedback about her use of tone of voice and body language.

If it is appropriate, *A* switches to the empty chair, and responds as she thinks the other would have responded. This conversation can continue as long as it is enlightening for *A*. It is a particularly effective way of dealing with 'unfinished business' with people who are dead or no longer in the life of *A*.

All of the above methods can result in very powerful experiences for the participants. For *B* and *C* the challenge lies in helping to support *A* to recognize and respect her emotional responses to the situation and to express them creatively and effectively. It is not important that all three people's scenarios are worked through. By dealing with one thoroughly, all are learning this method of working. But if there is time in hand, they could work on another example. (Time allotted: 45 minutes.)

3. Return to the large group for group feedback. Remember only to share your own experiences, or what has been agreed within the small group. If important issues have emerged in a sub-group, the individuals concerned may choose to work through these in the skills' practice session after lunch.

# DAY 5

## SPIRITUALITY (POEM) PM 21

When you find the light within you
You will know that you have always
Been the center of wisdom.
As you probe deeper into who you really are
With your lightedness and your confusion
With your anger, longings and distortions
You will find the true living god.
Then you will say
I have known you all my life
And I have called you by many names.
I have called you mother and father and child
I have called you lover
I have called you sun and flowers
I have called you my heart.
But never, until this moment,
Called you Myself.

Compiled by
Rodegast, P. and Stanton, J. (1987) *Emmanual's Book*.
London: Bantam Books.

## CHANGE (EXERCISE) PM 22

Consider three significant changes that have taken place in your life. They may be changes that you initiated or those that were beyond your control.

1.

2.

3.

What strengths can you identify which you needed to help you cope with these changes?

Consider the changes you have listed. What did you have to let go of to come to terms with the change? What did you gain from the change?

What I had to let go of:

What I gained:

## SPIRITUALITY (STATEMENTS)                    PM 23

Group discussion.     Time: 15 minutes.

WHAT DO YOU FEEL ABOUT THE FOLLOWING STATEMENTS?

These statements are provided to stimulate thought and discussion. Reflect briefly on each of them, and then share your thoughts and feelings with the group:

1. People with a religious faith find it easier to accept dying.
2. People without religious faith do not have spiritual needs.
3. Spiritual needs are only present in those facing death.
4. Spiritual needs can only be met through religious beliefs.
5. Psychosocial and spiritual needs are one and the same thing.

*Contributed by Kate Copp*

# SPIRITUALITY (SOME DEFINITIONS)     PM 24

SPIRITUALITY

'...relates to the inner essence of a person, is a sense of harmonious interconnectedness with self, others, nature and an ultimate other...' (Nagai–Jacobson and Barkhardt 1989).

MAN'S SPIRITUAL DIMENSION

'...is life giving and integrating. It transcends the physical and psychological dimensions...' (Granstrom 1985)

'...a fundamental part of every person's life...has always encompassed the need to contemplate and make sense of those things greater than himself...to be able to put his own existence into some greater perspective...to make sense of birth, death and, above all, the meaning of life itself.' (Cosh 1988)

'...encompasses the need for finding satisfactory answers to his ultimate questions about the meaning of life, illness, death. His deepest relationships with others, himself and with God are the center of his spiritual dimension.' (Highfield and Cason 1983)

'The spiritual component of an individual provides a sense of meaning and purpose in life, a means of forgiveness, and a source of love and relatedness.' (Petersen 1985)

Rumi (Levine 1989) the sufi poet speaks of: 'God's presence, our original nature, as always being in front of us'.

SPIRITUAL NEEDS

'1. The need for a meaning and a purpose to life.

2. The need to receive love.

3. The need to give love.

4. The need for hope and creativity.' (Highfield and Cason 1983)

*Contributed by Kate Copp*

REFERENCES

Cosh, R. (1988) 'Spiritual issues in cancer care.' In R. Tiffany (ed) *Oncology for Nurses and Health Care Professionals, Vol. 2: Care and Support.* London: Harper and Row.

Granstom, S.L. (1985) 'Spiritual nursing care of oncology patients.' *Topics in Clinical Nursing April 7(1), 39–45.*

Highfield, M.F. and Cason, C. (1985) 'Spiritual needs of patients: are they recognized?' *Cancer Nursing 6(3), 187–192.*

Nagai–Jacodson, M.G. and Burkhardt, M.A. (1989) 'Spirituality: cornerstone of holistic nursing practice.' *Holistic Nursing Practice 3 (3), 69–77.*

Peterson, E.A. (1985) 'The physical – The spiritual – can you meet all your patient's needs?' *Journal of Gerontological Nursing 11(10), 23–27.*

Rumi *Open Secrets – Visions of Rumi*, translated by John Mayne and Coleman Berks, cited in Levine, S. (1989) *Healing into Life and Death.* Bath: Gateway Books.

# ONE DEFINITION OF SPIRITUALITY (WITH EXAMPLES)　　PM 25

The spiritual experience is an aspect of human experience through which we discover that we are connected to, and participating in, the whole of Creation. It is the aspect of our experience through which we are united, and interdependent, with all other forms of life in the Universe. At the same time, in this union, paradoxically we remain essentially and most distinctly ourselves.

This last is very important, for we actually uncover this dimension of ourselves through very close attention to our individual experience, to its truth, moment to moment, and over time.

> Thomas Yeomans – from the introduction to his course, 'Spiritual Psychology'. Obtainable from The Concord Institute, Box 82 Concord, Mass 01742, USA Telephone – 508 371 3206.

EXAMPLE 1

The following poem illustrates spirituality in the act of holding on to life in the overwhelming presence of death.

> *On a sunny evening*
>
> On a purple, sun-shot evening
> Under wide-flowering chestnut trees
> Upon a threshold full of dust
> Yesterday, today, the days are all like these.
>
> Trees flower forth in beauty
> Lovely, too, their wood all gnarled and old
> That I am half afraid to peer
> Into their crowns of green and gold.
>
> The sun has made a veil of gold
> So lovely that my body aches.
> Above, the heavens shriek with blue
> Convinced I've smiled by some mistake.
> The world's abloom and seems to smile.
> I want to fly but where, how high?
> If in barbed wire, things can bloom
> Why couldn't I? I will not die!

> Anonymous, 1944. One of many life-affirming poems written by the children in Barracks L318 and L417, aged 10–16 years, in Terezin concentration camp

> Volavková, H. (ed) (1993) *I Never Saw Another Butterfly: Children's Drawings and Poems from Terezin Concentration Camp, 1942–1944*. New York: Schocken Books.

EXAMPLE 2

Spirituality can also be experienced in the acceptance of death. What follows are the words of a song in which the singer affirms life in his acceptance of death.

*The Joy of Living*

Farewell, you northern hills, you mountains all goodbye!
Moorland and stony ridges, crags and peaks, goodbye!
Glyder Fach, farewell, Cul Beig, Scarfell, cloud bearing Suilven.
Sun-warmed rock and the cold of Bleaklow's frozen sea,
The snow and the wind and the rain of hills and mountains.
Days in the sun and the tempered wind and the air like wine,
And you drink and you drink till you're drunk on the joy of living.

Farewell to you my love, my time is almost done;
Lie in my arms once more until the darkness comes.
You filled all my days, held the night at bay, dearest companion.
Years passed by and are gone with the speed of birds in flight,
Our life is a verse of a song heard in the mountains.
Give me your hand, then love, and join your voice with mine.
We'll sing of the hurt and the pain and the joy of living.

Farewell to you my chicks, soon you must fly alone;
Flesh of my flesh, my future life, bone of my bone.
May your wings be strong, may your days be long, safe be your journey.
Each of you bears inside of you the gift of love –
May it bring you light and warmth and the pleasure of giving.
Eagerly savour each new day and the taste of its mouth;
Never lose sight of the thrill and the joy of living.

Take me to some high place of heather, rock and ling;
Scatter my dust and ashes, feed me to the wind.
So that I will be part of all you see, the air you are breathing.
I'll be part of the curlew's cry and the soaring hawk,
The blue milkwort and the sundew hung with diamonds.
I'll be riding the gentle wind that blows through your hair;
Reminding you how we shared in the joy of living.

Composed by the British folk singer and political activist
Ewan MacColl in 1986. He died at the age of 79 years in 1989.

*Black and White. Ewan MacColl – The Definitive Collection.*
Cooking Vinyl CD (Cook CD 038)

## SETTING GOALS                                              PM 26

Setting goals occurs at every level of human activity: personal, domestic, professional and corporate. It also has a role to play in counselling. When people have explored and understood the issues that were confusing and distressing them previously, they then begin to realize that they can take action to change some aspects of their lives. Counsellors need to support them to do this in a way which will strengthen, rather than undermine, their confidence in themselves.

Locke and Latham (1984) describe some of the advantages of goal-setting:

1. Goal-setting focuses attention, and it gives direction to action.
2. Goal-setting mobilizes energy and effort. Planning and thinking about the goal is the first step towards its achievement.
3. Having a goal increases resolve to work harder and longer to achieve it. The clearer, more relevant and realistic the goal, the less likely that it will be abandoned.
4. By setting goals one is motivated to search for ways and means by which they can be achieved.

Egan (1986) refers to eight criteria for setting goals:

CRITERION 1

Goals should be formulated in terms of *accomplishments*, rather than forms of behaviour. For example, a woman who states that she intends to leave an abusive partner has thereby stated her goal. Her possible further statement, that she intends to join a 'Battered Wives Support Group', is not a *goal*, although it may be one way in which the goal might be achieved.

CRITERION 2

Goals need to be *specifically stated* if they are to motivate behaviour. For example, it is neither specific nor focused for a person to say that he needs to get more exercise. It would be more helpful to say something like, *'By my birthday I will have been swimming twice a week, every week'*.

CRITERION 3

Progress towards achievement of a goal should be *measurable*. For example, if a man who has had his leg amputated says, *'I'll be up and about soon'*, he cannot measure his progress. However, he can if he says, *'In five days' time I will have walked to the end of the ward and back with my artificial leg'*.

CRITERION 4

Goals need to be *realizable*. The resources required to achieve the goal must be available in practice. An unemployed woman with children may declare that she intends to have found work by the end of the month. If no child care facilities are available in her area, then this would be an unrealistic, unrealizable goal.

*© 1997 Fay W. Jacobsen, Margaret Kindlen and Allison Shoemark*

CRITERION 5

Goals need to be *adequate*. They should contribute directly to resolving or managing the problem that motivated the goal-setting. For example, a man may decide to marry a woman friend because he believes that this will help him feel better about himself. If the underlying problem is his 'shame' about his homosexual orientation, then he is not likely to achieve his goal.

CRITERION 6

Goals need to be the person's *own* goals. The manager who sets arbitrary time limits on tasks to be accomplished by his staff, is likely to be less successful than one who encourages his staff to set their own goals for streamlining their time management.

CRITERION 7

Goals need to be *in harmony with one's values*. A personnel manager who is feeling stressed by overwork may set herself a goal to introduce an appointments system for seeing staff on only one specific day of the week. However, if her view of her role is to be freely available to staff, to discuss personal issues affecting their work, then she might experience increased stress arising from the dissonance between her convictions and the goal she has set herself.

CRITERION 8

Goals need to be on a *clear time scale*. For example, '*I would like to work freelance*' does not generate a drive as effectively as, '*By this time next year I will have built up sufficient clients and training consultancies to be working freelance*'.
Note: some people have commented that criteria 2, 3 and 8 seem to replicate each other. In many cases this is true, but not in all.

REFERENCES

Locke, E.A. and Latham, G.P. (1984) *Goal Setting: A Motivational Technique that Works*. Englewood Cliffs, New Jersey: Prentice Hall.

Egan, G. (1986) *The Skilled Helper*. Third edition. Monterey, California: Brooks Cole, Ch. 9.

## EVALUATION FORM                                        PM 27

1. To what extent were the following broad aims of the course fulfilled for you? (Please circle the statement that best describes how you feel.)

    (a) To enhance existing counselling skills in working with people facing loss and bereavement.

    *Achieved*     *Partly achieved*     *Not achieved*

    Comments

    (b) To deepen self-awareness about living through loss.

    *Achieved*     *Partly achieved*     *Not achieved*

    Comments

    (c) To share your own experience of grief and bereavement.

    *Achieved*     *Partly achieved*     *Not achieved*

    Comments

    (d) To explore ways of looking after yourself and encouraging your colleagues to do likewise.

    *Achieved*     *Partly achieved*     *Not achieved*

    Comments

    (e) To explore some aspects of abuse.

    *Achieved*     *Partly achieved*     *Not achieved*

    Comments

(f) To identify relevant resources, including reading materials, which will support and inform you about living through loss.

                *Achieved*        *Partly achieved*        *Not achieved*

Comments

(g) To explain how learning can be taken back to the work place and can be incorporated into your life.

                *Achieved*        *Partly achieved*        *Not achieved*

Comments

Now please indicate whether you feel that:

2. The course content was…

                *Mainly relevant*        *Mainly irrelevant*

Comments

3. The teaching methods used in the course were…

                *Appropriate*        *Inappropriate*

Comments

4. The course would be improved if…

Signature_____     Date_____

# FOLLOW-UP DAY

## RETROSPECTIVE EVALUATION FORM      PM 28

Title and dates of the course_____

1.  In retrospect, what was the most helpful part of the course? Can you give reasons for this?

2.  In retrospect, what was the least helpful part of the course? Can you give reasons for this?

3.  What changes, if any, have you made in your personal and/or professional life as a result of the course?

4.  What have been the constraints in putting course learning into practice?

5. What have been the supports in putting course learning into practice?

6. What changes, additions or subtractions would you suggest to improve the course?

Signature_____    Date_____

## EXCERPT FROM WILLIAMSON (1992) *RETURN TO LOVE*                    PM 29

... our deepest fear is not that we are inadequate. Our deepest fear is that we are powerful beyond measure. It is our light, not our darkness, that most frightens us. We ask ourselves, 'Who am I to be brilliant, gorgeous, talented and fabulous?' Actually, who are you **not** to be? You are a child of God, your playing small doesn't serve the world. There is nothing enlightened about shrinking so that other people won't feel insecure around you. We were born to manifest the glory of the God that is within us. It is not just in some of us: It's in everyone. And as we let our own light shine, we unconsciously give other people permission to do the same. As we are liberated from our own fears, our presence automatically liberates others.

REFERENCE

Williamson, M. (1992) *Return to Love.* New York: Thorsons/Harper Collins.

# MATERIALS FOR USE WITH ADDITIONAL LESSON PLANS

## REFLECTION ON DEATH (EXERCISE)      PM 30

Thinking and talking about death is painful. The purpose of this exercise is to provide an opportunity for you to become aware of the fear and pain that you may have about your own death. Unacknowledged, this fear can obstruct efforts to help those who are facing their own death or that of a loved one.

Those who find that their fear of death is very powerful have two options. They can choose not to work with issues around death and dying, for the time being. Alternatively, they may seek support, to help them to deal with the origin of their fears.

*Complete the following sentences.* Once completed, it is important that you talk about your feelings.

1.  *To me, death is like…*

2.  *When I think of death, I…*

3.  *Being realistic, I think that I am most likely to die around the age of…years, as a result of…*

4.  *I have given this cause of death because…*

5. *When I think of my own death, I feel...*

6. *When I die, I hope that...*

7. *If I were to die, those I love would...*

8. *If everything was as it is now, except that yesterday, I had been told that I had about six months to live, the five things I would be most concerned about are...*

9. *If I had a young child who was about to die, I would...*

10. *The ways in which I could help a newly widowed relative are...*

(Adapted from Carr, A.T. 'Dying and Bereavement.' In A. Chapman and A. Gale
(1982) *Psychology and People: A Tutorial Text*. London: MacMillan Press.)

# IMPACT OF LOSS (EXERCISE)      PM 31

The purpose of this activity is to provide you with an opportunity to examine your response to loss.

1. List the ten things that are most important in your life at this particular time. You need not list them in any particular order, and what you write down may be tangible or intangible. Here are some suggestions of the kind of thing that you might choose: love; health; self-esteem; pets; security.

2. Now that your list is complete delete one item.

3. Delete two more items.

4. Delete another item (your options are becoming fewer).

5. Delete another item;… and another.

6. If you have been honest with yourself and have listed the things that you most value, you will now be feeling uncomfortable about what next you can delete. *What can you do without?*

   You may feel like cheating. You may even feel like not proceeding with this activity. Most likely it is becoming 'quite painful'.

7. Delete two more items.

8. You have two remaining items. Delete one.

This has been an attempt to bring to your awareness the feelings that you might have when confronted with loss or death. It is important that you now share this experience with another member of the group. You might want to consider the following points:

1. How easy or otherwise was it for you to make your list?

2. What were your thoughts, feelings and physical sensations during this activity?

3. How easy or otherwise was this activity?

Tear up your personal notes and return to the large group.

Adapted from Bower, F. (1980) *Nursing and the Concept of Loss.*
Chichester: Wiley and Sons.

# STAFF SUPPORT GROUPS (GUIDELINES)    PM 32

One way counsellors can help themselves to manage stress is to form a support group. However, this needs careful planning.

If you are not a member of a support group, then you may want to formulate a proposal, addressed to your agency, to establish one.

If you are already part of such a group, then this handout may still prove helpful. It could stimulate you to look again at how the group operates, and to consider whether it might benefit from any changes. It would also be helpful if you could share your experiences with others.

If a staff support group is not relevant to the type of work you do, then you may want to formulate a proposal, in the form of a letter or flyer, addressed to others in your organization who might benefit. This might suggest a meeting to set up an independent support group.

You may find it helpful to consider the following questions about support groups:

1. What is the precise aim of the group? Is it clear? Has it been recorded? (For instance, the aim might be: 'To provide an emotional support system to help staff deal more effectively with the stress of working with the dying and the bereaved'.)

2. How is the aim of the group to be achieved?

3. Is attendance to be optional or compulsory?

4. Is the group to be open or closed? (An open group allows new members to join, but this interrupts the development of group cohesion. A closed group can have greater intimacy, but new, and perhaps needy, members would be excluded. Another possibility is to open the group to new members every six or eight weeks.)

5. How many members should the group have? A small group (eight or less) allows great intimacy, but there may be more than eight members of staff.

6. Who would be members of the group? Would you include all counsellors, part-time counsellors, the boss, trainee counsellors, the receptionist, the telephonist, volunteers?

7. How often should the group meet, and for how long?

8. Where would the meetings be held? Would it be better to hold them somewhere other than the agency?

9. Would a group facilitator, someone to help discussions flow, be useful? Would it help if the facilitator came from outside the agency?

10. Would you want the facilitator to be someone who understood group dynamics, who understood what was going on, as distinct from dealing only with issues that are raised overtly at the meetings?

11. What safety guidelines would you build into the group culture? How would these be formulated, and by whom? For example, how would the group deal with confidentiality issues? If a colleague at a meeting reveals he is taking drugs or alcohol to help him through the work, would you, or should you, take this matter outside the group?

12. What issues are likely to arise in the group?

13. How would the logistics (for example, recording, providing coffee, arranging for the use of a room) be managed?

14. What about funding?

15. How would you like each group meeting to end?

# A BEREAVEMENT SUPPORT GROUP FOR CLIENTS (I: EXERCISE)    PM 33

EXERCISE

Use the following questions to collect, and share, your ideas about stages in organizing a bereavement support group for clients. Do not limit yourselves to just these questions if other important relevant issues arise (time: 30 minutes).

1. What would be the aim(s) of your group?
2. What sort of people or organizations would you contact to co-operate with you in setting up such a group?
3. What might be the advantages or disadvantages of involving others?
4. What practical organizational details would you have to address before the first meeting?
5. Suggest a rough outline for your first meeting.
6. Who might want to be members of the group?
7. How would you contact them?
8. Would it be a closed or an open group?
9. How many facilitators would there be, and what would be their role?
10. Would the group have any guidelines and, if so, how would they be determined?
11. How long after bereavement would you expect people to need the support of the group?
12. What are the advantages, to professionals working with bereavement issues, in facilitating such a group?

# A BEREAVEMENT SUPPORT GROUP FOR CLIENTS (2: GUIDELINES AND AN EXAMPLE)　　　PM 34

Bereaved people have similar needs, but they deal with them in different ways and at different times (if they deal with them at all). A fundamental need is to be able to talk with others who have had a similar experience. A participant in one support group said: *'The comfort that comes from the support of people who are dealing with the same emotions as you certainly helps us to see things more clearly, and thus we are able to cope'.*[1]

The value of such shared experiences is indicated by the diversity of issues that stimulate the formation of support groups, for instance, infant death, mastectomy, cancer and unemployment, among others.

Once a group has been set up, little is required in the way of resources. However, the initial practical preparations require attention.

## PREPARING FOR THE LAUNCH

1. Contact colleagues, hospice workers, those involved in pastoral care with local churches, synagogues, mosques and humanist groups. Outline proposals for setting up the group, and suggest a date and venue for a meeting of those interested in collaborating. In this way:

   - others who are interested will share their ideas and may become co-facilitators

   - there might be an offer to provide premises for group meetings

   - the contact network for potential users of the group will be widened

   - some individuals may be able to share the clerical load, offer help with stationery, photocopying facilities and so on, and perhaps contribute towards costs for postage and leaflets.

2. Plan the structure for the first meeting. Here is an example:

   (a) Introduction to the proposed programme and to each other (20 minutes).

   (b) Outline safety guidelines. These might include, for instance:

       - confidentiality in small and large groups

       - the need to listen to one another

       - letting everyone have a chance to speak if they wish

       - allowing expression of feelings

       - the value of keeping a journal to record feelings as the weeks pass.

       - Invite suggestions for other guidelines.

   (c) Choose a theme around which to conduct the first part of the programme (for instance 'Dealing with loneliness over the holidays'). This should be a fairly brief introduction (30 minutes maximum). It is helpful if you can provide a photocopied summary of what you plan to say.

(d) Arrange time to enable participants to share their experiences in small groups, followed by feedback to the large group (30–40 minutes).

(e) Invite suggestions for future meetings, timing between meetings, length of meetings and possible telephone support between meetings.

(f) Choose a closing exercise that provides some safe physical contact. (The closing circle described on day 5 of this course could be adapted for this purpose.)

3. Decide who is likely to want to join the group, and how they might be contacted:

(a) Decide on a telephone number or address where people can register their interest.

(b) Advertise in free news sheets. Write a letter to the press.

(c) Produce 'flyers' and send them to appropriate health care units, hospices and churches.

(d) Send sensitive letters to people who express interest. The letters might include information on the date, starting and finishing times, the venue (and how to find it) and the purpose of the evening; an outline of the programme and the name of the speaker, if any; the organizing agency or agencies; and contact name(s), telephone number(s) and address(es).

4. Plan to arrive early for the first meeting, to prepare the room and to greet people as they arrive. Provide some light refreshment for a mid-meeting break.

RUNNING THE GROUP

The initial discussion may provide ideas on how the group wants to conduct future sessions. However, people often need to meet a few times before they feel able to articulate how the group can help them. The basic structure of the first meeting may serve as a framework for subsequent meetings. You might decide to do without any formal input. Remind people about the group guidelines, and add any new ones as appropriate.

If there are enough facilitators, it helps to have one in each small group. Here they should feel free to share their own grieving issues, making sure that the available time is shared equitably. When reporting back to the larger group, facilitators must be circumspect regarding small-group confidentiality.

Participants respond differently to the group environment, not only because they are different personalities, but also because, generally, they will be at different stages of the grieving process. Group sharing helps to confirm for each individual that their particular pattern of grieving is normal and acceptable.

A frequent complaint from group members concerns pressure from others in the family to participate in some activity, such as sorting out a parent's wardrobe and deciding what to do with the clothing. The group member may feel distressed and resentful about being asked to deal with this at this stage, yet feel guilty at leaving it all to a sibling. It often helps in such situations to point out that people differ in the way that they respond to loss; each is doing what feels right for them at that particular time. If this can be accepted, a constructive dialogue between them becomes possible and the feeling of pressure and rancour may be reduced.

Gradually, as people move through their personal grieving processes, they recognize in others stages through which they passed earlier. A journal can make such feedback very specific (for example, '*I remember feeling just like that about two months ago. In fact, I used words very similar to yours, when I wrote about it*'). Such sharing tends to foster strong bonds between people. The longer that participants are witnesses to each others' experiences, the more likely it is that they (rather than facilitators or imported 'experts') will provide the supportive interventions.

New members of the group are sometimes uncomfortable with the absence of advice and instruction. Occasionally they attempt to fill that gap by contributing with '*If I were you…*' or '*You should/ought to do/say…*' type of comments. It helps, then, to affirm how right that course of action might be for them, but that it might not be helpful to someone else. After a little while, most people are able to distinguish between 'giving advice' and 'offering suggestions'. In any case, it is helpful to remind people, by examples, of the very different ways in which group members have dealt with their problems. A variety of different creative responses to difficult situations are thus provided by the group's own shared experiences. (Be careful not to name individuals when doing this, so that small-group confidentiality is respected. However, members may, of course, choose to identify themselves.)

Monthly meetings seem to work well, but it is important that people are offered support between meetings. If members recognize that someone is struggling with issues similar to their own, they may be encouraged to exchange telephone numbers. Facilitators may also choose to provide their telephone numbers.

The size of a group is likely to fluctuate; there is no prescribed period of time during which people 'should' attend; and there is no 'right' time for people to grieve. These general guidelines are illustrated below by some experiences at one support group, by way of example.

AN EXAMPLE

Over a 30 month period during which one facilitator was involved with two others in a particular group, attendance varied between 1 and 15. Two of the most satisfying meetings were attended by just one member and all three facilitators. On one of those occasions it was the member's first visit. As she unpacked her grief, the facilitators were humbled and excited. Every statement that she made expressed a problem – *and its solution*! For example, she was having difficulty in writing to her aunt about her mother's death. But she had no difficulty in telling the group why she had not written. The facilitators' role in this case was simply to point out that what she had said effectively constituted the text of the letter. It might read:

*Dear Aunt…,*

*I am so sad to tell you that mum has died. I wanted to tell you myself, as we are so close, but it hurts to give you such bad news. I wanted to write a long letter to tell you all you need and would want to know, but that will have to wait a while. I just feel I can't deal with the pain of recording that so soon.*

*© 1997 Fay W. Jacobsen, Margaret Kindlen and Allison Shoemark*

236

Several other issues that were distressing her were resolved similarly. This illustrates a common pattern experienced by people in distress. Problems are seen in their most extreme form: *'I need to do "x" but it hurts too much. But if I don't do "x" I shall also feel bad'*. The fact that there might be an interim alternative is obscured – until attention is drawn to it by someone else. One year later, the person concerned recalled her memory of that evening: *I didn't intend to say anything… The meeting didn't take away my sadness, but on my way home I felt less frantic and more hopeful.*

Two members of this group attended irregularly throughout a two-and-a-half year period. When they were present, they contributed so much of their experience to newer group members that they became the unofficial group elders. The facilitators suggested that they might become a resource for helping volunteers and professionals to supply more effective support for the bereaved. The 'elders' didn't dismiss the idea, but were not ready at that time to take on the task.

One of the facilitators has commented as follows:

> *As our group membership has changed over the course of the last three years, we continue to find that the need to talk with each other remains paramount. We asked the group recently if they would like to have a session on dealing with anger. We decided to have a speaker for at least some part of the evening. One of the members spoke up quickly and said that would be fine, but to limit the presentation to 20 to 30 minutes, so that there would be plenty of time to talk. This was from a gentleman who almost never says anything during the session!*[2]

Facilitators in such a group provide support *and they learn.* Theoretical 'models of grieving' unfold before their eyes. Watching the group evolve while minimizing intervention enhances an understanding of, and faith in, individual human beings and the group process.

NOTES

1. The examples throughout this section are based on one of the author's experiences at a support group in Morgantown, West Virginia, USA.
2. Sue Carpenter (1995) – personal communication.

## ALLEGATIONS OF ABUSE: CONFIDENTIALITY (EXERCISE)                          PM 35

This course is not a specialist training in how to deal with child abuse. Nevertheless, some of you will be in a job or role that means you are the person to whom others will turn if they suspect abuse. Your informant may have little concrete or specific information, but may have vague worries that are difficult to explain or put into words. It needs to be acknowledged, however, that all of us – whatever our professional roles or lack of them – may also be approached by a friend, a family member or a colleague *at a personal level*, often in relation to a child or adult known to both. These personal 'off the record' approaches are usually more difficult than those we may deal with in our 'official' roles, because we cannot simply respond according to principles of good practice – the people who might get hurt are people we know and care about. We are likely to 'get involved' whether we like it or not.

Sometimes an informant will ask for specific advice and/or action: '*I think something might be happening to Jacob, what do you think I should do?*'. Sometimes it will be less specific and more obscured: '*This person came to me last week. She's found out that her boyfriend has been interfering with her little girl. She wants to know what to do about it. What do you think?*'.

As ever, we cannot give you a simple set of rules to tell you how to respond to situations like this. All we can do is to help you consider some of the factors involved and the implications of various actions and outcomes, and offer some guidelines about good practice.

*Confidentiality* may become a problem. If one is to help, then it may be necessary to talk to others. It is better not to promise confidentiality in the first place than to break a promise.

Confidentiality raises a number of difficulties, which include:

- the possibility that people may not seek help or advice if they fear that their confidence will be broken

- commitments and oaths made within our role or profession (for example, the confidentiality of the doctor/patient relationship or of the confessional)

- strongly held cultural customs and group loyalties that would regard 'bringing in the authorities' as betrayal and disloyalty, particularly within minority groups that fear unfair treatment.

Balanced against these are:

- the need to stop the abuse if it is happening, and to protect the child from further abuse

- one's ability to offer help to the child, to the family and to the abuser

- the need to protect other children from future harm

- the need to protect yourself – from carrying a burden that you cannot cope with alone, and from getting into trouble if things go wrong.

None of these can be tackled unless you share your concerns with others, and seek help and advice from the full range of people who are able to offer it.

© 1997 Fay W. Jacobsen, Margaret Kindlen and Allison Shoemark

It is therefore better, in most cases, to make it clear from the beginning that you may need to consult others or to pass on information, if you believe the situation warrants it, *before getting involved in any discussion about another person's worries.*

Generally, in your professional or official roles there are likely to be guidelines which will clarify the situation and enable you to say to any informant something like, *'It's policy that I have to tell my superior about any worries – but I can assure you that whatever you say will be treated sensitively and passed on only to those who need to know'.*

You should check at your work place, or wherever you operate in an official capacity (if you do), what guidelines or codes of practice have been established about allegations of abuse, and how to deal with confidentiality. If there are no formal guidelines you may want to raise the issue – is it something that you and your colleagues need to work out together?

Keep a copy of any written guidelines readily to hand.

### EXERCISE (TIME: 30 TO 45 MINUTES)

Imagine that a friend comes round to your house and asks to have a private chat about something worrying her. Think of a specific person – it will make it easier to imagine.

Your friend says she knows you are likely to have had some contact with child abuse in your work and wants to talk to you 'in strict confidence' about the child of somebody you both know.

First, consider how you would feel about such a situation. Jot down some of the feelings you would experience and the concerns that would worry you. Then suggest some way you might explain to your friend about confidentiality and why it is not always possible.

Taking it in turns, role-play the situation with a partner. When each of you has had a turn, discuss the feelings evoked by this experience and how you dealt or failed to deal with them.

(Adapted from Open University Pack P554: *Child Abuse and Neglect.*)

# SEVEN STAGES OF TRANSITION (INFORMATION)                    PM 36

Hopson (1982) presents a seven-phase model of stages accompanying transition. As with other models presented here, the cycle is a general pattern rather than a rigid sequence of events. Some people will oscillate between stages, others may take differing amounts of time to complete the transition, and some will get stuck in certain stages. It is those who 'get stuck' who require assistance. The stages are:

1. *Immobilization*. A sense of being overwhelmed; of being unable to make plans; unable to reason, unable to understand – *frozen*. The intensity of the above feelings is proportional to the degree of unfamiliarity with the situation and is related to the strength of negative expectations that the person has. When expectations are positive, the immobilization phase is less intense or even absent.

2. *Minimization*. One way of moving out of the state of immobilization is to trivialize the change – deny it exists or project feelings of euphoria. Denial can be a positive and necessary stage in the process of adjustment. It is a normal response to a crisis which is too immediate or overwhelming to face head on. It allows for a temporary withdrawal from reality; to internalize, gather thoughts and begin to understand the changes that the crisis has enforced.

3. *Depression*. Eventually the realities of the change and the resulting stress become apparent. As people become aware of these realities, and the implications for them of the impending change in lifestyle, depression is a natural reaction. Depression is characterized by feelings of powerlessness and a loss of control of certain life events, sometimes magnified by a fear of losing control of emotions. There are swings in mood levels through a depression, from feelings of anger to periods of utter hopelessness. The depression signals that the person has begun to face up to the reality that a change has occurred. Frustrations arise in response to the difficulties encountered in deciding how to cope with new life requirements, for example, ways of being, or of any new relationships that may have been established.

4. *Letting go*. The first three stages characterize an attachment to the pre-change situation. Moving on requires a process of 'unhooking' from the past. The process of accepting change and letting go of negative feelings involves thoughts such as: *'Here I am now. This is what I have. I know I can survive. I'm not sure what I want, but I know I can sort things out. There is a future out there for me'*.

5. *Testing*. This stage might be described as bridge building. The person begins to test him/herself by 'trying out' new behaviours, new lifestyles and new ways of coping. There is a risk, perhaps, that the individual models himself or herself on a stereotyped image. Much energy is used up during this stage, and the heightened emotions may result in restlessness, irritability and anger.

6. *Search for meaning*. Following the burst of energy during the testing phase, there is a shift towards attempting to understand why and how things are different – the reason for the activity, the anger and the stereotyping. The understanding grows as the searching and the activity settles.

7. *Internalization*. Understanding the changes and acceptance of the new situation completes the process of transition. The pre-change situation has a new meaning, no less important, but significantly more comfortable to deal with.

REFERENCES

Hopson, B. (1982) 'Transition: understanding and managing personal change.' In A. Chapman and A. Gale (eds) *Psychology and People: A Tutorial Text.* London: Macmillan Press

# Extra materials

## HOW MUCH SUPPORT DO YOU HAVE?    PM 37

Working with people who are facing death, who are bereaved or who are otherwise traumatized can be very stressful. How many people do you have around you who can give you the emotional support which you need to be effective in your work, without depleting your emotional resources?

Record below your current support network by entering:

1.  The names of the closest friends with whom you can share anything.

2.  The names of close friends from whom you could seek emotional support on some things.

3.  The names of acquaintances, colleagues and peers who share your general approach to life and work; who are 'on the same wavelength'.

4.  Friends with whom contact is limited to Christmas and possibly birthday.

When you have recorded your network, consider the following:

1. Ten or twelve people are probably enough for the first two categories. How many have you?

2. How often do you contact the people in your support network? Is the support two-way?

3. Are there any people in categories 3 and 4 with whom you could develop closer reciprocal links?

# SUPPORTING ADULT SURVIVORS OF CHILD SEXUAL ABUSE (GUIDELINES)   PM 38

You may feel foolish crying over events that happened so long ago. But grief waits for expression. When you do not allow yourself to honour grief, it festers. It can limit your vitality, make you sick, decrease your capacity for love.

Grief has its own rhythms. You can't say, 'Okay, I'm going to grieve now'. Rather you must allow room for these feelings as they arise. Grief needs space. You can only really grieve when you give yourself the time, security and permission to grieve.

*Bass and Davis 1992, p. 120*

Bass and Davis (1992) suggest that, for survivors of child sexual abuse, the healing process is a continuum. They say this begins with survival and ends with thriving. The length of time between the extremes of the continuum varies enormously, depending on such factors as:

- the length of time over which the abuse took place
- the age of the child when the abuse began
- the presence or absence of emotional support in the child's environment.

They suggest the following stages on this continuum:

- the decision to heal
- the emergency stage
- remembering
- believing it happened
- breaking the silence
- understanding that it wasn't your fault
- making contact with the child within
- trusting yourself
- grieving and mourning
- anger – the backbone of healing
- disclosures and confrontations
- forgiveness?
- spirituality
- resolution and moving on.

What follows is a summary of guidelines suggested by Bass and Davis for those working with survivors of child sexual abuse:

- Believe healing is possible.
- Be willing to witness pain.
- Be willing to believe the unbelievable.

- Examine your own attitudes.
- Explore your own history and fears regarding sexual abuse.
- If you were not sexually abused as a child, explore those experiences which come closest.
- The survivor is the expert, not you.
- Validate her/his needs.
- Realize that your gender may be important to the client.
- Support your client in seeking other appropriate help if necessary.
- Remember that group work can be helpful in combatting feelings of isolation and shame.
- Believe the survivor.
- No one fantasizes abuse.
- Don't say or imply that the client is to blame for the abuse.
- If the client experienced pleasure, help her/him to let go of the shame.
- Incestuous abuse is a criminal act.
- Don't minimize the abuse.
- Don't spend time trying to understand the abuser.
- Never say or imply that the client should forgive the abuser.
- Check to see if the survivor has a drug or alcohol problem.
- Validate your client's ways of coping.
- Present a healthy perspective on what should be available to a child.
- Validate anger as a sane, healthy response to abuse, not something to be rushed through.
- Support your client in speaking out.
- Help to build the survivor's support system.
- Don't say or imply that anyone's sexual preference is a result of sexual abuse.

You should examine these ideas and their implications for your work in the light of your personal philosophy of life.

REFERENCES

Bass, E. and Davis, L. (1992) *The Courage to Heal (revised ed.)*. London: Harper and Row.

Davis, L. (1990) *The Courage to Heal Workbook*. London: Harper and Row.

# UNDERSTANDING WHY PEOPLE HARM THEMSELVES (INFORMATION)     PM 39

Self-harming, sometimes known as self-inflicted violence, covers a wide variety of practices, including severe skin picking, burning, scratching, carving and cutting the skin, hair pulling, anorexia, bulimia, abuse of alcohol and drugs, head banging and injecting urine. Some of these practices have received much attention, but others very little, particularly those involving the self-infliction of physical injury. Many people find this kind of activity the most difficult to understand because it does not appear to provide any short-term gratification (unlike the abuse of food, drugs or alcohol).

Self-harming often indicates physical, mental or sexual abuse during childhood, and the use of *dissociation* to cope with the trauma. Dissociation is a skill developed by those who are trapped in abusive situations. It enables a person to disconnect their feelings from the repeated abusive events. Such victims often describe how they 'leave the body' that is being abused, how they take the essential core of themselves to a safe place, to preserve it. But if someone is obliged to use this technique over a prolonged period, the feelings may remain disconnected; the person concerned may have great difficulty in responding at an emotional level to even nurturing relationships. Bear this in mind when meeting a client who dissociates from their feelings. Such dissociation should be recognized as a secondary issue, a likely indicator of more deeply buried problems.

Those who find that they are working with a self-harming client may be shocked and frightened to find that someone who appears to be a rational, articulate adult, regularly cuts or burns herself. However, a professional in a state of shock and fear is unlikely to use her skills and sensitivities as effectively as usual. Perhaps this is why self-harming clients report angry and judgemental responses when they attend Accident and Emergency departments. Wounds are often sutured without local anaesthetic; the patient feels treated as a pariah. Effective work with such clients requires that the counsellor tries to accept and understand the function of the distressing behaviour. Otherwise the self-abuse may remain a secret burden, to be coped with alone and unsupported.

People who inflict harm on themselves have reported that by doing this they feel they can:

- cut out the badness
- dig out the pain
- punish themselves for being such bad, loathsome people
- be in control of their punishment
- feel alive when they see the blood flow
- feel numb (due to the natural opiates stimulated by the injury) and thus cope with the pain of living, rather than killing themselves
- manage the physical pain rather than the emotional pain
- let the poison out.

These ideas are powerfully expressed in the following poem by a survivor:

My heart aches
A permanent pain
swirling inside
deep in my guts.
Empty in love
Vacant in life
The agony fills my body
polluting the blood that keeps me alive,
Hating myself
I try to excavate the pain.

Crashing my limbs against a wall
I try to break the ache,Bruises appear
Arms ache
Relief evolves
Outside aches now

Contented, I can deal with this pain,
until the other builds its way up again.

J.M.D.

The person who self-harms may often injure a part of the body associated with the original abuse, but without conscious awareness of the full significance of what they are doing. Bass and Davis (1992) report a woman who felt terror and severe vaginal pain every night. This was relieved only when she inserted objects into her vagina which hurt her. Then she was able to sleep. She experienced deep shame about this behaviour, until she recovered the memory of her father hurting her in this way. Having retrieved that memory, however, she was able to work on stopping her self-harming compulsion.

Mary Louise Wise (1989) suggests that self-harming is, '…a visible action which keeps alive the bodily memory path to the original abuse'. Wise writes of the 'victim/survivor', meaning, '…the person's physical and emotional survival of childhood abuse and the defensive abilities developed for on-going survival'.

In some people, the 'victim' may be dominant in the adult. The effect of this is that they may be immobilized; aware of their feelings and the effect of the victimization, but lacking the strength to initiate action on their own behalf. In others, the 'survivor' is dominant, powerfully committed to survival, but out of touch with most feelings other than overwhelming guilt and shame. This person may present to the world as a successful, competent, high achieving individual.

When young children are repeatedly abused, and repeatedly need to dissociate from those events, they sometimes create different personalities to contain the anguish of different types of abuse. This, it has been suggested, could explain the origin of Multiple Personality Disorder, more recently classified by the American Psychiatric Association's DSM IV as Dissociative Identity Disorder. It is argued that sharing the pain among several personalities may make bearable a level of anguish that would otherwise destroy a single individual. But those several personalities can then have no connection with one another.

If beating, drugs or hypnosis were used on the child, to reinforce admonitions to secrecy, then the adult survivor, when recovering her memories, is likely to experience extreme terror. She may become sleepy, appear as in a trance, have slurred speech, be unsteady on her feet or show any combination of these symptoms. As memories return and are revealed, self-harming can increase. (Perhaps this represents the punishment threatened if secrets are revealed.)

A counsellor can expect a client recovering from these types of experience to need long and patient support. Before committing oneself to continue working with a client who reveals such depth of abuse, one might consider some questions:

- Are my skills developed to a level where I feel secure to deal with these issues?

- Can I offer this person continuing support over a number of years?

- Do I have the emotional resources which will enable me to accept and witness this person's emotional and physical pain?

- Do I have support and supervision to sustain me through such work?

- Is there a colleague who the client might accept as a back-up counsellor, when I need to take a break from this demanding work?

If one feels unable to continue working with such a client, then it is vital to negotiate the change to an alternative counsellor together with the client, supporting her while she explores the possibilities. However, it would be a mistake to force oneself to continue to work with clients against one's better judgement. They will certainly detect any ambivalence and feel insecure, and this would sabotage the therapeutic relationship. A client needs to develop a growing trust: in herself, in the counsellor and in the relationship between them. On this basis the work may progress, until ultimately the client is able to relinquish her self-injury in favour of an alternative supportive strategy. One should recognize, however, that for some clients the damage may be so severe that they might never reach this stage. But even in these cases, one may at least minimize the severity of the self-harming behaviour.

ACKNOWLEDGEMENTS

Thanks to J.M.D. for allowing us to use her poem.

REFERENCES, FURTHER READING AND RESOURCES

American Psychiatric Association *Diagnostic and Statistical Manual of Mental Disorders – (DSM – IV)* (1994) Washington, DC: American Psychiatric Association.

Bass, E. and Davis, E. (1992) *The Courage to Heal (Revised ed.)*. New York: Harper Collins.

Casey, J.F. with Wilson, L. (1992) *The Flock: The Autobiography of a Multiple Personality*. New York: Ballantine Books.

Wise, M.L. (1989) 'Adult self injury as a survival response in victim/survivors of childhood abuse.' *Journal of Chemical Dependency 3*, 1, 185–201.

A leaflet, advice and a newsletter can be obtained from Bristol Crisis Service for Women, PO Box 654, Bristol BS99 1XH.

A booklet, *Self Harm – Perspectives from Personal Experience*, is available from Survivors Speak Out, 34 Osnaburgh St, London NW1 3ND.

## PLEASE HEAR WHAT I'M NOT SAYING (CENTRING)                    PM 40

Don't be fooled by me. Don't be fooled by the mask I wear. For I wear a mask; I wear a thousand masks, masks I am afraid to take off, and none of them is me. Pretending is an art that is second nature to me, but don't be fooled.

I give the impression that I am secure, that all is sunny and unruffled with me, within and without; that confidence is my name and coolness is my game; that the waters are calm and that I am in command and need no one. But don't believe it; please don't.

My surface may seem smooth, but my surface is my mask, my ever varying, ever concealing mask. Beneath lies no smugness, no coolness, no complacence. Beneath it lies the real me, in confusion, in fear, in loneliness. But I hide this; I don't want anybody to know it. I panic at the thought of my weakness being exposed. That's why I frantically create a mask to hide behind, a nonchalant, sophisticated facade to help me pretend, to shield me from the glance that knows. But such a glance is precisely my salvation. My only salvation. And I know it. It's the only thing that can liberate me from myself, from my own self-built prison walls, from the barriers that I so painstakingly erect. But I don't tell you this. I don't dare. I'm afraid to.

I am afraid that your glance will not be followed by love and acceptance. I'm afraid that you will think less of me, that you'll laugh and your laugh will kill me. I'm afraid that deep down inside I'm nothing, that I'm just no good, and that you'll see me and reject me. So I play my games, my desperate pretending games, with a facade of assurance on the outside and a trembling child within. And so begins my parade of masks, the glittering but empty parade of masks. And my life becomes a front.

I idly chatter to you in the suave tones of surface talk. I tell you everything that is really nothing, and nothing of what's crying within me. So when I'm going through my routine, don't be fooled by what I'm saying. Please listen carefully and try to hear what I'm not saying: what I'd like to be able to say; what, for survival, I need to say but I can't say. I dislike the hiding, honestly I do. I dislike the superficial, phony games I am playing.

I'd really like to be genuine, spontaneous, and me; but you have to help me. You have to help me by holding out your hand, even when it's the last thing I seem to want or need. Each time you're kind and gentle and encouraging, each time you try to understand because you really care, my heart begins to grow wings. Very small wings. Very feeble wings. But wings. With your sensitivity and sympathy and your power of understanding, I can make it. You can breathe life into me. It will not be easy for you. A long conviction of worthlessness builds strong walls.

So stay beside me and please hear what I'm not saying.

Contributed by a course participant

# ADVANCED DIRECTIVES (INFORMATION)   PM 41

A recent ruling in the Scottish courts has permitted a hospital to cease feeding a woman who has been in a 'persistent vegetative state' for a number of years. Clearly this raises a number of moral and ethical issues which deserve to be considered and discussed. One of these concerns the possible introduction of 'advanced directives' as a routine option for patients in British hospitals.

Two types of advanced directive are used in the USA, regulated by state law. One is the Medical Power of Attorney and the other is the Living Will.

## MEDICAL POWER OF ATTORNEY

A Medical Power of Attorney form permits a person (A) to appoint another person of their choice (B) to be their legally recognized representative if A should lose his ability to make health care decisions. A may also specify treatment preferences. By selecting someone who will talk to A's doctor on his behalf about his medical care, A is assured that his wishes are known and respected. B then becomes A's surrogate or proxy decision-maker or representative. The decision-maker chosen might be a spouse, parent, adult child or friend. It is important that B agrees to assume this responsibility and that B knows about A's beliefs and treatment preferences.

## LIVING WILL

A Living Will states a person A's wishes about medical treatment in case he is not able to do this himself. A Living Will may be either general or specific. It could include A's specific statements concerning treatments he does, or does not, want. It can direct physicians to withdraw or withhold life-prolonging treatment if A has a terminal illness or is in a persistent vegetative state.

Both of these forms have to be witnessed and signed by A, two witnesses and a Notary Public. The English equivalent of a Notary Public would be a Justice of the Peace (In Scotland, the documents could be witnessed by a Justice of the Peace or a Notary Public!). In addition to signing, the Notary Public has to state when the commission expires. Time to expiry date can vary, depending on the health of the client, perhaps allowing longer intervals for healthy people. The document ceases to be valid after the expiry date, but it can be renewed. This provides A with a stimulus to review and update his instructions, taking into account any changes in perspective which he might have had with the passing of time.

See **PM 43** and **44** for examples of a Medical Power of Attorney and a Living Will.

(Adapted from material published by
Morgantown Hospice, West Virginia, USA)

# MEDICAL POWER OF ATTORNEY (EXAMPLE) PM 42

To be completed by the person whose life decisions are represented below, who shall be called the Principal.

Dated_____ 199__.

I,_____of_____

_____

_____

[insert name, address, postcode and telephone number of the Principal], hereby appoint_____of_____
*[insert here the name, address, postcode and telephone number of the designated proxy or representative]*, as my representative to act on my behalf to give, withhold or withdraw informed consent to health care decisions in the event that I am unable to so do myself. If my representative is unable, unwilling or disqualified to serve, then I appoint_____as my successor representative.

This appointment shall extend to (but not be limited to) decisions relating to medical treatment, surgical treatment, nursing care, medication, hospitalization, care and treatment in a nursing home or other health care facility, and home health care. The representative appointed by this document is specifically authorized to act on my behalf to consent to, refuse, or withdraw any and all medical treatment or diagnostic procedures, if my representative determines that I, if able to do so, would consent to, refuse or withdraw such treatments or procedures. Such authority shall include, but not be limited to, the withholding or withdrawal of life-prolonging intervention when, in the opinion of two physicians who have examined me, one of whom is my attending physician, such life-prolonging intervention offers no medical hope of benefit.

I appoint this representative because I believe this person understands my wishes and values and will act to carry into effect the health care decisions that I would make if I were able to so do, and because I believe this person will act in my best interest when my wishes are unknown. It is my intent that my family, my physician and all legal authorities be bound by the decisions that are made by the representative appointed by this document, and it is my intent that these decisions should not be the subject of review by any health care provider, or administrative or judicial agency.

It is my intent that this document be legally binding and effective. In the event that the law does not recognize this document as legally binding and effective, it is my intent that this document be taken as a formal statement of my desire concerning the method by which any health care decisions should be made on my behalf during any period when I am unable to make such decisions.

*© 1997 Fay W. Jacobsen, Margaret Kindlen and Allison Shoemark*

In exercising the authority under this Medical Power of Attorney, my representative shall act consistently with my special directives or limitations as stated below.

*Special directives or limitations on this power* (If none, write 'none')

_____

_____

_____

*This Medical Power of Attorney shall become effective only upon my incapacity to give, withhold or withdraw informed consent to my own medical care.*

These directives shall supersede any directives made in any previously executed document concerning my health care.

Signature of the Principal_____

Witness:_____ Date:_____

Witness:_____ Date:_____

I, _____, a Notary Public of the County of _____ _____, do certify that _____, as Principal and _____ and_____ as witnesses, whose names are signed to the writing above bearing the date on the _____ day of _____, 19_____, have this day acknowledged the same before me. Given under my hand this _____ day of _____ 19____ My commission expires:_____ _____ Notary Public

(Based on the Medical Power of Attorney, State of West Virginia)

## LIVING WILL (EXAMPLE)                                    PM 43

Living Will made this _____ day of _____
19_____

I, _____, being of sound mind, willfully and voluntarily declare that in the absence of my ability to give directions regarding the use of life-prolonging intervention, it is my desire that my dying shall not be artificially prolonged under the following circumstances:

If at any time I should be certified by two physicians who have personally examined me, one of whom is my attending physician, to have a terminal condition or to be in a persistent vegetative state, I direct that life-prolonging intervention that would serve solely artificially to prolong the dying process or maintain me in a persistent vegetative state be withheld or withdrawn, and that I be allowed to die naturally with only the administration of medication or performance of any other medical procedure deemed necessary to keep me comfortable and control pain.

*Special directives or limitations on this declaration*: (If none, write 'none'.)

_____

_____

_____

It is my intention that this Living Will be honoured as the final expression of my legal right to refuse medical or surgical treatment, and accept the consequences resulting from such refusal.

Signed _____ Address _____

_____

I did not sign the declarant's signature above for, or at the direction of, the declarant. I am at least 18 years of age and am not related to the declarant by blood or marriage, entitled to any portion of the estate of the declarant according to the laws of intestate succession of the state of the declarant's domicile or, to the best of my knowledge, under any will of declarant or codicil thereto, or directly financially responsible for the declarant's medical care. I am not the declarant's attending physician or the declarant's health care representative, proxy or successor health care representative under Medical Power of Attorney.

Witness _____ Address _____

_____

Witness _____ Address _____

_____

County of_____

The foregoing instrument was acknowledged before me this _____ (date) by the declarant and by two witnesses whose signatures appear above.

My commission expires on: _____

Signature of Notary Public _____

(Based on the Living Will, State of West Virginia)

# STRUCTURED ROLE-PLAYS

## ROLE-PLAY I: ADULT RECALL OF CHILD SEXUAL ABUSE          PM 44

SUMMARY

A woman experiences terrifying flashbacks of violence of which she has no conscious memory.

CLIENT

You are June Pollack, aged 29 years and feeling very low just now. You have just come out of hospital after having some tests, and you were told that you would have to lose 20 lbs before the surgeon would operate to remove your gall bladder. He suggests that you see a counsellor to help you with the weight loss. You accept.

However, your health is the least of your worries. Your obesity and over-eating are a result of an overwhelming fear. For some years past you have been having flashbacks of violent incidents of which you have no memory. You were brought up by foster parents from the age of six years, and cannot remember your parents. You think you are going mad. The need to share your fear is so intense that the chance to see a counsellor has come just at the right time.

COUNSELLOR

You are about to have your first meeting with a woman referred to you by the local hospital. Ostensibly she has been referred because she needs to lose weight before surgery. But the surgeon has noticed that she seems to be under tremendous tension and feels that she will be unsuccessful in losing weight unless the cause of the underlying tension is addressed.

# ROLE-PLAY 2: A STUDENT WHO HAS RECEIVED BAD NEWS FROM HOME    PM 45

SUMMARY

A student has received a telephone call from his mother to say that she has breast cancer.

CLIENT

You are Philipa/Philip Judd, aged 20 years and a student living in lodgings, a considerable distance from home. Over the past year you have become increasingly alarmed at your mother's poor health, and you are concerned that she is neglecting herself and working too hard. She reared you as a single parent, and you are very close to her. You have no brothers or sisters. Your concern about your mother has affected your studies; your grades have gone steadily down.

Now you have received a telephone call from your mother, who sounded distressed and exhausted. She had just had confirmation from her doctor that a lump in her breast is cancer. Your initial reaction is to give up your studies, which under normal circumstances you love, and go home to be with her. You know your mother would be heart broken if you were to do this. A friend suggests that you talk to a student counsellor.

COUNSELLOR

This is your first meeting with Philipa/Philip Judd, aged 20, a student at the beginning of the third year of studies. S/he is described by her/his tutor as a quiet, private person, who was obviously happy and doing well at her/his studies until about six months ago. Then it was noticed that s/he was becoming depressed and her/his grades had been dropping.

## ROLE-PLAY 3: BEREAVEMENT AFTER A HAPPY MARRIAGE

**PM 46**

SUMMARY

A recently bereaved person has kept up the appearance of a happy marriage.

CLIENT

You are Jean/John Rank, aged 58 years. The funeral of your spouse was held recently, in the church to which you have both belonged since you married 40 years ago. The marriage has not been a happy one, but you stayed together while you reared your family, and then continued to stay together, partly through duty and partly due to the pressure of the religious community in which you were both active and respected. Often you felt that the pretence of being a devoted couple, in which you reluctantly colluded, was hypocritical. You felt very distressed by this, but you thought that it would cost you a great deal to give it up. You would lose the esteem of your children, who adhere strictly to the 'family values' philosophy of your brand of religion. You would also lose the friendship of many people whom you have come to value highly.

Now you have been offered the chance to see a counsellor. Will you keep up the pretence? Or might this provide an opportunity to establish an honest and open relationship?

COUNSELLOR

You have been asked by the minister of a local church or synagogue to see Jean/John Rank, whose spouse has recently died. He tells you that the Ranks have been active and respected members of the church community for a very long time. They were a quiet couple, who raised a fine God-fearing family and were always involved in 'good works' for the community. Jean/John had a stiff, mask-like expression on her/his face at the end of the service and remained dry-eyed throughout. This caused the minister to have some concern for her/him, and he was surprised when s/he accepted his suggestion for counselling. S/he has just arrived for the first appointment.

## ROLE-PLAY 4: HEALTH PROBLEMS
## TWO YEARS AFTER A BEREAVEMENT    PM 47

SUMMARY

A man, whom you counselled for a few sessions after his wife died two years ago, has been recommended to see you again by his doctor.

CLIENT

You are Donald Tedesco, aged 59 years. Your beloved wife Julia died 18 months ago. You had no children, so you were closer to her than anyone else in the world. Her death struck you like a hammer blow and left you numb. You saw a counsellor for a few sessions after Julia died. It was a comfort to have someone to talk to and you came to trust her/him. Your doctor has been pressing you to lose weight because of hypertension and has suggested a visit to the same counsellor.

Since Julia died you have had no interest in anything. Even your garden, once your pride and joy, has ceased to interest you now that Julia is no longer there to share it with you and praise your skill. You do your job as an electrician with the conscientiousness which has earned you a reputation as a respected craftsman, but you don't even get satisfaction from this any more. You can't be bothered to cook when you get home from work, so you eat out of tins or 'fast foods' in front of the TV, which you leave switched on all the time for company.

You have avoided speaking to anyone about how you feel since Julia's death, mainly because you don't feel close enough to anyone except your older brother Peter. He lives 200 miles away. You are not even sure how he would cope if you were to break down and weep; men didn't do this in your family. So you are holding all your feelings inside you, but the build-up is beginning to make you feel like a pressure cooker.

COUNSELLOR

Donald Tedesco, aged 59 years, first came to see you after the death of his wife, Julia, two years ago. The couple had no children and were very close. Donald was clearly bereft without his wife and had a permanently dazed look on his face. After a few sessions he said he didn't need to come any more. You were not too surprised when his doctor asked you to see him again to see if counselling would have any effect upon his high blood pressure. Now, you are shocked at his gross increase in weight and his red face. On your enquiry he admits that his doctor has been pressing him to lose weight.

## ROLE-PLAY 5: A MAN WITH TERMINAL ILLNESS PLANS BIG CHANGES      PM 48

SUMMARY

A man who is terminally ill becomes excited at the prospect of realizing a dream. But what of the consequences for his family?

CLIENT

You are Jim Delardo, aged 48 years and terminally ill with lung cancer. You have a wife, Josie, and four children: Brenda (20 years), a student; Jamie (18 years), about to start university; Sandra (15 years) and Justin (12 years). You have been accustomed to a good income as an architect, but haven't really hit the big time yet, although you have always been confident that you would.

Today you are feeling much better and are really excited. You have seen that the house of your dreams is for sale. It is literally the house of your dreams: when you were a rising young architect, you designed this particular house, in an idyllic setting, for a wealthy client. One day, you hoped, you would build one just like this for your family.

You share your excitement with your wife. She points out that it will triple your mortgage. You feel hurt that she doesn't share your enthusiasm, but you are due to see your counsellor whom you have already seen for several sessions. Perhaps s/he will share your enthusiasm.

COUNSELLOR

Jim Delardo, 48 years of age, is terminally ill with lung cancer. He has a wife, Josie, and four children: Brenda (20 years), a student; Jamie (18 years), about to start university; Sandra (15 years) and Justin (12 years). Jim has commanded a good salary in his profession as an architect.

You have seen Jim several times already. Today you find him in exceptionally good spirits. He tells you that he has seen an advertisement for a fine house in an outstanding situation. It is just what he has always dreamed about for his family. It will mean increasing the mortgage '...*a bit, but what the hell, why not go for it?*'.

## ROLE-PLAY 6: A CHILD IS DYING OF LEUKAEMIA; FATHER OPTS OUT PM 49

SUMMARY

Involves the parents of a child who is dying of leukaemia. The father never attends scheduled counselling sessions.

CLIENT

You are Alison Bujold, aged 30 years and mother of Jody, aged 10 years. Jody is suffering from leukaemia. You have been told that Jody has probably only about one month to live. This news weighs heavily on you, because you haven't yet told Jody and you don't know if you should. Your husband, Geoff, avoids discussing Jody's illness by working long hours. Apart from telephone conversations with your parents, who live in France, you have no one to talk to except the counsellor, whom you and Geoff were both invited to see. Geoff has not accompanied you to any of your previous four meetings with the counsellor.

COUNSELLOR

Alison Bujold, aged 30 years, is the mother of Jody, aged 10 years, and wife of Geoff Bujold. Both Alison and Geoff were invited to come to see you, but Geoff has never attended any of the four sessions which you have had so far. Jody is suffering from leukaemia and is not expected to live more than another month. Alison looks haggard and distressed. You greet her and comment about how exhausted she looks.

## ROLE-PLAY 7: A GAY MAN DYING OF AIDS HAS PLANS TO MAKE
**PM 50**

SUMMARY

A gay man dying of AIDS wants to talk about his funeral arrangements.

CLIENT

You are Vince Marshall, aged 42 years, a gay man dying of AIDS. You are cared for by your lover, Jos Vangelli, aged 40 years. Your relationship has been good for the ten years that you have been together, and Jos' tenderness to you during your illness has brought you even closer to each other. There is not much that you haven't been able to discuss. However, when you asked him to help you plan your funeral, he said he couldn't handle that.

You have strong feelings about what sort of funeral you want and this is weighing on your mind. You are atheist and Jos is Catholic. You don't want a religious funeral, but for his sake, you would like to include some appropriate religious music. You would also like to include some Jazz, which you both love, and you would like to leave a message on tape to say goodbye to your family and friends. Perhaps this is something you could talk about with the counsellor whom you have been seeing for the last few weeks.

COUNSELLOR

Vince Marshall, aged 42 years, is a gay man who is close to death from AIDS. He is cared for by his lover, Jos Vangelli, aged 40 years. You have been seeing Vince for several weeks now and have built a good relationship with him. Today, Vince asks you if you would help him with something that has been weighing on his mind.

# ALTERNATIVE EVALUATION FORMS

# ALTERNATIVE EVALUATION FORM (1)    PM 51

Please help us to measure the success of this course by completing the following sentences:

1.  On this course I was surprised at...

2.  I liked...

3.  I didn't like...

4.  The hardest activity for me was...

5.  The most enjoyable activity for me was...

6. I learned more about…

7. The course would be better if…

8. Overall I thought the course was…

Signature:                                    Date:

## ALTERNATIVE EVALUATION FORM (2)  PM 52

Please rate the effectiveness of the course with respect to the features listed below. '1' on the scale represents 'not good' or 'not effective'; '5' represents 'very good'.

|  | *Not good* |  |  |  | *Very good* |
|---|---|---|---|---|---|
| Venue | 1 | 2 | 3 | 4 | 5 |
| Organization | 1 | 2 | 3 | 4 | 5 |
| Content | 1 | 2 | 3 | 4 | 5 |
| Teaching methods | 1 | 2 | 3 | 4 | 5 |
| Appropriateness to your personal needs | 1 | 2 | 3 | 4 | 5 |
| Relevance to your work | 1 | 2 | 3 | 4 | 5 |
| Ability to involve you | 1 | 2 | 3 | 4 | 5 |

Did you enjoy the course?

|  | *Not at all* |  |  |  | *Very much* |
|---|---|---|---|---|---|
|  | 1 | 2 | 3 | 4 | 5 |

Signature:                          Date:

*© 1997 Fay W. Jacobsen, Margaret Kindlen and Allison Shoemark*

# PART 5

# References, Further Reading and Resources

## REFERENCES

American Psychiatric Association *Diagnostic and Statistical Manual of Mental Disorders (DSM IV)* (1994) Washington, DC: American Psychiatric Association.

Bass, E. and Davis, L. (1992) *The Courage to Heal* (Revised ed.). New York: Harper Collins.

Berne, E. (1971) *What Do You Say After You Say 'Hello'?* New York: Bantam Books.

Bion, W.R. (1968) *Experiences in Groups*. London: Tavistock.

Bond, T. (1995) *Standards and Ethics for Counselling in Action*. London: Sage Publications.

Bower, F. (1980) *Nursing and the Concept of Loss*. Chichester: Wiley & Sons.

Bowlby, J. (1969) *Attachment and Loss – Volume 1*. Harmondsworth: Penguin.

Bowlby, J. (1988) *A Secure Base: Clinical Applications of Attachment Theory*. London: Routledge.

Brandes, D. and Ginnis, P. (1986) *A Guide to Student Centred Learning*. Oxford: Basil Blackwell.

Bristol Crisis Service For Women, PO Box 654 Bristol BS99 1XH, produces a newsletter and leaflet and offers advice.

British Association for Counselling (1993) *Code of Ethics and Practice for Counselling*. Rugby: BAC.

Burnard, P. (1985) *Learning Human Skills: A Guide for Nurses*. London: Heinemann Nursing.

Carr, A.T. 'Dying and Bereavement.' In A. Chapman and A. Gale (1982) *Psychology and People: A Tutorial Text*. London: Macmillan Press.

Casey, J.F. with Wilson, L. (1992) *The Flock: The Autobiography of a Multiple Personality*. New York: Ballantine Books.

Cermak, T.L. (1986) *Diagnosing and Treating Co-dependence*. Minniapolis: Johnson Institute.

Chermin, K. (1985) *The Hungry Self: Women, Eating and Identity*. London: Virago.

Cherry, C., Robertson, M. and Meadows, F. (1990) *Personal and Professional Development for Group Leaders*. Edinburgh: Scottish Health Education Group.

Davis, L. (1990) *The Courage to Heal Workbook*. London: Harper and Row.

Douglas, T. (1978) *Basic Group-work*. London: Tavistock Publications.

Egan, G. (1986) *The Skilled Helper*. Third edition. Monterey, California: Brooks Cole, Ch. 9.

Engel, G.L. (1961) *Is Grief a Disease? A challenge for medical research*. Psychosomatic Medicine 23, 18–22.

Entwistle, N.J. (1981) *Styles of Teaching and Learning*. Chichester: John Wiley & Sons.

Ewles, L. and Simnett, I. (1985) *Promoting Health: A Practical Guide to Health Education*. Chichester: John Wiley & Sons.

Falshaw, M. (1985) *Self-Help Learning Groups: A Practical Guide for Organisers*. Cambridge: National Extension College.

Fisher, M. and Warman, J. (1990) *Bereavement and Loss: A Skills Companion*. Cambridge: National Extension College.

Hargie, O. (ed) (1986) *A Handbook of Communication Skills*. London: Croom Helm.

Harris, T.A. (1993) *I'm OK – You're OK*. New York: Avon Books.

Hayden, T.L. (1991) *Ghost Girl*. New York: Avon Books.

Health Education Bureau for Northern Ireland (1983) *Teacher Training Programmes in Health Education*. Dublin: Health Education Bureau for Northern Ireland.[Out of print.]

Herman, J.L. (1992) *Trauma and Recovery*. New York: Basic Books.

Holland, I. (1986) 'Head and neck massage.' In *Connections: Health and Arts in Scotland*, No. 7, 22–24.

Hopson, B. (1982) 'Transition: understanding and managing personal change.' In A. Chapman and A. Gale (eds) *Psychology and People: Tutorial Text*. London: Macmillan Press.

Horney, K. (1942) *Self Analysis*. New York: W.W. Norton. [Paper-back (1962): London: Routledge and Kegan Paul.]

Inskipp, F. (1986) *The Trainer's Handbook*. Cambridge: National Extension College.

Jacobsen, F.W. and Mackinnon, H. (1989) *Sharing Counselling Skills: A Guide to Running Courses for Nurses, Midwives and Health Visitors*. Edinburgh: Scottish Health Education Group.

Knowles, M. (1980) *The Modern Practice of Adult Education: Andragogy versus pedagogy*. Chicago: Follett.

Kolb, D.A. (1985) *Experiential Learning: Experience as a Source of Learning and Development*. New Jersey: Prentice Hall Inc.

Kubler-Ross, E. (1991) *On Death and Dying*. New York: Macmillan Publishing Co.

Lever, M. *et al.* (1985) *Learning Together: A Guide to Running Informal Learning Groups*. Cambridge: National Extension College.

Lindeman, E. (1944) Symptomology and management of acute grief. Cited in Worden (1988) Grief Counselling and Grief Therapy. London: Routledge.

Locke, E.A. and Latham, G.P. (1984) *Goal Setting: A Motivational Technique that Works*. Englewood Cliffs, New Jersey: Prentice Hall.

Luft, J. and Ingham, H. (1955) *The Johari Window: A Graphic Model of Interpersonal Relations*. Los Angeles: University of California Western Training Laboratory in Group Development.

Miller, A. (1986) *Thou Shalt Not be Aware*. London: Virago.

Miller, A. (1987a) *For Your Own Good*. London: Virago.

Miller, A. (1987b) *The Drama of Being a Child*. London: Virago.

Munsch, R. and McGraw, S. (1992) *Love You Forever*. Ontario: Firefly Books Ltd.

Murgatroyd, S. (1987) 'Evaluating change and development through workshops.' In *Coping With Crisis Research Group, Running Workshops*. Beckenham, Kent: Open University, Croom Helm.

Murray Parkes, C. (1972) *Bereavement: Studies of Grief in Adult Life*. Harmondsworth: Penguin.

Norwood, R. (1985) *Women Who Love Too Much*. New York: Pocket Books.

Orbach, S. (1979) *Fat is a Feminist Issue*. London: Hamlyn.

Perls, F., Hefferline, R. and Goodman, P. (1984) *Gestalt Therapy: Excitement and Growth in the Human Personality*. London: Souvenir Press.

Pinney, R. and Schlacter, M. (1983) *Bobby, the Story of an Autistic Child*. London: Harville.

Randal, R. and Southgate, J. (1980) *Co-operative and Community Group Dynamics: Or Your meetings needn't be so Appalling*. London: Barefoot Books.

Reich, W. (1961) *The Function of the Orgasm*. New York: Farrar, Straus and Giroux.

Reich, W. (1980) *Character Analysis*. New York: Farrer and Giroux Incorp.

Rodegast, P. and Stanton, J. (1987) *Emmanual's Book*. London: Bantam Books.

Rogers, C. (1983) *Freedom to Learn for the 80s*. Columbus, Ohio: Merrill.

Survivors Speak Out. *Self Harm – Perspectives from Personal Experience*. Booklet available from Survivors Speak Out, 34 Osnaburgh St, London NW1 3ND.

Southgate, J. (1989) 'The hidden child within us.' In W.S. Rogers, D. Hervey and E. Ask (eds) *Child Abuse and Neglect: Facing the Challenge*. P554 Child Abuse and Neglect. Milton Keynes: Open University.

Thomson, G. (1978) *The Prehistoric Aegean: Studies in Ancient Greek Society*. London: Lawrence and Wishart.

Tuckman, B.N. (1965) 'Development sequence in small groups.' *Psychological Bulletin 63*, 6, 384–399

Van Ments, M. (1983) *The Effective Use of Role Play: A Handbook for Teachers and Trainers*. London: Kogan Page Ltd.

Volavková, H. (ed) (1993) *I Never Saw Another Butterfly: Children's Drawings and Poems from Terezin Concentration Camp, 1942–1944.* New York: Schoken Books.

Ward, B. and Associates (1993) *Good Grief 2: Exploring Feelings, Loss and Death with Over Elevens and Adults.* London: Jessica Kingsley Publishers Ltd.

Williams, M. and Lockley, P. (1989) *HIV/AIDS Counselling: Trainers' Manual.* Edinburgh: Scottish Health Education Group.

Winnicott, D. (1971) *Playing and Reality.* Harmondsworth: Penguin.

Wise, M.L. (1989) 'Adult self injury as a survival response in victim/survivors of childhood abuse.' *Journal of Chemical Dependency 3*, 1, 185–201.

Woolfe, R. (1987) 'Experiential learning in workshops.' In *Coping With Crisis Research Group, Running Workshops.* Beckenham, Kent: Croom Helm.

## FURTHER READING

### Young children and death

Perkins, G. and Morris, C. (1996) *Remembering Mum.* Huntingdon: A.C. Black.

Varley, S. (1992) *Badger's Parting Gifts* [Animals mourn Badger's death]. Glasgow: Collins Picture Books.

Wilhelm, H. (1988) *I'll Always Love You* [A beloved dog dies]. London: Hodder.

### Young children, child abuse and strangers

Elliot, M. (1987) *The Willow Street Kids – It's Your Right to be Safe.* Basingstoke: Pan MacMillan.

Gil, E. (1986) *I Told My Secret: A Book For Kids Who Were Abused.* Rockville: Launch Press.

Hollick, H. and Cope, J. (1994) *Come and Tell Me* [Importance of telling parents where you are going]. Overton: Dinosaur Publishing Co.

Watcher, O. (1986) *No More Secrets for Me* [Situations which threaten children]. Harmondsworth: Penguin Books.

### Older children and death

Grollman, E. (1993) *Straight Talk About Death For Teenagers.* Boston: Beacon Press.

Mayled, J. (1986) *Death Customs* [Customs in major religions]. Hove: Wayland.

Sieff, J. and Traisman, E. (1995) *Flowers for the Ones You've Known: Letters from Bereaved Teenagers.* Omaha: Centering Corporation.

Smith, D.B. (1987) *A Taste of Blackberries* [A sensitive account of the death of a friend due to allergy]. London: Puffin.

### Older children, sexual abuse and violence

Bain, D. and Sanders, M. (1990) *Out in the Open: A Guide for Young People Who Have Been Sexually Abused.* London: Virago Press Ltd.

Davis, D. (1983) *Something is Wrong at My House. A Book About Parents Fighting.* Seattle: Parenting Press.

Levy, B. (1992) *In Love and Danger: A Teen's Guide to Breaking Free of Abusive Relationships.* Seattle: Seal Press Feminist.

### People working with bereaved children

Ayalon, O. and Flasher, A. (1993) *Chain Reaction: Children and Divorce.* London: Jessica Kingsley Publishers.

Couldrick, A. (1987) *Grief and Bereavement – Understanding Children.* Headington: Sobell Publications

Couldrick, A. (1991) *When Your Mum or Dad Has Cancer.* Headington: Sobell Publications.

Kubler-Ross, E. (1985) *On Children and Death.* New Jersey: Macmillan Publishing Co, Inc.

Kubler-Ross, E. (1992) *The Grieving Child: A Parents' Guide.* New York: Simon and Schuster.

Noonan, E. (1990) *Counselling Young People.* London: Methuen Childrens Books.

Smith, S.C. and Pennels, Sister M. (1994) *The Forgotten Mourners: Guidelines for Working with Bereaved Children.* London: Jessica Kingsley Publishers.

Smith, S.C. and Pennells, Sister M. (1995) *Interventions with Bereaved Children*. London: Jessica Kingsley Publishers.

Ward, B. and Associates (1993) *Good Grief: Exploring Feelings, Loss and Death with Under Elevens*. London: Jessica Kingsley Publishers.

Wells, R. (1988) *Helping Children Cope with Grief – Facing a Death in the Family*. London: Sheldon Press.

People working with abused children

Aldgate, J. and Simmonds, J. (1988) *Direct Work With Children – British Agencies for Adoption and Fostering*. London: B.T. Batsford Ltd.

Cattanach, A. (1994) *Play Therapy: Where the Sky Meets the Underworld*. London: Jessica Kingsley Publishers.

Oaklander, V. (1988) *Windows to Our Children*. New York: Center for Gestalt Development.

Salter, A.C. (1988) *Treating Child Sex Offenders and Their Victims*. Beverley Hills: Sage Publications.

## People with disabilities

Corker, M. (1995) *Counselling – The Deaf Challenge*. London: Jessica Kingsley Publishers.

Fitton, P. (1994) *Listen to Me: Communicating the Needs of People with Profound Intellectual and Multiple Disabilities*. London: Jessica Kingsley Publishers.

Goldsmith, M. (1996) *Hearing the Voice of People with Dementia: Opportunities and Obstacles*. London: Jessica Kingsley Publishers.

Lovett, H. (1996) *Learning to Listen: Positive Approaches and People with Difficult Behaviour*. London: Jessica Kingsley Publishers.

## People suffering from terminal illness

Buckmann, R. (1988) *I Don't Know What To Say*. London: Macmillan Press.

Buckman, R. (1993) *How to Break Bad News*. London: Macmillan Press.

Faulkner, A. (1992) *Effective Interaction with Patients*. Edinburgh: Churchill Livingston.

Faukner, A. and Maguire, P. (1993) *Talking to Cancer Patients and Their Families*. Oxford: Oxford University Press.

## People who are bereaved

Bright, R. (1996) *Grief and Powerlessness: Helping People Regain Control of their Lives*. London: Jessica Kingsley Publishers.

Faulkner, A. (1995) *Working With Bereaved People*. Edinburgh: Churchill Livingston.

Klass, D., Silverman, R. and Nickmann, S. (1996) *Continuing Bonds: New Understanding of Grief*. Hemisphere Publishing Corp.

Rando, T.A. (1995) *How To Go On Living When Someone You Love Dies*. New York: Bantam Books.

Raphael, B. (1992) *The Anatomy of Bereavement*. Northvale: Routledge.

## Counselling and group work –practice, training and background reading

Corey, G. (1995) *Theory and Practice of Group Counselling*. Pacific Grove: Brooks Cole Publishing.

Dwivedi, K.N. (1993) *Groupwork with Children and Adolescents*. London: Jessica Kingsley Publishers.

Dynes, R. (1988) *Creative Writing in Groupwork*. Bicester: Winslow Press.

Dynes, R. (1990) *Creative Games in Groupwork*. Bicester: Winslow Press.

Evison, R. and Horrabin, R. (1990) *How to Change Yourself and Your World*. Sheffield: Counselling Phoenix. [Text specific to co-counselling].

Faulkner, A. (1992) *Effective Interaction With Patients*. Edinburgh: Churchill Livingston.

Faulkner, A. (1993) *Teaching Interactive Skills in Health Care*. London: Chapman and Hall.

Fromm, E. (1989) *The Art of Loving*. New York: Harper Collins.

Fromm, E. (1994) *The Art of Listening*. London: Constable and Co Ltd.

Fromm, E. (1996) *To Have or To Be*. New York: Continuum Publishing Co.

Gersie, A. ((1992) *Storymaking in Bereavement: Dragons Fight in the Meadow*. London: Jessica Kingsley Publishers.

Glassman, U. and Kates, L. (1990) *Groupwork: A Humanistic Approach*. London: Sage Publications.

Kennedy, E. (1984) *Crisis Counselling: The Essential Guide for Non Professional Counsellors*. Dublin: Gill and Macmillan Ltd.

Kubler-Ross, E. (1986a) *Death: the Final Stage*. New York: Simon and Schuster.

Kubler-Ross, E. (1986b) *Working it Through*. New Jersey: Macmillan Publishing Co, Inc.

Lieberman, M. (1990) *Art Therapy for Groups: A Handbook of Themes and Games*. New York: Routledge.

Macout, M. (1989) *How Can We Help You? Information, Advice and Counselling for Gay Men and Lesbians* [For helpline workers]. London: Bedford Square Press.

Pedersen, P. (1995) *Counselling Across Cultures*. New York: Sage Publications Ltd.

Raphael, B. (1986) *When Disaster Strikes: A Hand Book for Caring Professionals*. London: Unwin.

Raphael, B. and Wilson, J. (1993) *International Handbook of Post Traumatic Stress Studies*. New York: Plenum Press, Chapter 40.

Scott, M. and Stradling, S. (1992) *Counselling for Post Traumatic Stress Disorder*. London: Sage Publications.

Worden, W. (1991) *Grief Counselling and Grief Therapy*. New York: Springer Publishing Co, Inc.

Wright, B. (1993) *Caring in Crisis: A Handbook of Intervention Skills*. Edinburgh: Churchill Livingston.

## Physical, sexual, ritual, cult and satanic abuse

Adams, C. and Fay, J. (1989) *Free of the Shadows: Recovering From Sexual Violence*. Oakland: New Harbinger Publications.

Braswell, L. (1989) *Quest for Respect: A Healing Guide for Survivors of Rape*. Ventura: Pathfinder Publications of California.

Oksana, C. (1994) *Safe Passage to Healing: A Guide for Survivors of Ritual Abuse*.New York: Harper Collins Publishers, Inc.

Sakheim, D. and Devine, D. (eds) (1994) *Out of Darkness: Exploring Satanism and Ritual Abuse*. New York: Macmillan Publishing Co, Inc.

Statman, E. (1995) *Battered Woman's Survival Guide: Breaking the Cycle*. Dallas: Taylor Publishing Co.

## RESOURCES

### Games

The following four board 'life games' are intended for 6 to 16-year-old children. They could be adapted to cover a wider age range. These games are based on a model which integrates systemic, cognitive-behavioural, humanistic and psychodynamic therapeutic orientations. They should be used only in the presence of a therapist. They provide a safe space where children may explore their inner feelings, and they can be used to answer questions which children may be afraid to ask.

Searle, Y. and Streng, I. (1996a) *The Grief Game*. London: Jessica Kingsley Publishers.

Searle, Y. and Streng, I. (1996b) *The Anti-bullying Game*. London: Jessica Kingsley Publishers.

Searle, Y. and Streng, I. (1996c) *The Social Skills Game*. London: Jessica Kingsley Publishers.

Searle, Y. and Streng, I. (1996d) *Bereavement; Private Game*. London: Jessica Kingsley Publishers.

### Teaching/learning packs

#### LIVING WITH PROGRESSIVE DISEASE

*Clair: Living with Cancer (Janette Weir)*
Video-assisted distance learning pack
This pack explores the issues of staff–patient interactions.
Available from

University of Glasgow
Media Services
64 Southpark Avenue
Glasgow G12 8LB

*Death and Dying K260 Tutors' Pack*
Video- and audio-assisted teaching pack
The contents contain workbooks, audio cassettes and videos.

- Workbook 1 – Life and death
- Workbook 2 – Preparing for death
- Workbook 3 – Caring for dying people
- Workbook 4 – Bereavement: private grief
- Audio cassette 1 – Discussion on euthanasia
- Audio cassette 2 – On a dying person's perception
- Audio cassette 3 – Coping with a dying child
- Audio cassette 4 – Dramatic scenarios in a
  - residential home
  - hospice
  - hospital
  - home
- Video 1 – One of the many facets: a multicultural perspective on death and ceremonies surrounding death
- Video 2 – Death and bereavement issues surrounding
  - sudden death
  - cancer
  - people with learning difficulties.

Available from:

Open University
Walton Hall
Milton Keynes K7 6AA

*When a Pet Dies*
A learning pack for people who support pet owners.
Available from:

SCAS
10b Leny Road
Callender FK17 8BA
Scotland

## BEREAVEMENT

*Bereavement and Loss (Maggie Fisher and Jane Warman)*
A training manual
This pack does not provide general training in counselling skills. It includes guidelines for the use of counselling skills which are specific to loss and bereavement.

Available from:

National Extension College
18 Brooklands Avenue
Cambridge CB2 2HN

*I wish I could have told you so*

A video-assisted training pack

Consists of three videos between 35 and 55 minutes long and a comprehensive training manual providing all the materials required for a three day training course.

- Video 1 – An introduction to bereavement
- Video 2 – Basic counselling skills – a person-centred approach.
- Video 3 – Helping others and helping ourselves.

A promotional video is available to help you assess the value of the package

Available from:

University of Portsmouth Enterprise Ltd
The Television Centre
Museum Rd
Portsmouth
Hampshire PQ1 2QQ

## VIOLENCE

*Child abuse and neglect p554*

A training pack for people working with adults and children. Comprises:

- Videos – 1. Triggers; 2. Setting basic standards; 3. Investigating abuse; 4. Helping and healing.
- Course reader – with sections covering theories and models; social and cultural contexts; legal context; recognizing and responding to suspected abuse; the effects of abuse; responding to child abuse
- A set of pictures – as triggers
- Course booklets – course introduction and study guide.
- Groupwork guide and exercises
- Resources guide
- Audio booklet – 1. Making sense of child abuse; 2. Recognizing and responding; 3. Coming to terms with child abuse.
- Wall charts – Local services and contacts; Legal wall chart – England and Wales; Legal wall chart – Northern Ireland; Legal wall chart – Scotland.
- Assessment pack audio tapes – 1. Introduction to the course; 2 to 4. Audio components for activities.

Available from

The Open University
Walton Hall
Milton Keynes MK7 6AA

A number of education resources are available from

Glasgow Women's Support Project
31 Stockwell Street
Glasgow G1 4RZ

## COUNSELLING SKILLS

*Counselling Skills (Francesca Inskipp)*

A self-study resource intended to help learners develop an understanding of counselling skills.

*Counselling: the trainer's manual (Francesa Inskipp)*
A resource for those involved in counselling training. Contains material which can be freely photocopied for use in workshops.

Available from:

> National Extension College
> 18 Brooklands Avenue
> Cambridge CB2 2HN

*Multi racial video scenes*
A video-assisted training pack.

Available from

> The Centre for Educational Technology and Development
> De Montford University
> Leicester LE1 9BH

### AIDS

*Careful Communication*
A training package on communication for doctors working with people with HIV/AIDS.

Available from

> Maggie Davis
> Health Promotion Manager
> Health Promotion Department
> Weald of Kent Community NHS Trust
> Blackhurst, Halls Hole Rd
> Tunbridge Wells
> Kent TN2 4 RG

## Videos

### VIOLENCE

*Aftermath (10 mins)*
This video deals with issues of rape and its effects.

Available for hire or purchase from

> Concord Video and Film Council Limited
> 201 Felixstowe Road
> Ipswich
> Suffolk IP3 9BJ

*Prime Suspects (25 mins)*
A Granada *World in Action* programme which looks at suspected child murder by parents. One case is explored where the father is responsible for the death of his child but no case can be brought.

Available for hire or purchase from

> Concord Video and Film Council Limited
> 201 Felixstowe Road, Ipswich
> Suffolk IP3 9BJ

*Suspicion of Abuse (52 mins)*
A hypothetical film looking at how decisions are made when child abuse is suspected. In this film a six-year-old child discloses alleged sexual abuse. Police, social workers, parents, rights campaigners and journalists have 48 hours to decide on their response.

Available from

> Academy Television
> HealthWatch
> YITM Customer Services
> The Television Centre
> Leeds LS3 1YY

*The Secret of Castle Hall (50 mins)*
This feature film gives an account of institutional abuse, both physical and sexual, at a British special school.

Available from

> Academy Television
> HealthWatch
> YITM Customer Services
> The Television Centre
> Leeds LS3 1YY

*When Women Kill (48 mins)*
This video asks the question: 'What would make an ordinary woman kill her husband?'. It features three women who suffered domestic violence over a prolonged period. They killed when in fear of their own lives.

Available for hire or purchase from

> Concord Video and Film Council Ltd
> 201 Felixstowe Road, Ipswich
> Suffolk IP3 9BJ

## LIVING WITH ILLNESS AND DISEASE

*When it Happens to You (50 mins)*
A BBC *QED* programme featuring a couple dealing with the news that the husband has a one month prognosis.

Available from

> Hopeline Videos
> PO Box 515
> London SW15 6LQ

*Facing Chronic Illness and Death When the Patient is a Child (58 mins)*
This video targets children in an effort to help them come to terms with what is happening to them.

Available on hire or for purchase from

> Graves Educational Resources
> 220 New London Road
> Chelmsford
> Essex CM2 9BJ

*Dementia (26 mins)*
This video from the ITV series *From the Cradle to the Grave* features a family dealing with the issues of dementia in a 67-year-old woman living with her daughter and family.

Available from

> Academy Television
> Healthwatch

YITM Customer Services
The Television Centre
Leeds LS3 1YY

*Siamese Twins (53 mins)*

A *First Tuesday* documentary tells the story of Katie and Eilish, three-year-old Siamese twins, and the agonizing decision facing their parents to go ahead with an operation to separate the twins.

Available from

Academy Television
Healthwatch
YITM Customer Services
The Television Centre
Leeds LS3 1YY

## BEREAVEMENT

*Breaking Bad News (15 mins)*

This video deals with sudden death and the task facing the police when breaking the news to relatives.

Available for hire or purchase from

Concord Video and Film Council Limited
201 Felixstowe Road, Ipswich
Suffolk IP3 9BJ

*Merely Mortal: Whatever it takes (40 mins)*

This video explores bereavement with a number of people, some recently bereaved.

Available for hire and purchase from

Concord Video and Film Council Limited
201 Felixstowe Road, Ipswich
Suffolk IP3 9BJ

*The Bereaved Teenager: Life goes on (32 mins)*

Four teenage girls discuss their experiences, feelings and reactions following the death of a parent.

Available from

Education Department
St Margaret's Hospice
Heron Drive
Bishops Hull
Taunton
Somerset TA1 5HA

*The Life That's Left (25 mins)*

A study of bereavement, featuring different people talking about their responses to the deaths of elderly and middle aged spouses, children, parents, siblings and stillbirth in both sudden and unexpected circumstances.

Available from

CTVC Churches Television and Radio Centre
Hillside
Maryhill Road
Bushey WD1 1DR

*Cot Death (29 mins)*

This video is designed to assist in the training of professionals who come into contact with a bereaved family after cot death.

Available for hire or purchase from

> Concord Video and Film Council Limited
> 201 Felixstowe Road
> Ipswich
> Suffolk IP3 9BJ

*A Kind Goodbye*

This video provides a guide to sensitive management of euthanasia and animal death.

Available from

> SCAS
> 10B Lenny Rd
> Callander FK17 8BA
> Scotland

*Drug Addiction (30 mins)*

This video is in two parts. The first discusses the psychological and physical reasons why people start and continue to use drugs. Part two offers practical and pragmatic guidelines for treatment.

Available for hire or purchase from

> Concord Video and Film Council Limited
> 201 Felixstowe Road, Ipswich
> Suffolk IP3 9BJ

*Solvent Abuse: The first time unlucky (20 mins)*

This video sets out the key issues of concern about solvent abuse. What users do, how they do it, the risks they run, the symptoms to look for and how to cope with the aftermath.

Available for hire or purchase from

> Concord Video and Film Council Limited
> 201 Felixstowe Road, Ipswich
> Suffolk IP3 9BJ

*You and Alcohol – Just Good Friends (20 mins)*

This video is aimed at 15-year-olds and older. It is an account of alcohol, how it works on the body and the brain, and the different effects on men and women. It poses the question – what is sensible drinking?

Available for hire or purchase from

> Concord Video and Film Council Limited
> 201 Felixstowe Road, Ipswich
> Suffolk IP3 9BJ

### ISOLATION

*Somebody's Wee Nobody (20–25 mins)*

This video deals with schoolgirl pregnancy, using music and drama to convey its message, and it was made involving young, single parents from the start. It shows the experience of one young mother, including reactions to her pregnancy, her experience of having the baby and life afterwards.

Available from

> Scottish Council for Single Parents
> 13 Gayfield Square
> Edinburgh EH1 3NX

*A Proper Job (12 mins)*
A London agency looks at employment for people with learning difficulties.

Available for hire or purchase from

> Concord Video and Film Council Limited
> 201 Felixstowe Road
> Ipswich
> Suffolk IP3 9BJ

*Counselling Skills in Practice (22 mins)*
This is a demonstration of counselling skills in the work place. Nine identified skills based on Egan's three-stage model illustrate how a typical work-based problem can be helped.

Available for weekly hire or purchase from

> RELATE Southampton
> 3 Kings Park Road
> Southampton SO1 2AS

*Why Won't They Talk to Me?*
A series of videos dealing with issues related to caring for people who are seriously ill or dying. Each video lasts for approximately 25 minutes.

- Video 1 – Introduction and objectives
- Video 2 – Opening dialogue
- Video 3 – Coping with problems part 1
- Video 4 – Coping with problems part 2
- Video 5 – Putting it together.

Available from

> Linward Productions Ltd
> Sheperton Studio Centre
> Studios Road, Shepperton
> Middlesex TW17 0QD

*Can We Help You? (37 mins)*
This video is designed to help people develop skills of handling enquiries, managing information, solving problems and communicating information and advice.

Available for hire or purchase from

> Concord Video and Film Council Limited
> 201 Felixstowe Road, Ipswich
> Suffolk IP3 9BJ

## Organizations

### CANCER SUPPORT

*Cancer Relief Macmillan Fund*
Anchor House
17–19 Britten Street
London SW3 3TZ

Provides pump-priming for a range of health care professionals' posts. Financial grants for cancer patients and a range of education and patient information leaflets.

*Marie Curie Cancer Care*
28 Belgrave Street
London SW1 8QG

Provides a range of health care professional services, education and patient information resources.

*Cancer Link*
17 Britannia Street
London WC1X 9JN

Provides a resource centre for cancer self-help, support groups throughout Britain and a telephone information service on all aspects of cancer.

*Bacup*
3 Bath Place
Rivington Street
London EC2 AJR

Provides a cancer information service.

### COUNSELLING

*British Association for Counselling*
1 Regent Place
Rugby CV21 2PJ

A membership organization for those involved in counselling. It provides a counselling and psychotherapy information service for the general public.

*Co-counselling Network UK*
John Parlbut
The Laurels
Berryhill Lane
Donninton-le-Heath
Claville LE67 2FB

### BEREAVEMENT

*Compassionate Friends*
6 Denmark Street
Bristol BS1 5DG

An international organization of bereaved parents offering friendship and understanding to other bereaved parents.

*Cruse*
Cruse House
126 Sheen Road
Richmond
Surrey TW9 1UR

Provides counselling and support for widows, widowers and their families. Offers training for their volunteers.

*Foundation for the Study of Infant Deaths*
5th Floor
4 Grosvenor Place
London SW1 7HD

Offers advice and support to parents bereaved by cot death.

*Critec*
Accident and Emergency
Leeds General Infirmary
Leeds LS1 3EX

Offers a debriefing and counselling service for those working with sudden death, critical incidents and other life crises.

*Society for Companion Animal Studies: Pet Loss support*
10b Lenny Road
Callander FK17 8BA
Scotland

Offers advice, support and education to owners of companion animals.

## VIOLENCE

*National Association of Victim Support Schemes*
34 Electric Lane
Brixton
London SW9 8JT

An organization which aims to promote victim support schemes and to identify the needs of the victims of crime.

## OTHERS

*Samaritans*
consult your local telephone directory

A UK organization which offers emotional support and befriending to the lonely, suicidal and despairing.

*Gingerbread*
35 Wellington Street
London WC2E

Provides help for single-parent families who need information, advice or companionship.